The Challenge
of the Resource
Exchange Network

From Concept to Action

Seymour B. Sarason
Elizabeth Lorentz

The Challenge
of the Resource
Exchange Network

Jossey-Bass Publishers

San Francisco • Washington • London • 1979

THE CHALLENGE OF THE RESOURCE EXCHANGE NETWORK:
From Concept to Action
by Seymour B. Sarason and Elizabeth Lorentz

Copyright ©1979 by: Jossey-Bass, Inc., Publishers
433 California Street
San Francisco, California 94104
&
Jossey-Bass Limited
28 Banner Street
London EC1Y 8QE

Library of Congress Catalogue Card Number LC 79-83579

International Standard Book Number ISBN 0-87589-407-0

Manufactured in the United States of America

JACKET DESIGN BY WILLI BAUM

FIRST EDITION

Code 7907

The Jossey-Bass
Social and Behavioral Science Series

Preface

T hrough the course of this book, the reader will understand that we are indebted to many people for their ideas, collaboration in everyday action, and for encouraging us to report what we and they have experienced and learned. We refer particularly to the members of the Essex network, too numerous to mention here. Richard Sussman, a coordinator in that network, must be mentioned because in diverse ways he has been unusually helpful, and we are grateful.

We did not expect that we would be publishing a second book on resource exchange and networks two years after the first one. Why we wrote the present book is explained in the first chapter. Although there is thematic overlap, this book is very different than the first one (*Human Services and Resource Networks*, 1977).

Unlike the first book, in which emphasis was on the network concept and process, in this book we give more attention to the features of human services agencies that have been remarkably successful in subverting changes public policies and legislation have deemed desirable. This is not because they have willed self-defeat or because they are any less moral and socially conscious than people generally. A good part of the answer lies in invalid assumptions about the nature and extent of human and natural resources, assumptions that have long been at the ideological core of our society. The task of our times is not how to define resources but how to redefine them, and there is nothing in human history to suggest that people willingly or graciously take to the redefinition process. That process has begun in our society, but we make no prediction about its present and future pace.

Some readers may conclude that we do not have an optimistic outlook; others may conclude that we are victims of utopian thinking not in tune with the social realities. We hope most readers will resist name calling, will see something in this book that helps them clarify what they have observed and experienced, and will be stimulated to pursue actions that will enable them and others to capitalize on the fact that, by becoming part of each other's world, their sense of excitement from learning and productive achievement will quicken. There is nothing in the statement that human and natural resources are limited that should occasion despair or passivity, and, we trust, no one will conclude that we are advocates of scarcity. The major value in accepting that statement is that it liberates the imagination and places the emphasis where it belongs: not on what we cannot do or do not have but on what we possess and can do. To an increasing extent, the entire human services area has become defect oriented, and countless professionals spend their time telling us about people's deficits and problems and usually end up telling us that we need more professionals, thus raising false expectations and setting the stage for future disillusionment. Obviously, we do not deny that people have deficits and problems, but we do argue that riveting on these characteristics exacerbates rather than dilutes the consequences of limited resources. As we point out later, nowhere is this point more validated than in the assumptions behind and the consequences of the Medicare legislation.

The resource exchange rationale is not a "solution." In the realm of social problems, there are no "solutions" in the natural science sense. It is a rationale that propels self and others into the redefiniton process and dramatically expands the universe of alternatives for thought and action.

February 1979

SEYMOUR B. SARASON
New Haven, Connecticut
ELIZABETH LORENTZ
Armonk, New York

Contents

The Authors

SEYMOUR B. SARASON is professor of psychology at Yale University. He founded, in 1962, and directed, until 1970, the Yale Psycho-Educational Clinic, one of the first research and training sites in community psychology. He has received awards from the divisions of clinical and community psychology, as well as two awards from the Ameican Association on Mental Deficiency.

Sarason is the author of numerous books and articles and has made contributions in such fields as mental retardation, culture and personality, projective techniques, teacher training, the school culture, and anxiety in children. His last three Jossey-Bass books, *The Creation of Settings and the Future Societies, The Psychological Sense of Community,* and *Human Services and Resource Networks* (1972, 1974, and 1977), contain themes that are elaborated on in the present volume.

ELIZABETH LORENTZ supervises new coordinators of resource exchange networks in the New York metropolitan area. She also brings network concepts to bear on organizations on whose advisory boards she serves, including the Institute for Responsive Education (chairman of the board), the Bank Street College of Education, the College for Human Services, the Rene Dubos Forum, and the Public Education Association.

Lorentz gained a generalist background by doing research and reports for directors of government agencies and magazine editors who wanted briefing on developments in various fields of human service. In the process, she became convinced that services by specialist professions and agencies would only be integrated if the lay citizen got involved.

The Challenge
of the Resource
Exchange Network

From Concept to Action

1

Resource Exchange: Problems and Issues

Three years ago we and some colleagues (Sarason and others, 1977) were impelled to write a book, *Human Services and Resource Networks*. That we felt we had to write the book was a response to two troublesome factors. For the previous three years, we had been part of an informal network of individuals, spanning three states, that was based on a resource exchange rationale: what in that book we called a *barter economy principle*. The network had no specific or restricted purpose; that is, resource exchange could take place around any substantive concern, and any concern was an opportunity to mobilize and exchange resources in relation to other concerns that on the surface appeared unrelated. Central to that story was Mrs. Dewar, a private citizen with one of those scanning and integrating minds, who could see connections where most people see unconnectedness. She could look at the needs of, for example, high school students, senior citizens, daycare children, and environmentalists, and weave a web in which meeting the needs of one group would, to a certain extent, meet the resource needs of all groups. It was an educating, stimulating, and instructive experience for all of us, especially as the network expanded in size and substantive foci. Today, the Essex Network continues to flourish. Much of its activities deal with fostering networks spawned and coordinated by its members.

The first troublesome factor we encountered was how to respond to the question "What is the Essex Network?" This was not the conversation-starting cocktail party question "Tell me about your research, or, what book are you writing now?" The question was being put to us by people who were seriously interested in the Essex Network because of what they had heard about it or on whom the activity of the network had impinged. And, no less important, they usually were people who had something to give to us and to whom we (or someone in the network) had something to give in return. On the one hand, we could give simple answers because the resource exchange rationale is not a complicated one; on the other hand, we also knew that developing and sustaining the Essex Network was no easy affair and that its resource exchange rationale, however simply it could be stated, was alien to the places in which people worked. In our society, the resource exchange rationale has a utopian, pie-in-the-sky ring to it. The trouble was not only "out there" but in ourselves as well, because we were by no means secure in our understanding of why the Essex Network developed and flourished and of the different meanings that its different members gave to it. The second troublesome factor was that the literature was amazingly deficient in descriptions of how networks developed, were sustained, or withered away. We could not say to our questioners: "Here are some descriptions of 'networking,' or "Here are descriptions of our kind of network." We knew that activators of resource exchange networks are usually activists; that is, they do not write to communicate the whys, hows, and whats of network development. We also knew that, if anyone had been disposed to take on the task, that person would quickly learn that meaningful description was quite a difficult business because wrapped up in it are the thorny issues of subjectivity and objectivity, a changing cast of characters, widely differing perceptions among participants, and the pitfalls of retrospection, introspection, and circumspection. But we felt we had to make the effort.

That book had two major purposes. The first was descriptive, and if we had any doubts about the complexity of that task they were dispelled in the effort, although it is a source of comfort that many people told us either that the description was helpful or that what we described in terms of process, dilemmas, and outcomes squared with their experience. It is not modesty that requires us to say that the problems of description were not handled in exemplary fashion by us. The second major purpose was selectively to review the literature on networks in different academic disciplines. Beginning in the mid 1950s, the concept of networks came to the fore in such diverse fields as geography, psychology, sociology, anthropology, mental health ("network" therapy), and the administrative sciences. It did not surprise us that what was being conceptualized and studied in one discipline was for all practical purposes unknown to the other disciplines. That review confirmed our perception that the concept of networks was in the academic air no less than it was in the air of the larger society. It also confirmed us in our belief that we should describe our experiences in the Essex Network.

The truth is that there was a third purpose stemming from our concern: that precisely because the concept of networks had become fashionable—in everyday parlance and in governmental and human services rhetoric—the concept's practical significance would get lost in slogans, labels, and hortatory proclamations about the need for more efficient and coordinate use of available resources.[1] The network concept has indeed become fashionable and trendy, and that, of course, is a mixed blessing. If we had any contribution to make, we concluded, it was in the effort to make concrete what we meant by a resource exchange network.

In writing a book, the writers and their substantive focus inevitably change, and that happened to us. Some things became clearer, others more complicated and fuzzy, and new dimensions emerged. Indeed, this happened to us to such an extent that there were times we felt we should not proceed because we felt unprepared to do jus-

---

[1]The popularity of the network concept not only is seen in its frequency in everyday conversation, or in policy statements, or in the scores of formal and informal new organizations that have the word *network* in their titles. In 1977, the International Network for Social Network Analysis was formed, issued a directory, and started a bulletin of research abstracts. In 1978, Volume 1 of *Social Networks* was published by Elsevier Sequoia in Lausanne, Switzerland. We have also learned that at least two other groups are planning an annual publication on networks.

tice to the emerging complexity. Our major purposes would, as in an embedded-figures test, alternate between being figure and ground. We made the conscious decision to stick primarily to our main purposes, although, contained in that first book, albeit briefly and oversimplified, are all the issues with which we deal in the present book.

The publication of that first book had enormously instructive consequences for us. For one thing, we heard from many people, near and far, about their efforts to develop and sustain a resource exchange network. There was no room for doubt that the resource exchange rationale not only was in the air but also had inspired people to action. And there could no longer be any doubt that a crucial question was, "Could the resource exchange rationale be developed in and among formal organizations, or was it viable, as in the case of the Essex Network, only on an informal, voluntary basis where people participated as individuals and not as formal representatives of formal agencies?" Equally instructive was that, as we became familiar with people who were instrumental in developing a network, the question of their cognitive characteristics, which they seemed to share to a far greater degree than they did personality status or educational characteristics, became an increasingly intriguing and pressing one. To understand why some networks live and others die, why some remain consistent with their purpose while others are transformed inconsistently, requires that we look into diverse sources—but surely the characteristics of those who play obviously key roles in the development and sustenance of the network are important. Finally, the publication of the book stimulated others to bring published and unpublished writings (many of which would be unknown or inaccessible to most people) to our attention and from which we have profited greatly. It is to no end frustrating to know that there are articles and books from whose titles one would be hard put to discern very much relevance to networks. For example, how would one know that the last quarter of a book titled, *Public Planning: The Inter-Corporate Dimension* (Friend, Power, and Yewlett, 1974) would be a penetrating analysis of networks in formal agencies in the public sector and would contain a description of the role and cognitive characteristics of the "reticulist" (network maker) similar to our description of the coordinator of a resource exchange network?

Our decision to restrict the focus of the first book turned out to have been a sound one, at least from the standpoint of furthering our own knowledge. In the meantime, the Essex Network continued to develop, and after five and a half years it remains a loose, informal, growing, voluntary affair that continues to raise new questions and require rephrasing of old ones. In the years since the first book, we came to see that a second book should be written, in which what was important, but muted or even absent, in the first book could be given the attention the restricted purposes of that book denied them.

The present book is related to the first one, but it can stand by itself and be judged independently. Chapter Two deals at length with the fact of limited resources or, put in another way, the myth of unlimited resources. As long as people cling to the belief, long a part of our culture and national ideology, that resources are limitless and that the wondrous achievements of science guarantee that ways will be found to satisfy all the material needs of all of us, they court disappointment. They also put an insuperable obstacle in the way of recognizing the potentialities of a need for a resource exchange rationale. It really makes little difference if one says resources are *limited* or *seriously limited,* as long as one recognizes that the usual ways in which we mobilize and allocate resources drastically underestimates the degree of limitation and deflects the imagination of people away from the importance of redefining what we mean by resources and how the process of redefinition casts the issues in a very different light. We give numerous examples of what happens when people redefine themselves as resources. Ordinarily, when people talk about resources, they mean natural resources. The degree of limitation in human resources is highly related to the way people are, so to speak, taught to define themselves, and we show that one of the distinguishing characteristics of the post-World War II world is the refusal of many groups (such as nurses, students) to stay within the confines of traditional definitions of their roles. They actively strove to redefine themselves as resources, with impressive results. Still another distinguishing characteristic of this period, also based on the redefinition process, is the rise of the highly differentiated self-help movement, a movement that—at the same time that it is a reaction to the perception of the inadequacies of large, bureaucratic, insensitive, ponderous public agencies and of self-serving professionalism—is also a breaking out from the confines of the stance of being passive recipients of what others think these groups are and need.

When one looks into these different instances of human resource definition, it is not surprising that in some of them a resource exchange rationale comes into center stage; that is, individuals not only redefine themselves as resources but also seek to use each other's resources in a mutually satisfying way, in a way that dilutes the consequences of an individual's limited resources. The exchanges serve not only a compensatory function but a social psychological one as well, in that each person can potentially become part of another person's "environment" in a way that can sustain and even increase the variety of exchanges. There is no logical or necessary relationship among recognizing limited resources, engaging in the process of redefinition, a resource exchange rationale, and the development of networks. The thrust of this chapter is to show why we have to learn how to put these factors together as one way of dealing with the current social malaise.

The beginnings of that conceptual integration are reflected in different ways in different groups and places, albeit with differing degrees of scope and clarity. In Chapter Three, we give several detailed case presentations illustrating attempted integration. All instances have in common the process and consequences of resource redefinition. Some of them deal very clearly with the fact of limited resources. All of them accept the principle of resource exchange, although they differ widely in how that rationale determines action. They differ even more widely in how they tie a concept of networks to the other factors. Beyond all these considerations, however, these case presentations will give the reader a feel for the diversity of ways in which widely differing individuals and groups struggle to forge a new way of thinking, living, and working. They are not only reactions to perceived defects in our public and private institutions but also a movement toward something. And for all of them it has been, is, and will be a struggle. In Chapter Three, we have let these people speak for themselves, because our effort at paraphrase took the warmth and complexity out of their phenomenology. More instructive to the reader than our summary of the accounts of these people is how they came to have the courage to redefine themselves and others as resources. It is one thing for us to say that a feature of these instances is the importance people attach to their need to empower themselves; that is, to actively seek to gain more control over their lives. It is another thing to hear it in their own words. We are all familiar with the energy powering the actions of diverse minority groups who seek empowerment (Sarason, 1978a). But the need for empowerment, the need to feel active, responsive, and responsible for one's life, is a general one in society today, and it is a mistake to think it is only at work in the political arena. We think it would not be hyperbole to say that, among the many factors responsible for the resurgence of interest in resource exchange (as a rationale or as a stimulus to action), the need for empowerment as a reaction to feeling socially and intellectually passive and confined is one of the most important.

In Chapter Four, we focus on professionals or, more correctly, the spirit and traditions of professionalism. This focus is necessary because in our experience what we have termed *resource exchange networks* have usually been formed by a nonprofessional individual or group. Or, in the few instances where professionally trained individuals played a formative role, it was because they saw themselves in extreme disagreement with established modes of organization. Also, in regard to this type of network, the professional has usually adopted a disdainful attitude. The reasons for this are many, and in this chapter we explore the major ones: the emphasis and consequences of specialization, the presumption that formally acquired expertise entitles a person to a position of "leadership" over less credentialed individuals, the unease of the professional in participating with others on a basis of parity, and, most obvious of all, the relationship between professionals' education and training, on the one hand, and their extraordinarily narrow definition of people as resources, on the other hand. The issue of professionalism as an obstacle to developing and participating in resource exchange networks cannot be avoided, if only because of the simple fact that professionals either dominate, or control, or mightily influence human services policies and agencies. More subtly and powerfully, they seek to shape the definition, mobilization, and allocation of human services and resources. We did not write this chapter in a spirit of indictment, as if professionals (and their emphasis on increasing specialization and credentialism) were engaged in a deliberate conspiracy to exploit others. If that were the case, the outlook would be more optimistic, because the evil would have been located, and ways to rectify matters could be undertaken. The problem is more difficult than that, because the professional's stance is the outcome of years of education and training geared to making him or her feel special, different, and apart from others. That stance is inhospitable to participation in a resource exchange network. If anything is clear about the viability of these networks, it is the willingness of the members to redefine themselves *and* others as resources in an ambience of voluntary participation in which the universe of alternatives is not restricted by undue concern for titles and status. It is fair to say that, in the critical questioning of all kinds of institutional authority (so prominent a feature of recent decades), the stance of the professional was an easy target. It should go without saying that the rationale for a resource exchange network is not inimical to the participation of the professional who has unlearned the habit of defining a problem in a way so that dealing with it will require more and more specialized professionals, thus aggravating rather than lessening the degree of limited resources.

In Chapter Five, we look at a resource exchange network from the standpoint of the individual (individuals) considered crucial to its development and maintenance. Phenomenology is never easy to reflect in words, and the process becomes even more problematic when the person one is trying to understand is in a role and context that has hardly been studied and is unfamiliar to most people. Here, too, we have restricted our scope primarily to the question, "What are some cognitive characteristics that these people seem to share?" The capacity to scan their environment, to distinguish between appearance and reality, to see potential linkages and commonalities among people seemingly diverse in work, site, and concerns—these are some of the cognitive characteristics the actions of these people reflect. But there is more to it than that; for reasons we are far from understanding, they have conceptualized relationships among resource redefinition, resource exchange, and a differentiated conception of how networks can be the vehicle for action. In brief, they have a thought-through resource exchange rationale, quite the opposite of sloganeering, glib labeling, and diffuse actions. They are more than network coordinators, unless one also means by that term that by force of their ideas they stimulate and attract others to their network. They do not see themselves as leaders, but they are looked to by others for direction. From one perspective, they are correct in not seeing themselves as leaders, because in practice they are able to perform two feats, the second of which is harder than the first (although they are both hard). They are able to get people to see how their diverse self-interests can be met in ways that make each valuable to the other, that makes each person an expander of another person's resources and of his or her knowledge of the environment, and, significantly, does this with the earnest wish that the new interpersonal system will be self-propelling and not dependent on the coordinator. From the standpoint of the coordinator, the best of all possible outcomes is that the new subsystem is not only self-sustaining but also enables some of these individuals to learn to play the coordinating role for other people in other parts of their personal network. This point was illustrated in a general meeting of the Essex Network, over five years after its development. A stranger at that meeting would never have guessed that Mrs. Dewar, who was there, was the prime mover of the Essex Network. So, when we use the term *leader-coordinator* it is because, alone, each part of the term simply does not convey what we are trying to describe.

Until Chapter Six, we use the network concept without defining it, a practice we have criticized in others in these days when the concept is in fashion. This omission was deliberate because our interest is not in networks in general but in a very specific type: the resource exchange network. We felt it would not be helpful to the reader to define at the outset what we mean by a resource exchange network before we discussed at length the significance of limited resources, the process of redefinition of resources, people's disillusionment with the countless and fruitless efforts to coordinate resources more efficiently for the purpose of more humane services, and the varieties of ways in which countless groups (usually informal) have assumed responsibility for dealing with these issues in their locales. Without this background discussion, the reader might view our attempt at definition as arbitrary, unrelated to experience as well as to the major cross currents and upheavals in our society. We see our experiences, and those of others, in the context of our times, and, therefore, whether one agrees or not with our approach, it should occasion no surprise that we were drawn to the ways we define human resources. Chapter Six is less an attempt at definition than a way of bringing together values, principles, and action.

The discussion in Chapter Six, emphasizing as it does the informal, voluntary nature of a viable resource exchange network, sets the stage for Chapter Seven, where we give representative examples of the staggeringly self-defeating way in which formal human services agencies define resources, are unable to consider (let alone engage in) meaningful exchange with each other, are in competition with each other for resources and survival, and, to cap it all, manage

to subvert efforts at coordination even when those efforts are powered by sizable amounts of money. Nobody wills these disasters, and
yet nobody, neither the money givers or takers, derive any constructive conclusions from the experiences. *Ad hominems* abound. In
each example, we raise questions about how the effort at
coordination would have been approached if it was based in a resource exchange rationale. And the conclusion to which we come is
that without the carrot of federal or foundation money some (not
all) of the objectives could have been attained. We are not advocates
of scarcity, or mindless partisans of fiscal integrity (whatever that is),
or gleeful proponents of creating necessities from which we can then
derive virtues. But the examples we give in Chapter Seven, and a
good-sized library could be filled with similar case descriptions, give
force to the conclusion that a resource exchange rationale and network within and among formal agencies would encounter mammoth obstacles and that the obstacles become insuperable the more
one resorts to money as an incentive and to legislative or administrative fiat as the stick. The reader may draw different conclusions, but
he or she cannot be familiar with past and present efforts at
coordination among formal agencies and remain wedded to any of
the traditional conceptions of institutional change.

When you are seeking new ways of thinking and acting in relation to seemingly intractable problems, it is no end comforting to
learn that there are people who are moving in similar directions,
even though they are in different fields, work contexts, and countries. In Chapter Eight, we present and analyze two such instances.
The first is an unpublished paper by Sheane (1977) in Ulster, Northern Ireland. Viewing the fratricide going on in that tragic setting,
Sheane comes to three major conclusions: One concerns "the creative minority" who bear marked similarities to our description of the
leader-coordinator; a second concerns the almost complete inability
of formal institutions to engage in meaningful exchange; and the
third advocates resort only to informal networks. Sheane, an industrial executive, is no less pessimistic than we about the compatibility
of the resource exchange network with formal organizations. The
second instance is *Public Planning: The Inter-Corporate Dimension*, by
Friend, Power, and Yewlett (1974). Most of that book is a very detailed description of the planning and implementation of a public
policy (in England) that had major consequences for a particular

small town and adjoining districts and urban areas. It is difficult reading, but not because the scene is foreign or because it is another example of two countries divided by a common language. It is difficult because Friend and his colleagues have a very sophisticated conception of formal and informal networks in the public sector that prevents them from oversimplifying the complexity of the scene. The last part of the book is about the role and cognitive characteristics of the reticulist, and this discussion is amazingly similar to what we say about the network leader-coordinator. Friend and his colleagues, no less than Sheane and us, have few illusions about the feasibility of the role of the reticulist in the formal organization. So, from different experiences and backgrounds, we find people arriving at conclusions quite in conflict with the current wisdom.

In light of the tone of the preceding chapters, the contents of Chapter Eight may come as a surprise, because they contain a concrete recommendation of a way in which the resource exchange rationale might be introduced into formal organizations of government. The recommendation is based on the concept and role of the ombudsman in the Scandinavian countries, as described by Gellhorn (1967). The word *ombudsman* has become familiar in our country but its use rarely, if ever, reflects a knowledge of the strange mixture of responsibilities, independence, formal powerlessness, and informal power of the ombudsman (the "citizen's protector"). Nor does it reflect the realism and courage of the legislative body in creating the role as it did. Our recommendation is for a resource exchange ombudsman. The recommendation is certainly not a panacea. It is one way by which a note of sanity can begin to be introduced into formal organizations in regard to resource exchange. It is basically an informal approach subject to the advantages and disadvantages of such an approach, but past experience suggests that the former far outweigh the latter.

In this book, the term *resource exchange* refers to more than what people "give and get" in a material sense. That is to say, it should not be viewed in the context of a market economy in which people, in a relatively impersonal and transient way, engage in a "barter" and then go their own ways. That kind of bartering is by no means infrequent, as the following statement from an article in a nationally syndicated Sunday supplement (Michaels, 1978, p. 18) suggests: "Bartering is the art of putting your mouth where your money isn't. Its possibilities are limitless, and millions of Americans are taking advantage of them—a housewife doing inventory for a local grocer in return for a week's food; a dentist trading work for a new suit from a tailor; a car-repair shop bartering a lube job and tires on a radio station's news car in return for advertising time." And, from the same article (p. 20), " 'Everyone has something that someone else wants,' says Connie Stapleton (1978) in her book *Barter*. 'Find out what the other person needs and match your need to his vacuum. Decide ahead what you are willing to trade for what. Strike when the need is greatest to make the best deal. Don't take "no" seriously. Relax and enjoy it!' She suggests beginners start close to home—among family members, in the neighborhood, through newspaper ads or notices on church and supermarket bulletin boards."

When we use the term *resource exchange* or *resource exchange rationale* in the context of the development of a network, our focus goes beyond a narrow conception of exchange to one in which people learn to see themselves and each other as very differentiated resources that literally expand not only knowledge of one's environment but the possibilities for influencing and changing it as well. At its best, the resource exchange network creates an ambience that empowers people, in the sense that the process of redefinition is one in which our usually restricted sense of the universe of alternatives for the thought and action is challenged and changed and in which we feel less impotent to direct our lives. And, crucially, what is learned goes beyond the personal or the interpersonal to the cognitive stance that allows one to see ways whereby the needs and resources of groups ordinarily seen as differing from each other (possessing different labels that tell us to shift the structure of our thinking as our attention goes from one group to another) can now be seen in relation to each other.

This book is about individuals and groups, differing widely in status, role, social class, and site, who came to similar ideas and actions in response to dissatisfactions either about themselves, their society, or both. We endeavor to describe and understand similarities and differences among them in order to gain greater clarity about the potentials of and the obstacles to the implementation of a resource exchange rationale. Indeed, this book should be looked on as part of a continuing effort to learn, through doing and observing, what the important issues are in the relationship between rationale and action. The challenge of the resource exchange rationale has a Janus-like character: It directs one's gaze to what people have done and thought about the rationale at the same time that it draws our attention to the perceived features of the society "out there" that propelled these people to act in ways new for them. It would be shortchanging the significances of the rationale to focus exclusively, or even primarily, on what people have done with it. No less important is what these actions say about the nature of our society. That is why our gaze alternates, in the course of this book, between the internal workings of resource exchange networks and certain aspects of the larger society.

2

The Significance of Limited Resources

In the past half century, our society has experienced four major crises: the Great Depression, World War II, the upheavals of the 1960s, and, more recently, the realization that we not only do not control resources we thought were limitless and on which we depended but also that some of these resources are limited and under the control of other countries. Each of these crises involved, among other things, the nature, definition, and use of resources.

During the Great Depression, the question was, "How can a country so blessed with resources of all kinds find itself with upward of 20 percent of its people unemployed, many of them without sufficient food to sustain life?" With the onset of World War II, the paramount question was, "Can we, quickly enough, develop and husband our bountiful resources to defeat the fascist threat?" It was during the turbulent 1960s that the first real doubts about limitless resources began to be expressed. Could we sustain a war in Southeast Asia at the same time that we wanted to explore outer space and decrease the number of people living in poverty?

And then, in the 1970s, came the Arab oil embargo and in its wake the realization that we had to examine our accustomed ways of defining and utilizing resources. This is not to say that *we* refers to many people. On the contrary, there is every reason to believe that most people continue either to bypass, or ignore, or deny the issue. It would be surprising if it were otherwise, because attitudes that have had continuous support in our society from its very beginnings will not easily change. (The discovery of America was considered the new Garden of Eden and that imagery has been part of our national rhetoric ever since.) Furthermore, the resource crisis is not yet a "real" crisis in the sense that the Great Depression, World War II, and the sizzling 1960s were. It is not until a crisis is both obvious and sustained—until we are as a society, so to speak, hit over the head and hospitalized—that we begin to redefine the nature of our world; more correctly, we are then willing to entertain new ways of thinking. But even then, once we think the crisis is over we revert to the old ways, albeit not completely.

World War II is an especially clear example because it required radical redefinition and use of human and material resources, not only in regard to the needs of the armed services but in civilian life as well. Criteria for selection for different roles, how people would be trained, and the length of training changed quickly. Older people, physically handicapped people, mentally subnormal people, and women suddenly were seen as important "resources." As important as what people had (or had not) done was what they could quickly learn to do. Necessity required that individuals be viewed not as *a* resource, not perceived in terms of the narrow confines of work labels (such as lawyer, medical internist, accountant, businessman, farmer), but potentially capable of being and doing many different things. Over the course of the war years, literally millions of people were doing things that they never had expected to do and, in many instances, with little or no "training." And the lives of many of these people were positively affected as they discovered in themselves new interests and capabilities. It is perversely strange that it takes a total war for a society to recognize how narrowly people are defined and utilized as a resource.

Once the war was over, our society reverted to its accustomed narrow ways of locating and training people as resources. But World War II planted seeds of rebellion against the "old ways" that have flowered in the last decade or so. Women, handicapped people, older citizens no longer are content to be "slotted"—that is, to accept the implications of labels that constrict what these people are supposed to be capable of, at the same time distorting what they would like to experience.

The concept of human resources has two aspects: (1) society's impersonal and conventional definition and (2) people's subjective perceptions. It used to be that these aspects were not dramatically in conflict with each other but that is far less the case today. They were less in conflict during World War II because of the dictates of necessity. Today they are in conflict because the rigidities of conventional definitions, formalized in institutional concrete, seem to be becoming stronger as people's needs and perceptions of themselves are increasingly incongruent with these conventional definitions. The reduction of conflict between these two aspects is as much a necessity today as it was during World War II, but, unfortunately, necessity is not always the mother of invention.

The ways a society defines a human resource is rooted in everything we mean by that society's social history. So, for example, if one wants to understand our society's emphasis on and support for professionalism—what Bledstein (1976) in his illuminating book has called the "culture of professionalism"—one has to comprehend what our society was, the forces of change, and the often unverbalized values and ideologies that were at work. Bledstein's analysis not only indicates how the desire for professional status and recognition (for legal and administrative recognition by society of a group's distinctiveness and expertness) was a notable feature of the nineteenth century and became even more general in the twentieth, but also, and no less fateful, how laypersons began to give up any claim to possessing resources or the ability to define them. It is only somewhat of an exaggeration to say that as the concept of "expertness" and the role of the expert intruded into almost every area of living, laypersons no longer felt able to do anything for themselves or about anything.

Not until one confronts that social history can one begin to understand how, wittingly and unwittingly, the nature of human resources was being defined in ways that, however understandable for the time, have become maladaptive in the present. Only in recent years have the glamor and high status associated with specialization been questioned on numerous grounds, not the least of which un-

derlies the question, "Has the seemingly inexorable trend to specialization reached the point where it is defeating of societal needs?" Implied in that question is a new note in our social history: Our
resources are not limitless (needs, however, may be!), and we may no
longer be able to afford to allow human resources to be defined in
very narrow ways. The very fact that this is a new note, albeit a muted
one, and has already begun to influence the substance of public policy as well as thinking about our educational system is of great significance. But that new note is being heard and voiced by the
consuming public.

How do the specialists view the issue? Although professional
associations either ignore, or give lip service to, or disagree with the
implications of the new note, there is reason to believe that an
increasing number of specialists feel themselves to be victims of their
own narrowness, of the constricted range within which their personal resources can be given play (Sarason, 1977). As one highly educated and successful middle-aged specialist said, "What amazes
and upsets me is that when I look back at when I entered my field, I
had no realization how narrowly I was allowing myself to be defined
even though I feel I should have known that there was a lot more to
me that would never be used. And as I learned more and more about
less and less, getting a lot of rewards in the process, I felt there was a
lot in me that was wasting and shrinking. As for your question about
the societal consequences of specialization, there is no doubt in my
mind, or in my experience, that it aggravates rather than dilutes the
serving of societal needs. I would go so far as to say that it creates resource scarcity." And then, with laughter and as an afterthought, he
went on: "But scarcity of a resource can be quite lucrative to those
who possess it, as I well know."

The significance of the example of specialization, for our
present purposes, is less in suggesting how it may aggravate the consequences of limited resources than in illustrating how what is considered a "good thing" is defined by society (and its institutions) as if
it had no implications for existing limited resources. René Dubos
(1978) said, "There are no 'natural' resources. There are only raw
materials of nature and the forces of nature. These materials and
forces become resources only after techniques have been developed
to transform them and to use them to some human end." The pro-

cess of transformation, be it in relation to human or material resources, is a social process in that it defines, or rather asserts, a desirable human end, a way of producing the resource to achieve it, and
thereby raises the question of the degree of availability of that resource.

There is, of course, no ethical or moral problem if the transformed resource is limitless, but in the realm of human resources
that is rarely, if ever, the case. So, when a human resource is judged
as desirable for some human end, that judgment must confront the
fact that the resource is limited and simply not available to all those
who, by social definition, need it. But, unfortunately, that kind of
confrontation tends to take place after the disjunction between desirable human ends and limited means has become glaring. The societal context within which a desirable human end is asserted is not
one conducive to the recognition that the human resources necessary to meet those ends may not only be limited but also may become
more limited over time precisely because the assertion creates increased needs for those resources. If this is the truth with *one* asserted socially desirable end, it is obvious that the fact and consequences of limited human resources become exponentially more
complex and difficult to face when, as is always the case in the social
arena, there are many asserted socially desirable ends.

Let us take a familiar example. Today we are all aware that
there is a surfeit of teachers for available positions in our schools,
colleges, and universities. One would be tempted to say that we have
more teachers than we "need." A dozen years ago, we had fewer
teachers than we "needed," to such an extent that regulations were
eased to make it easier and speedier to become a teacher (similar to
what happened in World War II). Is the "need" that produced a
shortage the same as the "need" that has produced a surfeit? Did
society discernibly change its definition of desirable educational
ends within a matter of a few years? In the 1960s, public policy was
relatively unambiguous about what were the desirable ends of
education; for example, changing outmoded curricula, improving the preparation of teachers, reducing class size, increasing the
number and quality of specialized personnel, and developing compensatory programs for those from disadvantaged backgrounds
(with special emphasis on the ubiquitous "reading problem"). Those
were the days when one heard much about individualized instruc-

tion and the overarching aim of "helping each student develop his or her potential."

It did not take long before it became obvious that these ends had been asserted as if the human resources necessary to meet these ends were or could be made available. For example, if Congress had decided that class size would be reduced by half, it could not become a reality. It is conceivable that we could have doubled the number of schools, but it was impossible to train twice the number of teachers. Our teacher training centers were already overcrowded, and if, in accord with desirable educational ends, the raising of the quality of educational personnel was to be a criterion, the result would not be in doubt. Quantitative goals always have implications for, and frequently founder on, the qualitative factor. But the assertion of educational ends was only one of many desirable human ends that gave the 1960s a distinctive stamp. They were not necessarily substantively or morally in conflict with each other, but from the standpoint of resources they were in competition.

Today, when we talk about a surplus of educational personnel, it is not because there has been a change in educational goals that in turn has altered conceptions of needed resources but rather because of adverse and complex national and international economic dynamics. The surplus, currently, cannot be accounted for solely, or in large measure, by the decline in the student population. Many people have argued that the decline in the student population presents the opportunity to use the "surplus" to make a serious effort to meet desirable educational goals. That is to say, from the standpoint of these ends the surplus is a specious one.

Let us take another example of how societal assertion of a desirable end can founder on the failure to examine closely the quantity and quality of available and potential resources. One can characterize the post-World War II period as the Age of Psychology or the Age of Mental Health. During the war, and with ever quickening speed after its close, our society was made aware of large numbers of people who were in need of some form of personal counseling or psychotherapy. Unlike earlier times, when "going for help" was kept a secret because of the fear that others would consider the individual "crazy" or "strange," people were now encouraged to regard their personal problems much as they regarded physical symptoms and to seek appropriate help. It was obvious, however, to policy makers and their advisers that in order to make such help available a large number of helpers would have to be trained.

And so began a series of programs to develop the resources to meet stated goals. It was as if psychotherapy was akin to a mental aspirin, and therefore the task was, as in the case of "real" aspirin, to develop the manufacturing process. No one seriously asked if it was possible to train professionals in numbers appropriate to the defined dimensions of the mental health problem, or, assuming we could do that, if we knew how to select the qualitatively most able people.

The fact is that everyone seemed to agree that the training of such a professional was a long and arduous affair and that not everyone who wanted such training was appropriate for that kind of work. And yet the implied contradiction between the numbers that were said to be needed and the paltry numbers that training centers could graduate was either not recognized or was given the silent treatment. It was not until the mid 1950s that that contradiction surfaced in a way that could not be overlooked (Albee, 1954). The contradiction may have surfaced, but even today policy makers and spokespersons for professional associations seem unable to face up to it. Apparently it is much easier to assert a desirable human end and to initiate a process to transform "materials" into resources to achieve those ends than it is to confront the possibility either that the "materials" are limited in supply or that the selected transformation process, far from creating sufficient resources, may aggravate the problem, if only because it has the effect of increasing the need for service.

When a society in the form of a public policy asserts a desirable human end, it is almost always after important and numerous segments of the citizenry have urged such a policy. The process by which these pressures then become realized in a formal public policy (involving as that process does the legislature, the executive, lobbying, the mass media) tends to have the effect of increasing the number of people who are supposed to benefit from the policy, with the further consequence of increasing the resources that will be required. It is a process in which what is controversial is how to phrase the public policy, how to decide who will be affected by it, and how it shall be funded and administered. What gets less attention is whether the resources exist or can be developed to the extent required by the stated desirable ends. The issue of resources does not become controversial until after implementation of the policy has exposed the centrality of the issue, and even then a frequent reaction does not center on the implications of the fact of limited resources but on heightening the national resolve to create more of these resources.

As we shall see later, the seriousness of the problem is exponentially aggravated by the failure to see that the way in which desirable human ends are phrased and defined already dictate the techniques by which the necessary resources will be obtained, a relationship that usually and inordinately constricts the resources that will be made available. When in the 1960s desirable educational goals were formulated in a public policy, that policy explicitly dictated that many more teachers would have to be trained, overlooking the possibility that this would not be feasible on quantitative and qualitative grounds. Only in wartime, or in the face of other societal catastrophes, is the relationship between the phrasing of the goals and its bearing on resources quickly confronted and altered.

In relation to any desirable goal, the definition of an appropriate resource is societally determined and, thus, will vary as a function of societal changes. So, for example, up until the early 1960s college and high school students were no more than that—students. Their role was to conform to and absorb the values and contents of the school's curriculum. Their place was in the classroom. They were a *future* resource, and schooling was a way of developing that resource for use at a later time. But the societal changes that surfaced in the 1960s changed that view of students, and they came to be seen, and to see themselves, as possessing resources that could be applied to current social problems; for example, tutoring disadvantaged children and developing recreational and summer educational programs for them, as well as participating in therapeutic programs for various institutionalized populations. If this redefinition of college and high school students as resources was not always greeted with enthusiasm and acceptance, the evidence that the students were a valuable resource is very impressive (see reviews in Zax and Specter, 1974; Cowen and others, 1975; Rappaport, 1977). No less impressive are the findings of research studies in the consequences of redefining parents of retarded children as resources in the training of their children (for example, see Baker and others, 1972, 1973; Baker, 1977; Heifetz, 1976).

Another example from the 1960s is contained in the idea that people who were to be affected by the policies and actions of agencies should play a role in the formulation of those policies. Support for this idea, which became incorporated in legislation, was powered by ethical, moral, constitutional, and political considerations, but implicit (and, frequently, explicit) in it was the belief that people had resources to contribute in the form of information, new ideas, and organizing talents. They were not to be considered passive, dutiful, respectful receptacles of the ideas of others. They had "something" to contribute independent of any abstract right to do so. The formulation and implementation of policies were too important to be left to the professionals, the experts. The "nonexperts" were not without relevant resources; that is, they had something valuable to contribute. Indeed, the simmering and sometimes seething rebellion on the part of the public to the *noblesse oblige* stance of professionals has to be seen in part as an effort to redefine what a resource is. Needless to say, this effort, despite legislative support, has encountered strong resistance. It would be strange if it were otherwise, because what is at issue is not only how one defines people as resources but also how they can be productively utilized.

Still another example from recent years is the emergence of the self-help movement. Here, too, the emergence of this movement has diverse sources reflecting widespread societal changes, but certainly one of its roots is the belief people have more resources to help themselves and each other than they have been taught. One might say that basic to the self-help movement is the need to get people to redefine themselves as resources, thereby being better able to use the resources of others. And the movement is not understandable unless it is seen as a reaction to the perception that the customary, institutionalized ways by which helping services of almost all kinds are rendered have two characteristics: They make people unduly dependent on these services, and they are constantly and unsuccessfully coping with limited resources.

It needs to be noted that one of the stimuli to the self-help movement came from experiences in our foreign aid programs. Initially, the phrasing of the goals of these programs determined the kinds of resources that would be needed, and they were strikingly similar to the kinds of resources we use in our own society. Briefly, our vision for underdeveloped countries was to get them started on the road to industrialization and big technology, for example, steel mills, factories, complex farm equipment. That our vision was, so to speak, "bought" by leaders of these countries says more about the role of experts and political power than it does about anything else. The resources we made available, far from being syntonic with the resources of these people, frequently had adverse consequences. Schumacher (1973), whose book *Small Is Beautiful: Economics as if People Mattered* continues to have an impact on people's thinking about the definition and use of human and material resources, was one of the first people to see the self-defeating nature of foreign aid programs. Let us listen to a succinct account of his ideas and actions as reported in the *New York Times* (October 26, 1975, p. F5):

> Because of plentiful fossil fuels and an abundance of labor willing to do mindless work without complaining "We've created a technology of superhuman size," he explained.
>
> Mass production units, operated by managers and engineers seeking economies of scale, have been situated near large population centers, thereby causing migration from the countryside, the depopulation of rural areas and unemployment and overcrowding in the cities.
>
> "Big technology has also been unkind to nature," Dr. Schumacher went on. Its massive energy requirements exhaust the world's resources while its reliance on machines reduces "the skillful, productive work of human hands."
>
> None of this implies that technology is a bad thing, Dr. Schumacher is quick to point out, but it has taken a wrong turn. Now that the cheap fuel and labor that made bigness possible are vanishing, it is time to create a new kind of technology on a smaller, more human scale. . . .
>
> Dr. Schumacher first conceived of the notion of an "intermediate technology"—on a level between the hoe and the tractor, as he puts it—as a solution to the problems of unbalanced growth in the developing countries. He achieved the insight twenty years ago while serving as economic adviser to the Prime Minister of Burma, where he observed a rich culture that was based neither on heavy industrialization nor on high consumption rates.
>
> It was in Burma, too, that he discovered Gandhi, whom he has called "the greatest economist of the twentieth century," for his recognition that development must be based on simple technology in the hands of the people of the villages. . . .
>
> Following Gandhi's lead, Dr. Schumacher's essential idea was to encourage the establishment of miniplants in rural areas, and to utilize local resources in producing the basic necessities of life. ("All you need is simple materials," he insists. "The Taj Mahal wasn't built with Portland cement.")
>
> To accomplish this end, Dr. Schumacher set up the Intermediate Technology Development Group in London ten years ago. Today the pri-

vate, nonprofit corporation and its three subsidiaries compile and make available inventories of existing low-cost, labor-intensive technologies; develop such equipment when it does not exist; and publish manuals on how to do everything from building a small foundry, to setting up a bookkeeping system for farm cooperatives and to designing simple farm machinery or hospital equipment that can be produced locally for a fraction of the cost of more sophisticated imports.

The group has helped Sri Lanka locate small-scale sugar-refining equipment, so the industry could be distributed throughout the island. It has enabled the Sudanese to stop importing boats from Italy by building their own ferrocement craft on the banks of the Nile. It has found miniturbines for Pakistan, to harness the power of 1,000 small streams pouring out of the Himalayas.

Most importantly, the group has helped establish similar organizations in a number of poor countries, including India, Pakistan, Ghana, and Nigeria, to pursue the search for cheap, homegrown answers to development problems. "Extreme poverty isn't caused by a lack of money or hardware," argues Dr. Schumacher. "It's mental. It must be overcome by education, organization and discipline."

Today, after years of funding massive, capital-intensive projects, international development experts are beginning to share this perception. It is now generally recognized, as Edgar Owens, director of rural development for the United States Agency for International Development noted at the Houston conference, that "there is an economic justification for small producers." "We now know that a two-acre farm can be more efficient than a very large farm in a developing country, and that a small enterprise can be more productive than an assembly-line factory. And the techniques used will be the same ones Dr. Schumacher has been talking about."

That people in developing countries have resources, that they are capable of helping themselves and each other, that they do not have to become unduly dependent on or prisoners of big technology, that they cannot be regarded as primitive ciphers waiting eagerly to be told what is good for them—these lessons derived from foreign aid programs were seen to be applicable to our own society, and they informed the self-help movement. If people take pride in the fact that ours is a "developed" society, there are other people who look with ambivalence on the price they pay for having to deal with or work in big, impersonal organizations (private and public) on whom they have become dependent and toward whom they feel impotent to exert any influence. The very label *self-help* conveys clearly the intended message: People have the resources to develop their capabilities to become more differentiated and adequate, and this can and should happen in mutual ways with other individuals, a process or dynamic that increases the resources available to all. There is, of course, nothing new in the philosophy and procedural rationale of the self-help movement. They are centuries, if not millennia, old. What is noteworthy about the movement today are the myriad ways and places in which it is being articulated and implemented, and the centrality of its concern for redefining human resources.

It is a risky business to predict how people half a century from now will describe and understand our present era. Such predictions, inevitably perhaps, bear the stamp of thinking characteristic of our own day, and there is every assurance that that stamp will be different, in whole or in part, than that which future historians will put on it. This is particularly the case when the predictions are specific. There is one general prediction we would make: One of the ways that future historians will describe and understand our era is in terms of an emerging sensitivity to the possibility that human and material resources are not limitless, that traditional conceptions of resources began to be challenged, and yet the weight of tradition permitted us only a glimpse of the problem and its dimensions. The outcroppings of social change are springing up in the form of new ideas and new types of relationships reflecting, on the one hand, a disillusionment with conventional means of providing human services, and, on the other hand, a willingness to break out of imprisoning categories of thinking. But one should never underestimate the weight of tradition and the power residing in its institutionalized forms.

Take, for example, the changes that have occurred in the field of nursing and the obstacles those changes are encountering. It is a fact (not bruited about) that nursing has declared its independence of physicians. It is one of those outcroppings that does not receive recognition. The declaration has many sources, and there can be no doubt that autonomy, power, and professionalism are among them. But what can be too easily overlooked is that behind these sources, antedating them, were conflicting views of nurses as resources for the care of sick people. The popular view was, and physicians did nothing to challenge it, that nurses were like pharmacists: They did what physicians told them to do and there was (and should be) little or no room for independent judgment. Nurses, of course, saw it quite differently. They saw physicians as people who visited their patients for a few minutes and then left the nurses to cope with patients for the rest of the day. More to the point, nurses saw themselves as coping with problems that required knowledge and independent judgment, without which the health of patients would be endangered. And few nurses did not feel that the resources of nurses frequently compensated for the deficiency of physicians. From the standpoint of nurses, they not only possessed and utilized resources that were not given recognition but also, and more significant for our present purposes, they could increase the resources available for the care of patients if the resources of nurses could be independently developed and applied. The supply of nurses was limited, needs seemed limitless, and one way to deal with the problem was to redefine nurses as a resource.

Following World War II, and probably as a result of nurses' experiences in the war, the process of redefinition began and, as physicians will attest, hospitals have not been the same since.[1] In recent years, the logic of that redefinition has been pursued further, and we now find leaders in nursing education advocating the training of nurses for private practice. Here again the argument is based, conceptually at least, on the recognition of limited resources. That great sage, Woody Allen, once said, "Not only is God dead, but try getting a plumber on Sunday!" What the nursing educators are saying is that people have health needs that can and should be met in the home but are not because there are not enough physicians who, in any case, are as available as Woody Allen's plumbers. There are needs, these educators contend, that nurses are capable of learning to deal with in the home if we redefine nurses as resources. Physicians, of course, are aghast at any such development and are as strongly opposed as nurses are in favor to including nurses as health

[1]Three or more decades ago, there was little ambiguity about who ran hospitals. With the subsequent changes in nurses' definition of themselves have come changes in their administrative roles, participation in policy and decision making, and autonomy, with the result that, today, nurses and physicians experience the hospital and each other in ways that "old-timers" characterize as revolutionary. And revolutions are stormy. The changes in the nurse-physician relationship must, of course, be seen in the context of other changes that have occurred in hospitals; for example, the professionalization of hospital administration and the emergence of the nonphysician hospital administrator.

providers in the proposed National Health Insurance, because if nurses are given such status they would be eligible for direct government payment for services, ensuring their independence from physicians.

The process of redefining resources is always a complicated, controversial social process not only because it threatens the customary boundaries, status, and prerogatives of guilds, or because there are conflicting opinions about the scope and substance of the redefinition, but also because the pressure powered by societal recognition that needs far outstrip resources requires that some change take place. What frequently happens is that, as the controversy heats up, as the protagonists hurl invectives at each other, and as different compromises are offered and debated, the fact that resources are limited tends to be obscured. Very often the compromises arrived at are presented as "solutions," and it is not until after the compromises are implemented that people become aware that the disparity between needs and resources had not been realistically posed or confronted. And, it must be noted, there are times when those participating in the process of influencing policy are quite aware of the disparity but for reasons of strategy (political or professional) choose not to emphasize it.

Obstacles to the Recognition of Limited Resources

Of all the obstacles to the recognition of limited resources, none is more powerful than "great expectations." In countless ways, both in the past and present, we have been taught that our society can do anything it decides to do. This has been a land of opportunity. Our streets may not have been paved with gold but we had all the resources for which one could wish or need. We were a divinely favored land unencumbered by the stifling, oppressive traditions of the rest of the world. And we had boundless resources that only required ingenuity and hard work to develop and to be made available to everyone. From the standpoint of individuals, the only restriction on their partaking of the good life was the strength of their motivation to better themselves. There was enough of everything to go around; that was and would never be a problem. And, if some people got less than others, it said more about their lack of ambition, or the impersonal workings of Lady Luck, than it did about how much there was to go around. There could be doubt about the fate of individuals to get what they wanted but not about the fate of the larger society. It was onward and upward, because there were no limits to what we possessed. We were a nation of individuals, and the more rugged we were the better. Individuals should look to their resources and not depend on those of others. And individualism was so important that the most healthy thing a government could do was to stay out of the lives of people. We had a supply and demand market economy—the most thriving the world had seen—and only cynics or fools could doubt that supply could keep up with demand. "A chicken in every pot and a car in every garage"—that was only a small sample of all that people could expect. To expect less was simply to misunderstand what had made the country great and would make it even greater.

Rhetoric alone cannot explain the hold of great expectations on the minds of people, nor can any concept of indoctrination. The fact is that there were kernels of truth in the rhetoric. Comparatively speaking, this country did seem to have boundless resources as well as opportunities "to better oneself." Individual freedoms existed (not for blacks, of course), and it did not take long before education was available to all. The standard of living rose steadily, and scientific and technological advances provided a basis for the belief that our society could (and would) make a heaven on earth or a reasonable facsimile thereof. The inevitability of progress and the belief in endless growth were regarded as facts and not the stuff of fantasy. The inscription on the Statue of Liberty was both fact and rhetoric. If the rhetoric was a kind of hard sell, there was, nevertheless, something of value to sell. Not everyone bought the rhetoric, least of all Henry Adams ([1906] 1974) who questioned the belief in progress as well as the identity between quantity and quality, and who was prescient about the consequences of the twin evils of rootlessness and materialism. One of those rare books that is as illuminating of a society as it is of the writer is *The Education of Henry Adams*. It is history, autobiography, social commentary, and foreboding prediction. What comes through in that book is the inexorable hold that the ideas of growth, expansionism, and progress had on nineteenth-century America. Limitless growth could be counted on as a fact. Even Henry Adams—pessimistic, dysphoric, questioning, and questing soul that he was, gripped and disheartened by his view of a future soulless society—had no doubt about limitless resources. One might say that it was the boundless riches of the country that Adams saw as a contributing factor in leading the society down wrong paths.

We live each day as if we are immortal. The way we structure our days, the phenomenological substance of our experience, are based on the unverbalized assumption that there will be a tomorrow, an infinite number of tomorrows, and no death. The fact of our mortality holds too much terror to permit us to confront its implications for today and the finite tomorrows (Becker, 1973). Consequently, when circumstances remind us that what we believe is a fact is instead a fiction, the forces of denial and avoidance assert themselves, and everything in us wants to be allied with these forces. The strength of these internal obstacles to perceiving reality has to be seen in relation to the countless external reminders that we are mortal. Analogously, when a society has been reared, so to speak, to believe in the existence of limitless resources and growth, it will experience powerful obstacles to altering its treasured assumptions. The power of these assumptions is not understandable only in terms of an individual psychology (just as the denial of death is not comprehensible only in terms of the individual psyche). The belief in limitless resources has been institutionalized in the nature, structure, and future thrust of our economy and political institutions. It is part of an outlook that has suffused almost every aspect of our society's functioning. It is not hyperbole to say that the possibility that limitless resources is a fiction strikes terror in the minds of individuals and those responsible for institutional policy and continuity. After all, if it is a fiction, it will require a radical redefinition of purpose and direction.

In addition to outright denial rooted in our social history, there is the reaction that accepts the possibility of limited resources but considers it dramatically overdrawn. With some people who hold this view, it turns out that they strongly believe that science and technology will somehow manage to come up with discoveries that will obviate any need for radical redefinition of resources and social outlook, much as in the song from World War II: "We did it before, and we can do it again." But when these people talk about resources they obviously mean material resources. It does not occur to them that human resources may be no less limited than material ones—that for the major social problems with which our society is wrestling, defined as they are and dictating the human resources they would require, there are qualitative and quantitative resource limitations. In fact, in today's discussions about resources the emphasis is almost exclusively on natural or material resources. We hear a great deal about preserving the environment, learning how to use natural resources more efficiently, and giving up our habits of wasting these resources. So we are (rightly) bombarded with pleas and plans for the efficient use of energy. In regard to the efficient uses of human resources, discussion tends to be scanty and hortatory. There is recognition that whatever we do or should do in regard to natural resources has obvious implications for the quantity and quality of human resources: availability, shifts from one work sector to another, and, fatefully, the degree to which funding of social programs is effected. But that recognition has not led, as it has in the case of material resources, to creative, bold thinking, let alone to any change in public policy.

We have long prided ourselves on being a highly sophisticated, technological society capable of producing products efficiently and in great quantities. When Henry Ford set up his assembly line, it was regarded as quintessentially American in its level of efficiency. Today we know that the assembly line was not all that efficient in terms of its effect on the physical and human environment and in its bedrock belief that the future was a carbon copy of a present in which the supply of oil was limitless and cheap. If that lesson has been learned, it is one that needs to be learned again and again, and applied no less to human as well as to material resources.

It is by no means easy to explain why it has been so difficult to confront the possibility that human resources are limited in the ways natural resources are. Put in another way, faced with mammoth social problems, why are we unable to entertain the possibility that one of the many sources of difficulty in coping with these problems is in restrictions in the quantity and quality of available human resources?[2] When we talk about natural resources, we are referring to

[2]This question is relevant to any industrial or would-be industrial society regardless of whether it is considered capitalist, socialist, or mixed, developed, or underdeveloped. What has powered political revolutions in modern times is the promise that they will free and alter human resources to eradicate, once and for all, persistent social problems. It has not worked out that way.

concrete, measurable things the characteristics of which we can study, manipulate, and even drastically transform. More than that, we can combine resources. We can transform and combine them in ways nature cannot. We can, for example, by a process of either splitting or imploding atoms create vast amounts of energy. All of this is obvious enough, but it is not explainable by technology. If one had to pinpoint the decisive factor, it would be that part of the traditions of science that says, "Seek knowledge, never let your imagination rest, try anything that gives promise of illuminating the nature of our world, do not take anything for granted, especially those cautions that say that something cannot be done or will not work." Among scientists, as among other groups, there are great differences in imagination, the capacity to combine ideas and things and to come up with something new.

If you show a random sample of the population a pencil and ask these people what it is, we would have no doubt how many "right" answers there would be. If now you were to show them a pencil and ask about all the different uses to which it could be put, we would find a small number of people who could come up with scores of ways for which the thing we call a *pencil* could be utilized. Most people are so tied to the familiar and concrete that when they are asked to perceive the familiar differently, to redefine it, they are unable to do so. It is our impression that people have less difficulty in altering their thinking in regard to things as resources than to people as resources. Whether or not this is the case is not decisive. The fact is that when it comes to thinking about people as resources in regard to major social problems, "imagination" seems remarkably absent, with two results: Not only is the possibility of limited resources diverted from recognition but also, and of more immediate import, the extent of the limitation is enormously increased. But here too we run the risk of trivializing the issue by explaining it in terms of variations among human psyches. The influence of culture, social structure, and social history are always omnipresent. For example, we applaud scientists who can "dream up" new combinations of things and forces, especially if these combinations will provide society with what it wants. We have always been ambivalent about people who are "playing around" with problems of no immediate practical import. We have never been ambivalent about the "practical" scientist and inventor. We respect imagination in the service of coping with "real" problems. But when it comes to dreaming up new ways of defining people as resources, new ways by which heretofore unused human resources can be applied to major social problems, our track record is poor. More correctly, our record is poor when attempts to implement these new ways are made. The obstacles reside not only in the difficulty of redefining human resources and dreaming up new combinations among people that will dilute the consequences of limited resources but also in the threat that poses to the established order (as in our example of nurses and physicians). Oil is more than oil, in the sense that the human mind was given free play by society to figure out the different uses to which it could be put and the different ways it could be transformed. And so we have a mammoth petrochemical industry that transforms oil into myriad products. But that kind of "figuring out" runs a mined obstacle course when the issue is how to define and transform human resources. Transforming oil gores the oxen of few people; transforming human resources gores the oxen of many people. The differences between the two types of transformation are noticeably decreased during periods of crisis.

There is another obstacle, no less powerful for its subtleness, that also has its roots in our culture. Up to this point, we have been talking about people whose roles make them influential in the definition of social problems and, therefore, in defining the nature of available resources. But what about people generally? Let us put the question more concretely: Why did it take so long for nurses to see themselves as more capable and differentiated than society generally saw them? Why did it take so long to redefine themselves as resources now and in the future? For that matter, why did it take so long for women generally to liberate themselves from the narrow confines assigned to them by society? We ask these questions not because we are prepared to answer them (that would take at least one good-sized volume) but because they are suggestive of the rigid way in which people are "slotted"; *more important for our present purposes, they suggest that people come to accept society's narrow definitions of them as resources.* It is understandable that if you enter roles in which by tradition and training your functions are clearly defined, and often these definitions have a legislative and judicial basis, the tendency is to believe that you are not capable of going beyond the stated boundaries. (Of all the horrors accompanying the institution of slavery, none rivals the acceptance of inferiority, the sense that one is unworthy or incapable.) Indeed, when one studies training programs of all sorts, one is struck by the effort to define rigidly what students can do and, by implication, what they are incapable of doing. And when one adds to this the obvious fact that as a society we are in our working and social lives very sensitive to the implications of differences in status, and the consequences of going beyond one's assigned role, it should occasion no surprise if most people accept society's view of them. This is not to say that most people passively accept society's view, because fantasy and reality so often stimulate us to think of ourselves as more capable and differentiated than our existence suggests. But between these thoughts and action is a chasm too intimidating for most people, and they retreat. It is safer to believe that one is incapable of managing the feat. The obstacles to acting on these thoughts are both external and internal. The obstacles are real.

It could be argued that a great deal of public attention has been given to the nature of human resources—witness the scores of studies of and programs for manpower development and witness how no self-respecting city or federal department would be without a department of human resources. Of the different factors behind these developments, three must be mentioned. The first is the recognition that a lot of people are not receiving the quantity and quality of services public policy says they should receive. The second is that more resources are needed, and by resources is meant additional money to hire more personnel. The third factor, and the most fateful, is the belief that a major obstacle to providing more services is inefficient and uncoordinated modes of "delivering." The popularity of the phrase "delivery of services" well reflects an engineering way of thinking: to put the pieces together in a way that maximizes the smooth flow of services and ensures that each part will be used efficiently and will facilitate the efficient functioning of all other parts and that resource waste will be drastically reduced. Order will replace diffuseness of effort, cooperation will dominate competitiveness, and optimization of use of existing resources will give us a "bigger bang for our buck."

From one standpoint, this concern with inefficient use of existing resources is undeniably valid, especially as one tries to comprehend the relationships, or lack of them, among the myriad agencies (voluntary and public) in human services. Regardless of people's social class or ethnic or racial background, they share a conception of the bureaucracy in human services as proliferating, bewildering, unpredictable, and seemingly mercurial. In the mass media as well as in daily social conversation (and, of course, in humor), stories abound with the irrationalities of "rational" bureaucracy. As someone once said, "It is wrong to say that the left hand does not know what the right hand is doing because that metaphor implies a central nervous system and a recognizable body. The point people are really trying to make is that they feel they are in a mammoth, disorganized parts warehouse totally beyond comprehension. It looks like a warehouse, each part has a recognizable form, but what each part is for and how it relates to the others is beyond our ken." One can, of course, show people administrative charts indicating the function of each part of the bureaucracy by a label, and then, with connecting lines and arrows, one can picture how the parts relate to each other, but in the phenomenology of those who have actual commerce with bureaucracy the rationality of the administrative chart is absent. This sense of being like a snowflake in a storm is by no means peculiar to the outsider dealing with the insiders, as the accounts of Blatt (1970), Fill (1974), and Wildavsky and Pressman (1973) painfully indicate. (The novels of Franz Kafka decades ago were literary harbingers of the contemporary scene.)

It is too easy to make public bureaucracy the scapegoat. When one turns to voluntary agencies in human services, the situation is not much different. An unpublished study by London (1977) is instructive in this respect. Her interest was in the number of and interrelationships among agencies serving mentally retarded individuals. In an area containing about a quarter of a million people, London found twenty agencies and programs providing some sort of explicit service. In each of these agencies, she interviewed an administrator in relation to four questions: what services were they rendering, how well informed were they about other services and programs, how much cooperation and sharing of information and staff existed among these agencies, and what was the quality of agency interrelationships? The results were staggeringly discouraging. Here are some of the clearest findings:

1. Less than a handful of these agencies had any kind of meaningful relationship to the state department of mental retardation

and its satellite offices, programs, and settings. And those agencies had surprisingly little knowledge of the nature and scope of the state's programs, resources, and responsibilities. One could, of course, look at that finding in another way: The state department did not seem to have taken the initiative to establish some kind of cooperative arrangement between it and the agencies.

2. Not one community agency had any real knowledge about more than three or four other community agencies, and some of that knowledge was either obsolete or wrong. Some community agencies, amazingly, had no real knowledge of *any* other community agency or program.

3. Cooperation of any kind among agencies was, for all practical purposes, nonexistent. This was also true for the relationship between school system personnel and programs, on the one hand, and community agencies, on the other hand.

4. Agencies tended to be very critical of each other.

5. Every agency bemoaned the lack of cooperation.

6. Every agency uttered the universal complaint. They did not have the resources either to meet the demands made of them or to give service according to the highest qualitative standards.

It would be illegitimate to come to any conclusions about the quality of services and the programs. That was not the point of London's study. The major significance of her findings is the picture we get of fragmentation, unrelatedness, and ignorance of existing community services.

The response to the perception of bewildering complexity and of rigid boundaries within and among agencies (public and voluntary) has taken two major forms: administrative reorganization and legislation intended to facilitate, and sometimes to require, a coordinated network of relationships. It would be hyperbole to say that these are "solutions" by fiat, although the element of "Thou shalt coordinate and cooperate" is there. But it is not hyperbole to say that neither of these forms address some crucial questions: "What is the size of discrepancy between asserted goals and available resources? Do we have to redefine our conception of resources? What are the incentives that would begin to induce agencies to use each other's resources not only to avoid waste and duplication but also to enlarge the horizons, experience, and skills of their person-nel? Why should agencies used to protecting their autonomy, used to scrambling competitively to sustain and enhance their resources at the expense of other agencies, used to emphasizing their differ-ences with rather than their similarities to other agencies change their accustomed stance and seriously try to become part of a 'two-way street' type of network?"

The cogency of these questions is not on a theoretical plane—they are not questions dreamed up in an armchair or the outcroppings of utopian schemes—but stem directly from the fail-ures of corrective efforts. And behind these fruitless efforts that confuse the rationality of administrative charts with the culture of agencies and their traditional perceptions of each other is the inabil-ity to confront implications of the fact of limited resources. More correctly, these efforts are not based on an examination of how we have come to define human resources the way we do and how those definitions illuminate the obstacles to desired change. The obstacles at their roots are not philosophical or moral or even political (al-though their consequences are) but are in some basic categories of our thinking that are deeply embedded in us to such an extent that we cannot see that what we consider "natural, right, and proper" may be self-defeating. As we indicated earlier, once the nature of these obstacles is comprehended, however dimly, and the process of redefinition of human resources begins, the objections have very much of a philosophical, moral, and political cast. Let us illustrate this point by again looking at the effort to change school-community relationships.

Until the 1960s, schools were walled enclaves under the direction of teachers and administrators. The legal control was vested in a board of education, but for all practical purposes what went on in schools was determined by educators. This seemed "natural, right, and proper" both to the educators and the com-munity. If there has always been an undercurrent of tension and conflict between the professionals and the community, it was muted and rarely surfaced. Then came the post-World War II population explosion and, as we indicated earlier, the "solution" to the problem was put in terms of training more teachers. The tradi-tional nature of the school-community relationship was not ques-tioned. But in the late 1950s and picking up a head of steam during the 1960s several developments began that called that relationship into question.

Initially, it was the teachers (like the nurses) who came to redefine themselves as resources, as people who had something to contribute to educational policy making, quite in contrast to their accustomed "hat-in-hand" passivity toward the educational administrator and board of education. Although it is correct to see the rise of teacher unions in terms of changing power relationships, that view should not obscure the fact that teachers first had to redefine themselves as resources who had something to contribute to decisions affecting the substance and process of education. And in those earlier days teachers sought and received community support against boards of education and public officials who looked on teacher unions as a threat to their accustomed prerogatives.

As the sizzling 1960s generated heat in the cauldron of the civil rights movement, racial conflict, the War on Poverty with its theme of community participation, and rebellious youth, the redefinition process became more general, aided by legislation. Parents and other community groups now saw themselves as having something to contribute to the educational process; that is, they no longer were content to be just parents on the receiving end of the educator's thinking and decisions. And, especially in our high schools, students were adopting precisely the same stance. Students said they were more than students, more than receptacles into which information is poured. They had experiences and perceptions that should, had to, inform decisions that affected their lives. Here, too, one can see the changing roles of students and community as a struggle for power, as indeed it was (and is). Nevertheless, these developments could not have taken place if they were not founded on a redefinition of human resources. The struggle for power was a struggle to legitimate these new definitions.

Needless to say, these new definitions continue to meet serious objections on philosophical, moral, and political grounds. But during the entire controversy one crucial question never was clearly raised: "Given the stated goals of the educational process and the resources that would be required to meet them, what further redefinitions of resources would be necessary to reduce the gulf between goals and existing resources?" The fact is that neither teachers, students, nor community groups could entertain the possibility that, despite their redefinition of themselves as resources, they were still left with the consequences of limited resources. Indeed, the consequences were exacerbated by the rising expectations their redefinitions helped stimulate.

The Popularity of the Network Concept

One of the ways in which issues of human resources, bigness and bureaucracy, coordination of services, inefficiency, and duplication has been formulated is from the standpoint of the concept of networks. It is not surprising that the concept of networks has gained popularity both in technical literature and general parlance. Precisely because it is a concept concerned with the extent, substance, and form of human relationships in a world in which everybody (and everything) seems interrelated, actually or potentially, it seemed to have the potential for a better understanding and resolution of the thorny problems of improving resource utilization, intra- and interagency coordination, and information sharing. In a world increasingly sensitive to and cynical about the barriers to relationships and information, the concept sounded an optimistic note, if only because it might provide new bases for ameliorative action. The concept accented an obvious feature of contemporary life, paying attention to and contrasting the different features and consequences of formal and informal networks. It is obvious enough that everyone belongs to a variety of networks and that experience in them is not of a piece. The attractiveness of the network concept resides in the sharp contrasts it suggested between the quality of experience in formal and informal networks.

The very distinction between formal and informal networks suggests what many people believe: The basis, quality, productiveness, and personal satisfactions experienced in networks within formal organizations tend to compare unfavorably with what we experience in our informal, voluntary networks. The informal network is perceived as being based on some sort of mutual, voluntary exchange of resources, information, and shared values—a kind of willing "giving and getting" that may not run a smooth course but that the parties strive to maintain. The formal network (such as most people are part of in their work setting) is perceived as not being voluntary and suffused with competitiveness and a "dog eat dog" ambience.[3] If there is an element of exaggeration in people's perceptions of formal and informal networks, it is not of a degree that invalidates the contrast. It is a contrast accepted by people, having almost the status of a cliché. And the popularity in recent decades of the concept of networks is in large part accounted for by the pithy way it sums up what people know, believe, and hope.

At the same time that the concept and theory of networks began to become popular, so did systems theory. Far from being antithetical to each other, the two have many points of overlap. And yet systems theory has never captured the minds of people as the concept of networks has. There are several reasons for this, but the one we would stress here is that, whereas systems theory tends to center on the structure and function of interrelationships within and among large *entities* (sometimes including the entire earth and biosphere), the network concept tends to emphasize *individuals*. Systems theory has been applied to the structure and functions of large governmental and private organizations in an effort to raise efficiency and productivity, but it is precisely because it is not concerned, except in indirect ways, with individuals that it is viewed in some quarters with scepticism and even hostility. The word *system*, unlike the word *network*, has come to have pejorative connotations, engendering as it does imagery about bloodless planning that will make large, bureaucratic, impersonal organizations even more so. Both system and network theories speak to thorny issues in contemporary society, and, if the latter more than the former seems to have caught people's imagination, this says less about the validity of either than it does about people's perception of themselves in mass society.

When we turn to the uses and meanings the network concept has gained in practice, the picture is both heartening and disheartening, confused and clear. Take, for example, how the concept is

---

[3]Formal settings, of course, always spawn informal networks that serve numerous purposes; for example, as a subversive counterpoint to the formal network or as a vehicle through which "things get done." Just as in a formal setting one must distinguish between formal and informal power, one must also distinguish between its formal and informal networks. Far more often than not, the informal network in a formal setting sees itself, and is seen by others, as in conflict or at variance with the procedures and goals of the formal network. As a result, these informal networks remain small, encapsulated, and vulnerable. Formal networks in formal settings are allergic to informality.

employed in governmental policy and regulations. There is no doubt that its popularity in government stems from an awareness of (and public clamor about) interagency conflicts about turf and resources, scores of similar programs scattered among scores of agencies, astounding lack of knowledge by one agency about other agencies seemingly having programmatic communalities, and, fatefully, the feeling of frustration from past failures to change this state of affairs. These past failures had at least one characteristic in common: They were reorganizational schemes, centrally planned and directed, possessed of the superficial rationality conveyed visually in administrative charts, and, far from having any new incentives that would spur the reorganized parts to relate more effectively with each other, they tended to have the opposite effect of creating a new stage for conflict and controversy. And frequently the argument was made that, although the new reorganizational scheme might initially require additional resources, in the long run the reduction in resource waste would more than compensate for the increase, and there would be, of course, a vast improvement in the services rendered to the public. The results of all of these past efforts have been such as to make policy makers gun-shy about any new efforts, and, just as some people have said that New York City is unmanageable, there are those who feel the same way about the federal bureaucracy. Nevertheless, committees, commissions, and task forces are appointed with monotonous regularity to look into new ways of using governmental resources to provide better public services.

Sarason recently served temporarily on a task force in the U.S. Department of Health, Education, and Welfare to review and make recommendations about how to improve the dissemination of information and materials in the field of education. It turned out, not surprisingly, that literally scores of different parts of this galaxy-sized department were disseminating educational materials of diverse kinds, and one needed a score card just to keep the names and functions of these parts straight. That score card did not exist. The point of this experience is not in the degree of diffuseness of the dissemination function but in the total absence of incentives that would make it "profitable" for these parts to form a mutually beneficial network among themselves. As we shall be stressing throughout this book, the act of cooperation, of exchanging resources, can only take place (or be sustained) where participants perceive the possibility of "giving and getting." It cannot take place by fiat or high-sounding rhetoric.

What, then, is the basis for the assertion that network concepts are frequently employed in governmental policy and regulations? The answer is that they have been incorporated in legislation affecting scores of programs to be carried out by states and municipalities in regard to housing, education, hospitals, aging, and so on. Avoidance of duplication of facilities and programs, display of cooperative arrangements, sharing of resources, decentralization and regionalization of planning and control, increased diversification and representation of community groups in policy and planning—these are some of the ways by which new networks of association are to be forged with the aims of more efficient use of resources and providing more and better services. And, if these aims seem indirectly related to network concepts, one has only to read administrative guidelines, speak to agency heads, and attend conferences to hear the word *network* used repeatedly to describe a desirable process and goal. One can expect to find at many of these conferences visual representations of the network of agencies that has been created. The charts are impressive and complicated. They bear resemblance to the interconnectedness of telephone networks. Unfortunately, the appearance is discrepant with the realities. Far more often than not, agencies (public and voluntary, and sometimes private) are functioning as independently as before, exchanging neither information nor resources with each other, and remarkably free from the feeling that they belong to a network. They may or may not have superficial knowledge about some of these agencies, but they do have the sense that they are increasingly controlled by federal and state policies and directives that impinge on their financial support and limit their autonomy. And, fatefully, they continue to see themselves in competition with each other. In every instance of which we have knowledge, we could not find a single instance of meaningful (let alone sustained) resource exchange.

One could sum up this state of affairs by saying that, although there is the intent in federal and state legislation to create networks to increase resource exchange and better public service, the concept of networks employed lacks substance, direction, and a methodology. How to foster resource exchange, the kinds of incentives that would stimulate such exchange, the type of leadership required and by whom, how to confront creatively the fact that resources are limited, how to broaden people's definition of themselves as resources—these questions, which should inform one's concept of exchange networks, are not even in the background. And yet each agency is poignantly aware that it does not have the resources to meet needs as the agency defines them but is unable to entertain the possibility that its resources will always be limited, and that therefore it must depart radically from accustomed ways of thinking. The concept of resource networks appeals to them—it does have the sound of virtue and common sense—but without being able to ground the context in a set of explicit values and actions appropriate to those values the concept remains on the level of rhetoric.

Let us offer an illustrative experience. A section in a federal department was created to stimulate research on and the creation of resource networks in a particular problem area. The people in the section were an unusually thoughtful group, quite aware that past efforts to create resource and informational networks in this field had at best been minimally effective and at worst had wasted a lot of money. They knew well that one of the most ambitious efforts to develop networks (described in Sarason and others, 1977, pp. 67–70) had foundered, and some of the reasons why. One of the authors of this book was asked to consult with this group about research and action strategies. His relationship to this group began to sour when he pointed out that they were trying to get people "in the field" to do what they themselves could not do, did not know how to do, in their own bailiwick. That is to say, the people in this small section were a cohesive enclave with very limited resources surrounded by and administratively related to a score or two of other sections with whom they competed for funds, recognition, and even survival. They had a sense of wariness, even beleaguerment, and were fearful that their functions would be taken over by others or simply eliminated. The fact was that some of these other sections were also interested in networks in their own ways. It was not a situation where there was no overlap in ideas, strategies, and programs. The author said to them, "You want to create resource networks among agencies in the field who are faced with the same situation your section is here. What advice do you have to offer these agencies that would aid them to extricate themselves from this state of affairs? How would you go about trying to remedy *your* situation *here*? What makes you think that people in the field will be able to do what you seem unable to do?"

The point of these questions was not "Physician, heal thyself" but rather that there was a need to clarify the relationship between one's particular concept of network and the known obstacles to a productive resource exchange network. There are many kinds of networks with differing purposes, but if resource exchange was the type of network sought then one would have to be clear as to what the obstacles were. For example, the obstacles that the development of an informational network would encounter are not the same as those of a resource exchange network. Similarly, if one wants to go the route of developing informal networks, the obstacles are not the same as when one develops a network within and among formal organizations; that is, the difference between a network of individuals and a network of organizations, between a voluntary and contractual arrangement. And, as we shall see in later chapters, the leadership or coordination function varies considerably with the purpose of different types of networks. If the concept of networks has become popular, especially in regard to human services, it is obviously not a source for unalloyed satisfaction.

In this chapter, we have stressed the popularity and ambiguity of the network concept. In the next chapter, we give several case descriptions that, among other things, implicitly or explicitly deal with the relationships between a network concept and the issue of resources, more specifically, the process of redefining resources. The purposes of these case presentations are several, but chief among them is the concrete opportunity they give us to raise questions about the meaning of networks in relation to the definition of resources. Thus far we have not attempted a definition of a resource exchange network, nor shall we until a later chapter. Definitions and typologies are not hard to come by, as our review of the literature demonstrated (Sarason and others, 1977). However, given our interest in networks *and* the issues surrounding limited resources, it seemed that more important than definitions and typologies was the need to pursue this interest from the different perspectives that case materials permit. As the next few chapters endeavor to demonstrate, the development and maintenance of a resource exchange network, however defined, is a process that encounters the consequences of some formidable traditions in our society.

In our previous book, we devoted two long chapters to a review of the theoretical and research literature on networks. One of the characteristics of that literature is the typologies proposed for distinguishing among networks. Some of these typologies have more than a surface plausibility, and their heuristic value cannot be denied. But these typologies have several limitations: They are not based on anything resembling a large number of instances; most of these instances are neither described nor understood in clinical detail; and very little is known or described about how these networks developed. Networks are not created, they exist, and what is so fascinating about them is how and on what basis they grow, are transformed, and wither. A danger in applying any typology is the tendency to emphasize differences, and in the process overlook similarities and overlappings. Similarly, we often attribute to identically labeled instances a degree of similarity that they rarely possess. So, we have talked about informal, resource exchange networks as if they were highly similar to each other, whereas in truth we cannot justify such an implication. Some of these networks are not legal entities and have no agreed-on structure, although there may be an unwritten agreement about their functioning and goals. Others may be a legal entity and therefore they may be highly similar to the first kind. But that comparison tells us little about the "appearance versus reality" issue and how to account for differences that may appear over time. If there is anything we can say about networks, it is that they are constantly changing relationships mightily influenced by dynamics from within and without. This is especially true for resource exchange networks that grow up outside of traditional institutions and that so often are efforts to supplant or compensate for the deficiencies of such institutions.

In the next chapter, we shall describe a number of instances that are heterogeneous in a number of ways but appear to have some common characteristics. Our descriptions will serve several purposes: to impress on the reader the frequency and recency of resource exchange efforts; to emphasize their heterogeneity; and, most important, to serve as a basis for raising and discussing issues that we consider crucial not only for a better understanding of resource exchange networks but also for their practical import. Our interest in resource exchange networks does not stem from theory but from a concern with problems we face daily, as individuals or a society. Most theories die either because they do not square with "data" collected to prove their validity or because initially they were conceived by people who had little firsthand experience with the social context they sought to illuminate (Sarason, 1978b). In the realm of social behavior, the latter has been a more frequent cause of death of a theory than the former. At this time, theorizing about networks in general and resource exchange networks in particular should be informed by modesty of goal and expectation. We know far too little about the realities of networks to be too respectful of our theories. Implied in that caveat is still another consideration: Resource exchange networks are galvanized by values, the shoulds and oughts of living, that have the effect of redefining the participants' perception of themselves as resources, and it is that relationship between values and redefinition that too often is ignored by theory. Theorists tend to be more comfortable with overt behavior and processes than with the internal transformations without which what we see can be misleading or incomplete. We are dealing with issues that are compounded of values and facts. The descriptions that follow are intended as ways to explore as many different facets as possible of the ways in which people are breaking out of confines of institutions, roles, and definitions by inventing new structures, new mechanisms, and new systems for empowering themselves at the same time they empower others.

A word about the detailed descriptions that follow. Initially, we resorted to paraphrase, which had the virtue of brevity and also what we can only call the defect of "coldness." That is to say, our summaries of what people reported they felt and did, and why, were valid but somehow failed to convey that sense of personal purpose and outlook, that sense of context, problem, and mission, that gives experience and action a distinctive stamp. After all, these people were not describing how to build a bridge, fix a car, or plant flowers, but rather transformations of self, others, and their human surroundings. We decided to let these people speak for themselves. For one thing, most of these materials are not easily available. For another, what will be excess for some readers will be grist for the mill of others. Finally, in subsequent chapters we will be referring to different concrete aspects of these descriptions, and, we thought, erring on the side of excess description would be more helpful to the reader than our own summaries.

3

Network Concepts
In Action:
Case Studies

A picture different from the one
painted in the previous chapter emerges when one turns away from
government and formal organizations and looks at other aspects of
our society; for example, informal and loosely constituted associations that may not even have a public name, label, or rules, although
many do. We refer in particular to a kind of "underground" in the
sense that they are explicitly a response to several perceptions: In a
mass society dominated by big government and big business, the individual counts for little; organizations that are supposed to meet
the needs of people (such as schools, social agencies, communication
media) do their job poorly either because they do not understand
how our society has changed or because their self-interest takes pre-
cedence over the needs of the people they are supposed to serve;
people must learn to rely on themselves, to form alliances among
themselves, to exchange information and resources with each other,
as much to enhance each other's options and capabilities as to protect themselves against further erosion of their values and worth;
the individual must assume responsibility for countering the forces

that make people feel lonely and apart, that constrict their understanding of their social and physical environment, that make them feel impotent.

These statements may have the ring of high-sounding rhetoric of the "for virtue and against sin" variety. The fact is, however, that in the past fifteen years such beliefs powered literally innumerable efforts of an informal kind (or of a minimally formal structure) having some or all of the characteristics of voluntary participation, some form of mutual exchange, an avoidance of hierarchy and of an exclusionary principle for participation, and a missionary zeal that frequently put the effort in an adversarial stance in relation to traditional institutions. These efforts are certainly not new in our society (we have long been a society of "joiners"), but what is distinctive about their dramatic increase in numbers is that they take place at a time of a societal malaise and change in which many people are redefining their relationship to each other and to their society, and prominent in that redefinition is the theme of people as differentiated resources. If people are seeking new roles, it is a consequence of a change in how people want to regard themselves and to be regarded by others. Whether it be in relation to the structure of marriage and the family, the experience of work, the purpose of education generally and adult education in particular, religious affiliation and experience, the quality of the environment, dietary practices, exercise, or attitudes toward experts—in these and other arenas, people are seeing themselves and traditional institutions in new ways (Sarason, 1977).

Although these new efforts or arrangements vary considerably in form, purpose, and size, one of their common characteristics is that they regard themselves as informal networks, and the word *network* is very frequently used, being part of the name or used descriptively in conversation. Precisely because these tend to be informal arrangements, developed less for public recognition and growth than for meeting the psychological and resource needs of its members, it is literally impossible to estimate how many of these informal networks exist. Interested as we have been in networks, it is not surprising that we have gained some knowledge of many of these networks that ordinarily would not receive recognition. The people who develop and participate in these networks tend not to see what they are doing as something that should be written up, which is another way of saying that people who write either do not participate in or do not have an interest in networks. On the contrary, the people who develop these networks are activists more than they are writers or conceptualizers.

For example, our previous book *Human Services and Resource Networks* (Sarason and others, 1977) was probably the first to be devoted to a description of the rationale and workings of an informal, "barter economy" type of network. That book stimulated many people to write us to say that our account was similar to what they were involved in. Ordinarily, there would be no way (certainly no easy way) to locate and study these informal networks. Nor is it possible at this time even to suggest a scheme for categorizing them. Here is a far from exhaustive list of some of the issues and themes around which these informal networks have developed:

1. Advocacy for children, the aged, and people hospitalized in state institutions
2. Environmental "watch-dogging"
3. Cooperative food purchasing
4. Informal newsletters to facilitate interconnectedness among people who may be able to help each other
5. Women helping women
6. Daycare arrangements for children
7. Facilitating self-help
8. Teachers helping teachers
9. New religion-based social and work arrangements for those disaffiliating from organized religion

In the next section, we describe several of these arrangements, less because they permit us to raise questions about their nature, structure, results, and viability than because they illustrate the perceptions that power them, perceptions that are shared by increasing numbers of people.

The Skills Exchange, A Learning Community

The Skills Exchange, A Learning Community, is a relatively new organization in Toronto. The following excerpt is from one of its handouts (1977, pp. 1–5):

Adult Education: Meeting the Challenge

The Skills Exchange of Toronto is a learning community that has been organized by people interested in creating a shared educational experience in response to the increasing need for alternative forms of continuing education for the *part-time adult learner*. This category of students figures as one of the most prevalent and most neglected student bodies in Ontario today. It is increasing at a percentage rate far exceeding that of the overall student population.

Enrollment statistics for *part-time* students in Ontario in the ten years between 1964–65 and 1974–75 show an increase of nearly 250 percent, while the population increased by only 22 percent over this period. During the same period, *full-time* student enrollment increased by only 190 percent, despite the fact that the population aged eighteen to twenty-four was increasing in that period at a rate twice as fast as that of the older generation.

As the eighteen to twenty-four age group declines relative to the older age ranges, so the ranks of the *full-time* adult student body will diminish and the ranks of the *part-time* adult student body will expand. With this increasing population of part-time students, it becomes necessary for the relatively limited number of continuing education courses to be expanded and enriched and for new alternatives to be explored. This is what the Skills Exchange of Toronto has set out to do.

The Skills Exchange is modeled after the Apple Skills Exchange, which was founded in New York in September of 1976. The Apple Exchange began with less than $1,000 capital and no more publicity than a two-page ad in the *Village Voice*, which listed the thirty-six courses available. In less than ten months, Apple was distributing 165,000 copies of its own monthly catalogue, which listed over 120 courses averaging two sections each. Student enrollment had grown to 3,000 per month.

The Toronto Skills Exchange anticipates a like response from Toronto area residents. Further, we are attempting to be sensitive to changing realities in the world of education, within the context of social environment. For example, due to a variety of reasons, there are increasing numbers of unemployed teachers in Ontario. A percentage of these, whose backgrounds and interests are in accord with the Skills Exchange's style and objectives, may very well find the opportunity to put their talent to work in this new format.

Most importantly, we seem to be approaching times of serious economic constriction, which makes the kind of high-cost, building-centered education of our current system extremely impractical. What seems to be required in future educational programming is a labor-intensive approach; that is, programs that are designed to employ large numbers of teachers to accommodate the needs of a growing student body of part-time adults, with a minimum of associated administrative and building costs.

Another dilemma in the field of adult education is the inordinately high dropout rate (61 percent). Since adult education is by and large voluntary and not compulsory, the opposite would be expected (that is, low dropout rates). What is it, then, in the present system that "turns off" the adult learner?

The context within which most adult education is offered is the most probable culprit. Most adult learners are attending night courses after having already put in a day's work. An environment that is not both comfortable and stimulating is certain to lose their interest and whatever initial commitment to learning was made. The traditional adult education environment—the classroom—happens to create just such an environment.

Length of courses is also likely a factor in the high dropout rate. The rigors and demands of academically oriented presentations within the usual academic time frame (semester, term, quarter, trimester) is bound to overburden the typical adult learner, for whom continuing education must compete with other responsibilities and priorities.

To meet the needs and demands outlined above, the Toronto Skills Exchange has begun to create a whole new educational structure, which may very well be relevant to many other levels of education. Below are listed a few aspects of the Skills Exchange that differentiate it from other types of adult education programs.

1. Classes offered through the Skills Exchange take place by and large outside of the traditional classroom environment. Classes are held in locations that are most conducive to mastering the desired subject or skill. For example, courses may be given in a writer's home, a potter's studio, a night court, an interior designer's office, and so on. The economic ramifications of this are that the Skills Exchange's budget will not be burdened with the overwhelming cost of renting or owning space, and thereby will help to maintain us in the business of providing a learning community.

2. The entire community becomes a potential for learning, exploration, and experiment at a minimal cost of time or money. Skills Exchange teachers are committed to make arrangements either through the Skills Exchange, or independently, to work with and direct students whose interests go beyond the initial introductory month.

The Skills Exchange, therefore, should not be considered just "another" adult education institution. Because of its willingness and commitment to take into account the demands of changing times and realities and create new and untried forms to meet them, the Skills Exchange approach could very well become an important model for future educational structure and innovation.

Note: The Skills Exchange of Toronto is a privately funded, nonprofit organization and is not affiliated with any other institution.

The staff of the organization consists of four individuals (there are no secretaries), including the person (Jeff Hollander) whose idea it was to begin the venture. Each is responsible for a different task: working with teachers; enrolling students; preparation and circulation of a free, eight-paged, tabloid-sized, monthly catalogue of courses with a circulation of eighty to a hundred thousand; financial matters. It is a very closely knit core group dedicated to each other and the purposes of the Skills Exchange. At the time this is being written, the breakeven point was in sight, and there had been periods when the salaries of the staff were not covered. Requests to teach come from as motley a group as one could imagine, ranging from a business executive who teaches his class in the board room to one who wishes to hold his class in his bar. The content of the courses vary from the straight academic to arts and crafts, calligraphy, drama, graphic design, mechanics, and so on. There have also been requests for the Skills Exchange to help individuals set up similar ventures in small towns in Ontario. One of the primary purposes of the Exchange is to bring the teachers into closer relationships with each other, which is behind the idea of allowing teachers to enroll free in any of the courses. Attempts are made to hold meetings with and among teachers, and, although this has met with some success, the heterogeneity of their backgrounds and interests is reported as a problem. If instructors are having problems in their teaching—and this may be known either by teachers requesting help or complaints by students—an effort is made to help them. Randomly selected students and teachers have recently been brought together to discuss their experience with the Exchange and to offer whatever advice or help they wish. Explicitly, however, the major effort is in relation to forging interrelations among teachers. However much the staff may wish to make similar efforts with students and between students as a group and teachers as a group, time is a constraint.

One of the motivations for starting the Exchange was to enlarge the core members' social network; that is, to bring them into contact with more people because they had a need to feel part of a larger network of relationships. It was also hoped that the Exchange would serve a similar purpose for teachers and students but, as we indicated, the major effort in this regard has been with the teachers. Unlike similar ventures with which the staff had experience, they had vowed not to grow much beyond where they hope to be in several months, to avoid the dilemmas of growth, bigness, and the lure of making a lot of money. They distinguish between their hopes and the realities of the social world; they know there is and will be a tension between economics and consistency with values and purposes, but they hope not to succumb. As it is presently conceived of and constituted, no one (staff or teachers) stands a remote chance of becoming affluent (some teachers are unemployed professionals on welfare).

How does the Skills Exchange illustrate our earlier discussions? For one thing, the Skills Exchange was a response to the perceived inadequacy of educational institutions to meet the needs of adult learners; that is, neither in ambience or substance were they sensitive to the needs of the adult community, and their structure and staffing incurred costs that made these institutions inflexible in responding to these needs. Second, the Skills Exchange has explicitly challenged the traditional view of resources; for example, who is "qualified" to teach and, not unimportant, who can start an educational institution? Third, the Skills Exchange takes into account the economic realities (unemployment, particularly among teachers) and seeks a way to deal with unused or underutilized talent, a way that tries synergistically to meet the needs of diverse individuals. Fourth, it attempts to avoid the dilemmas of growth; that is, to avoid becoming like those traditional settings against which the Skills Exchange is a reaction. Fifth, the venture is powered by, or seeks to be consistent with, the value of a sense of community.

In what ways is the Skills Exchange a network? What kind of network? The Skills Exchange is a "formal" organization in that it is incorporated, has paid staff (four)—one could say it is a business. But, obviously, to say that the Skills Exchange, Xerox Company, and the U.S. Department of Health, Education, and Welfare are formal organizations is not very illuminating. The Skills Exchange differs from what we ordinarily call a *formal organization* in the motivation for community on the part of its developers and in their desire to satisfy similar motivation in others. Although there is a central organizing node in this network, and direction emanates from it influencing the relationship between an individual and that node and between that individual and other individuals, there is a deliberate effort to encourage relationships and subgroupings that are little or not at all related to the central node. The emphasis on exchange—be it of the interpersonal, informational, or technical skill varieties—requires that in practice there can be no rules, roles, or constraints on when or how the exchange takes place. What is required is an agreement on values that makes exchange possible in a loose, informal network of individuals. If the Skills Exchange remains true to this goal, it will be because the central core can resist seeing the network as belonging to them or as a vehicle to enhance their power and status. Resource exchange can take place in a variety of ways among a variety of individuals, and optimization of the frequency and fruitfulness of these exchanges is lessened to the extent that efforts are made to set boundaries for the network, to formalize rules and roles, to put barriers before voluntary participation, and to put a high price on the predictability of outcomes of relationships. If there is anything that characterizes the formal organization and the types of networks that comprise it, it is in its annoyance with, resistance to, or avoidance of the unpredictable. When a new idea or possibility for change and exchange runs into a formal structure with its familiar ways of "doing things," it is running an obstacle course that usually destroys the new idea.

It was not our purpose to evaluate the Skills Exchange. That would require a special process and, as we shall be emphasizing in later chapters, one beset with some very thorny problems. The Skills Exchange may or may not be what it says it is; we do not know to what extent it is achieving its stated purposes; and although the core group sees the vehicle as a means of developing a resource and interpersonal exchange network (the word *network* crops up frequently in discussion), we do not know how many of the participants feel themselves part of such a network. Nor did we employ the Skills Exchange to contrast its structure and growth characteristics with those of other types of networks. For us, the significance of the Skills Exchange is that it is representative of countless other truly informal networks in the attitudes and expectations that power it, its redefinition of resources, its almost adversarial stance toward traditional, human services institutions, and in its goal of expanding the individual's sense of belonging and web of relationships.

We have said that there has been in recent years a dramatic increase in the number of these networks, reflecting a disenchantment with almost every major type of societal institution. A critic can validly say that we have no data to justify such a claim. Our claim is based on three grounds: the popularity of the word *network*, our experience and that of others, and (most persuasive) the thrust of legislation to foster the development of networks. Legislation is a reflection of the larger society, a reaction to what is already happening in it, as much as it is an effort to alter something about the society. It makes no difference where groups place themselves on the political spectrum, or what the age, sex, religion, or color of individuals are, the fact is that most people feel that a marked change has occurred in attitudes toward the legitimacy and sensitivity of our major social institutions. It did not begin fifteen or so years ago, but there is consensus that the social unrest that became blatant in the 1960s affected, and continues to affect, more people than ever before. Watergate was the icing on this cake of cynicism. But cynicism has been only one of the reactions to recent social history. Less obvious, because of their very nature, has been the spontaneous development of informal networks having the characteristics we described. These networks are not newsworthy, and some, in fact, avoid or do not see the need for recognition. Just as the frequency of bankruptcy is not low among formal organizations, one must expect that the same will at least hold for informal networks. However favorably one regards the rationale for these networks, it is no warrant to gloss over the gulf that exists between laudable intent and successful practice. We indicated earlier how within and among formal organizations (in government and the human services area) the popularity of the network concept too easily obscures its absence in practice. One of the aims of this book is to try to clarify the dilemmas of and obstacles to the development of networks in and outside of formal organizations.

In the previous chapter, we focused on the difficulty people have in accepting the fact of limited resources. We then went on to indicate that one of the characteristics of many informal networks is their redefinition of human resources as a way to increase existing resources for service. However, it would be erroneous to conclude that these networks are based on acceptance of the fact of limited resources. On the contrary, it is our experience that, although they are sensitive to the discrepancy between existing resources and needs and seek ways of reducing the discrepancy, there is no explicit recognition that resources are inevitably limited. We stress this point not because we have cast ourselves in the role of spoilsports or because of some quirks in our developments we became wet blankets and take easily to gloom and doom prophecy, but rather because, if one explicitly accepts the fact of limited resources, it can free one's imagination to entertain the myriad ways by which one can redefine and utilize resources. It has the immediate effect of forcing one to face the intrinsically self-defeating ways in which we conceive of human resources and the degree to which we are all victims of such conceptions. It would be surprising if it were otherwise, because in varying degrees we have, without ever thinking about it, assimilated the myth of unlimited resources (Sarason, 1972). Depending on time and circumstances, we become aware of a particular discrepancy between needs and resources and we endeavor to do something about it. But we confront the particular discrepancy not as an instance of the general axiom of limited resources but, so to speak, as an atypical departure from some imagined desirable state of affairs. It is the inability to accept the general axiom that sets constraints on how well we perceive a variety of discrepancies and deal with them concurrently in action. The acceptance of limited resources, far from being a source of dysphoria, can liberate us from the ruts of unthinking tradition. And it is that kind of liberation that not only exploits more of our capacities and interests but also expands our awareness of and knowledge of our interpersonal, social, and physical surroundings.

Uplift: What People Themselves Can Do

In 1974, a thick book titled *Uplift: What People Themselves Can Do,* by the Washington Consulting Group, was published. It contains 100 "stories" of the "most representative and successful" self-help projects chosen from almost a thousand instances of how disadvantaged groups helped themselves. Each instance in the entire sample was identified and written by someone in the community but not indigenous to the self-help effort. The preface (p. ix) states:

> The existence, let alone the success, of many such projects seems to have been largely unknown until very recently, not only to the public at large but also to people at all levels of government. What is more, there has been little communication among the self-help projects themselves, which means they have not had the opportunity to learn from one another's experience.
>
> The principal purpose of this book, therefore, is to make all segments of society aware of both the scope and success of the burgeoning self-help movement, as well as to spur the development of new self-help projects and to help bring about a dialogue among the existing ones.

And the following is from the introduction (pp. xvi–xviii):

A great many low-income and other disadvantaged people recognize the potential that self-help holds for them. And the actual number of self-help projects in existence points to a self-help movement that promises to be the basis for significant social change.

It is crucial, therefore, to make sure that this change can be brought about without destroying the essential self-help characteristics of local individual initiative and independence.

Both fostering and preserving the self-help movement are related directly to the need for increased awareness, understanding, and cooperation among the various segments of society. The people in positions to give outside assistance to self-help projects need to be aware of the self-help organizations in their community and to know what these groups are seeking to accomplish.

This also requires a new attitude on the part of the many people involved in social action who mistakenly view self-help as a process of "letting the poor fend for themselves." Self-help needs links to sophistication; it needs to be sophisticated itself.

For their part, many disadvantaged people need to learn what resources are actually available to them, as well as how to mobilize these resources and how to form effective alliances with service organizations, churches, business, and government. They also need to know more about other successful projects within the self-help movement and to develop means of sharing experience, knowledge, and ideas with those other projects—as well as with disadvantaged communities not yet active in the self-help movement. . . .

It is imperative that the self-help movement be neither organized nor wholly serviced by government or any outside organization. Self-help projects are not—and cannot be—a rigid network of identical programs imposed on or handed to the people. The worth of the projects rests in their individuality and independence and natural growth within their local communities.

Here are two typical descriptions. The first is of the Humphreys County Union for Progress Farmers Cooperative, Belzoni, Mississippi (Washington Consulting Group, 1974, pp. 4–7).

A farmers' cooperative that started in a tiny backroom office is helping rural blacks in the Mississippi delta break the chains of economic servitude that have been their lot since the Civil War.

Operating with little government aid, the Humphreys County Union for Progress and its cooperative have brought a previously unknown degree of economic security to almost a hundred farm families. They have provided the things that many Mississippi black farmers have been used to not having—credit, reasonably priced supplies and fertilizers, equipment and machinery, and a more stable market and earnings for their crops.

On the map, and in spirit, Humphreys County lies deep within the Mississippi delta, some seventy miles northwest of Jackson. Two thirds of its 14,600 residents are black and most of them live on farms or in small communities. The largest community, Belzoni, has only about 3,200 inhabitants. Agriculture is the main source of income for half of Humphreys County's people. According to the 1970 census, however, only 119 blacks are farm owners, and their land holdings average only forty to eighty acres per unit. These owners are supposedly on the top of the black economic ladder in the county, yet their median income was only $862 in 1969; a man could earn more working in the underwear factory in Belzoni or as a truck driver on a big plantation.

Twenty-five years ago, the economic opportunities for blacks in Humphreys County were even worse. In those days, soon after World War II, a number of blacks left the county to look for work in the cities, especially northern cities. But some men, such as Ernest White, remained, hanging on to the small farms they owned and struggling to keep their families together. White attempted to build up his farm, but fought against heavy odds. In 1954, at a time when many whites were still unwilling to see blacks participate in the electoral process, White registered to vote. The result was that he lost his bank credit and then had his name removed from the voter rolls. Despite these difficulties, he managed to develop his property into a well-run, 120-acre farm. But the white-controlled Humphreys County cooperative never asked him—or any other black farmer—to join.

Time passed, and conditions in Humphreys County did not improve appreciably.

So, five years ago, Ernest White and a few other black community leaders in the county decided to organize. In White's words:

"It was time to become a part of America. We wanted to have some voice in the community. We wanted to better our conditions. And by uniting together we felt like we might be able to."

Humphreys County blacks began organizing on a formal basis, with some help from the Mississippi Action for Community Education of Greenville, which helped train two fieldworkers to canvass the county and enroll members.

Some 850 members were enrolled by the end of 1969 in a new organization that became known as the Humphreys County Union for Progress (HCUP).

At the time that HCUP was organized, the black farmers in the county were having problems obtaining both farm supplies and loans. What is more, they were also being forced to pay very high prices for what supplies they did manage to get.

The members of HCUP discussed the problem at length. Ten of them, including Ernest White, met in December 1969 to discuss one possible approach: the creation of their own cooperative. They had many reservations and some fears about their business ability and lack of experience, but against those drawbacks they weighed the advantages to be gained from a collective effort that would help them acquire both economic and political power. The group sought legal assistance from the North Mississippi Rural Legal Services (funded by the Office of Economic Opportunity), and in March 1970 the cooperative was formally chartered as the Humphreys County Union for Progress Farmers Cooperative.

The cooperative began with somewhat limited resources—a $950 loan from the Greenville community group, 80 farmer members, plus an experienced fieldworker, an accountant, and an office manager. It carried on its business out of a backroom in a building rented by HCUP. Fertilizer, seed, and other supplies were kept in a member's barn.

With $450 from the first loan, the cooperative bought stock in the Mississippi Chemical Corporation of Yazoo, both to be able to purchase fertilizer and also to obtain the rebates that are part of the delta farming system—a part previously limited to whites.

Even with that small investment, the cooperative saved its members $6 a ton on ammonium nitrate, in addition to obtaining the patronage rebate. These kinds of savings were persuasive evidence. "We would go from community to community," recalls Ernest White, "and show the farmers what they could do if they united together and the savings that they could make if they combined their efforts."

The co-op had a remarkably successful first year. It handled sales of $35,000 in supplies and products to the farmers, and it ended the year with a $2,500 profit.

Determined to expand its activities, the co-op secured $20,000 from a private foundation and set about establishing its own storage and warehouse buildings, plus offices for the co-op and the Humphreys County Union for Progress. The members used $6,000 to buy a site in Belzoni, and then spent $10,000 to build a 5,000-square-foot structure for crop and fertilizer storage.

An arrangement was made whereby almost all the farmer members would keep half their rebates in the co-op to fall back on in a bad crop year. That decision paid off in 1972. With late rains and floods, the harvests of both cotton and soybeans were way below normal levels. The co-op had a paper debt of $22,000. Its fertilizer surplus provided the margin for survival. It sold $11,000 worth of fertilizer to co-ops in neighboring counties and so weathered the year with total sales of $46,518 and rebates and earnings of $5,487.

Despite the 1972 setback, the co-op's annual sales figures were good. The high point was reached in 1973, when the organization achieved a $7,100 profit on sales of $55,000. The profits, as usual, were distributed among the members, largely in patronage rebates.

Beyond the co-op's balance sheet are the individual co-op members. Consider, for example, the experience of a typical small farmer, Tommy Nalls.

A forty-year-old father of ten, Nalls has managed, thanks to the cooperative, to buy a mechanical cotton picker.

"If the cotton is just right," he says, "I can pick as much cotton in a day as we used to pick by hand in a month. My family appreciates it, too, because there's no more bending over. That's a job—bending over picking cotton."

For Farmer Nalls' account books, there are benefits, too. As he says, "I can get it much cheaper here [at the co-op]. I buy fertilizer, oil for my tractors and picker, cottonseed, and poisons.

"Fertilizer cost me $59 in the co-op, and then I get the $12 rebate. In town I would have paid $63 and no rebate."

Securely on its feet now, the co-op is branching out into other ventures. It has established a store in the predominantly black community of Louise, offering staple food items and vegetables at a five percent discount to co-op members. And it has set up a record shop in Belzoni, where young people can buy tapes and records at discount prices.

There are more ambitious plans for the future. The co-op, for example, hopes to launch a supermarket in Belzoni, and to build bulk liquid fertilizer storage facilities.

It will take time before the co-op can put together all the money it needs for those and other plans. What it has established in abundant supply now is self-assurance among its members.

And economic power has led to growing political power. The fear that made blacks take their names off the voting list twenty years ago is gone. Today, blacks are running for county and city offices, as well as voting for them.

"We haven't won," Ernest White says, "but we have a political voice now, and we expect to use it."

The second description is of Homeworkers Organized for More Employment, Orland, Maine (Washington Consulting Group, 1974, pp. 140–144).

Despite local jetports that put the area within an hour or two of most eastern cities, despite the lure of the interstate highway system's intersection-free efficiency and high-speed curves, many of Maine's summer visitors still prefer the leisurely drive up the coast along U.S. Highway 1. Following the rise and fall of the rocky landscape and maintaining a discreet distance from the sea, the coast road picks its way carefully from town to town, feeding secondary roads down to the shore as it goes.

To the summer visitor heading for Maine's stellar attraction, Acadia National Park, the highway promises the charm and beauty of northern New England, together with the temptation of those irresistible Down East antique stores, country inns, and gift shops. And to the visitor stopping in the small community of Orland, some thirty miles short of the national park, the highway offers a chance to glimpse a unique social experiment that is known as Homeworkers Organized for More Employment (H.O.M.E.).

The visitor pulling in at H.O.M.E. finds a trim collection of buildings that houses a well-stocked craft shop. He is soon inside, looking over the store's selection of quilts, toys, dried-apple dolls, and other handmade goods. Perhaps, if he has the time and curiosity, he wanders about the other buildings in the complex. A quick tour of them reveals a shoe-repair shop, a wholesale clothing operation, a pottery class, and a group of some twenty-five adults intent upon completing their high school education.

But such a tour does not reveal all the people touched by H.O.M.E.'s activities—unless it includes a trip to the austere, weatherbeaten, neighborhood farmhouses, where the rural families who make the store's crafts are working for a better life.

H.O.M.E., it turns out, is much more than a gift shop.

It was in the late 1960s that a group of Roman Catholic nuns moved to the Orland area to start their own hermitage. As they could not hope to find local work to support themselves in an area where jobs were and are in such short supply, they turned to another, novel way of supporting themselves. They arranged to do work at home for a shoe factory in Belfast, on the western shores of Penobscot Bay.

When the nuns began to receive more than enough work for themselves, they recruited additional workers from the Orland area to handle their increased workload. The program was a success, but it was not to last. The business downturn of 1970 struck throughout New England, and the Belfast shoe factory shut down.

This was a serious blow to the nuns and their helpers, but they did not give up hope. They had proved that it was possible to make money working at home. They had proved that there was an alternative to abandoning the land and looking for work in the big cities—a trend that has afflicted many areas of rural America.

The Orland community was determined to keep alive the idea of home production.

"It was like striking a match to a flammable material," recollects one of the nuns about the effect of the idea. "There was a real need in the community. We knew by the response to the home work that there was a great need of income. These people had skills and a contribution to make."

With property and a house donated by a relative of one of the nuns, the H.O.M.E. cooperative was started and incorporated in June 1970, with a charter that stated the aim of the organization: "To present an alternative to welfare living by improving the quality of life for rural families."

"We started selling a little bit of everything," says Sister Lucy, the director of H.O.M.E. "It was just a cut above a church bazaar."

That situation changed in time, though, as the store began to concentrate on its popular items and drop the others. Increasing numbers of tourists stopped off at H.O.M.E., and before long the "bazaar" image was a thing of past. In its first year of operation, the store grossed $16,000. Sales during the second year amounted to $39,000, and in the third year they topped $49,000.

In 1972, about two years after opening the store, the cooperative ventured into the wholesale clothing business, despite the fact that initially it had neither the experience nor the business knowledge to grapple with the complex marketing practices involved in such an operation. Optimism and hard work have paid off, though, for the wholesaling of women's dresses now grosses over $34,000 a year.

The Orland store proved so successful that the cooperative made efforts to expand its business by opening satellite stores elsewhere in coastal Maine. Expansion, however, resulted in a considerable increase in costs, so H.O.M.E. decided it would be wiser to close down the additional stores. Currently the group does operate one other store (in addition to the one in Orland) in Bangor, a major regional center some twenty miles to the north.

The sale of handicrafts benefits both H.O.M.E. and the homeworkers. By agreement, 75 percent of the sales price of each item sold goes to the maker, who is paid monthly. Depending on the store's sales and the worker's productivity, the amount of money a craftmaker receives each month ranges from $10 to $1,500. At last count, some 900 craftmakers had earned money through their cooperative effort with the store.

Being able to earn money rather than rely on meager welfare handouts has meant a great deal to the rural families living in the Orland area.

"It sure does help," says Annie Stethan, of nearby Bucksport. "I hadn't worked for years until my husband retired. Then we had to do without a lot of things, like a hot-water heater. Now we don't have to worry as much."

The worry has been reduced because Mrs. Stethan regularly earns money from the sales of her quilts. In 1973, for example, she made over $1,500. And the quilt making is now a family affair, occupying both her and her husband; he cuts the squares, and she sews them together.

So it is that working at home produces other benefits for such people as the Stethans, in that it helps give them a renewed interest in life, a rekindled pride in workmanship and production, and relief from the boredom of retirement or enforced inactivity.

The group of nuns found, in meetings with the crafters, that the Orland community had an interest in and a need for much more than a simple economic arrangement with a craft store. Like rural areas elsewhere in the country, Orland had been bypassed or ignored in many ways having to do with education and social welfare. Many people, especially women, in the Orland area had, for one reason or another, quit school before graduation. And some had never had an opportunity to learn about family planning or modern childrearing practices or health care. And what is more, it turned out, some of the people interested in trying their hand at making handicrafts and selling them through the H.O.M.E. cooperative store actually did not know how to make them. Consequently, before joining the enterprise, they would first have to learn the necessary handcrafting skills.

The people's interest and need could be summed up in one word: *education*. So H.O.M.E. began an education project.

At about the same time that H.O.M.E. was thinking about what to do to provide educational opportunities, a local Catholic priest and teacher named Father Claude Vachon was wondering what to do with a currently unused schoolhouse—unused because the parochial school had had to be closed down.

Arrangements were made, and Father Vachon began classes again—this time for the young adults and older people in the area.

The first classes were aimed simply at teaching craft skills to the people who wanted to participate in the craft store program. Gradually, though, other courses were added. These included "personal enrichment" courses, along with diploma courses, which were certified by the state department of education.

As Father Vachon would not be able to handle all the teaching load himself, H.O.M.E. recruited a number of volunteer teachers, including members of VISTA (Volunteers in Service to America).

The search for teachers was initially more successful than the search for students. As Father Vachon recalls, "We had forty-five more volunteers the first year than we had students." Although some local people had clearly expressed an interest in learning, and many needed it, only a few were actually willing to risk any of the noncraft courses at first.

"Remember," says VISTA volunteer Jacqueline Mitchell, "that these people basically distrusted any and all institutions. They considered them all useless."

Nevertheless the barriers of distrust were gradually torn down, and students came to outnumber their teachers. The school currently has about 400 students, most of them women, who range in age from sixteen to fifty-nine.

The H.O.M.E. school has managed to do more than simply offer instruction in a variety of prescribed subjects. On an informal level the students have also learned much about social relationships (after all, H.O.M.E. is a cooperative). And in particular they have gained a better sense of themselves. As Jacqueline Mitchell says: "Their self-esteem is established by accomplishing something."

And here is the summary of findings from the 100 projects (Washington Consulting Group, 1974, pp. xv–xvi):

To begin with, successful self-help projects may resemble federal and state antipoverty programs, but their origins are rooted in independence. They are not substitutes for government programs; they are unique alternatives that have evolved as a way of meeting continuing and unsolved needs within a given community.

Almost without exception, the successful self-help projects reported in this study began as a result of meeting internal needs, rather than responding to outside intervention. Self-help projects have evolved in disadvantaged communities, and they have done so in answer to disadvantaged needs and at the direction of disadvantaged people.

Some self-help groups completely shun government support and its attendant controls. Others incorporate minimal government grants into their projects but maintain a balance that heavily favors private support.

While government-instituted programs rely on paid staff, self-help projects more often rely on volunteers. (Analysis revealed that self-help projects utilize an average of seventeen volunteers for every paid worker.) And, when many volunteers are willing to give their time to a project, it is an indication that the endeavor is valued by the community. Moreover, most of these volunteers, as well as the paid staff, come from the local neighborhoods, which means the projects have strong ties within their own communities and they can create roles and responsibilities for the people themselves.

Nearly all the projects were organized by persons living within the community they served. Strong leadership and the quality of the staff are particularly important in projects that have to deal with the policies of local officials in order to succeed.

The average operating period of the selected projects is close to five years so far. This means that these projects as a whole have had time-tested experience in overcoming problems of planning and financing, as well as of meeting continuing needs within their communities.

The analysis also revealed that the successful self-help project tends to be one having the following features:

The enterprise is self-sustaining and is often a spur to the development of community programs.

There are tangible benefits for the community (that is, improved quality of life, more social services, increased employment opportunities, increased income, better health facilities, better housing).

The ratio of private to public monies is high.

The project was community initiated and remains community controlled.

There is significant cooperation and integration with other community organizations.

There is effective leadership, effective use of volunteers, and sound fiscal management.

If we avoid getting bogged down with the question of labeling the instances in the book—are they self-help projects, *or* cooperatives, *or* networks—several of their characteristics come to the fore. The first is the crucial role of an individual or small core group. That is obvious enough, but it implies a second characteristic that is also obvious but the significance of which is not: The leader or core group were, prior to the emergence of the project, embedded in a variety of formal and informal community networks. We have no basis for saying what the basis, quality, and extent of these networks were, nor can we say what it was in or about these networks that throws light on why the new project surfaced when it did and what that meant for changes in the existing networks. The descriptions assume that the changes were all positive, but that assumption should not be lightly glossed over. We can assume that transformations in the existing networks occurred, but it does not follow that all of them were desirable in terms of value and goals.

We shall return to this point shortly, but first we must note a third characteristic: *Necessary (but not sufficient) for the development of these projects was an explicit redefinition of the participants as resources; that is, they had to change their accustomed ways of viewing their capabilities and of their contributions to each other.* What is suggested in almost every description in the book is that in the early stages of the project, resource redefinition and exchange were taking place at a rapid rate among the participants at the same time that they were consciously striving to expand their network. And one also gains the impression that all of this was taking place in a context of face-to-face interactions satisfying the need for a sense of community.

This third characteristic permits us to raise an important developmental question: How did the network of loose, informal, resource exchange, face-to-face relationships change (if they did) as a consequence of the dynamics of becoming a formal organization having a structure, defined tasks, leadership roles and hierarchy, and the need to pursue financial support? This question in no way suggests that these projects did not accomplish a great deal for their members, but it raises a question of whether in changing over from an informal to a formal organization the process of redefinition of resources, as well as the frequency and quality of face-to-face relationships, may have suffered. Put in another way, in the changeover did the existing network become one in which members looked to the central leadership for direction and self-definition, reflecting an alteration in intranetwork relationships? Did the pursuit of funding have the effect, as it so frequently does, of short-circuiting imaginative thinking about redefining resources so that one is not unduly dependent on funding; that is, what are the trade-offs? Can the benefits of organizations, which have to do with structure, arrangement, orderliness, systemization, be separated from negative aspects of organizations? We raise these questions because, from the standpoint of the development of a resource exchange, self-help network these questions are crucial. They not only focus on the relationships between values and actions but they also require that one recognize that the question of how to sustain such a network, especially one that goes from an informal to a formal status, requires study and better understanding than we now have.

A key to the difference between a formal institution as we have heretofore known it and an organization based on self-help, mutual help, and resource exchange, lies in the locus of responsibility. No matter how modern a participatory management may be in a business, industry, government, or social agency, responsibility for management ultimately is at the top or in the center of a table of organization. In an organization whose objective is self-help, mutual help, and resource exchange, whether a coordinator is local, regional, or national, responsibility for all activity, all conduct of affairs, any participation in the organization, lies in each self. It is each self who is decision maker, evaluator, and manager of his or her actions and participation in the organization. Responsibility stays with the self no matter how elaborate the organization becomes. Where the fate of others in the organization is concerned, only positive contribution from an individual is possible—harmful effect is not. The least positive act toward the organization is not to participate. But any harm, or failure of benefit, affects chiefly the self.

From the perspective of network rationale, it is unimportant how one categorizes the instances in *Uplift*. What is important is that from such a rationale one can ask questions that are of the most practical import for how one deals with limited resources, and there are no issues more important than that. The issue arises in another form in *Uplift* (Washington Consulting Group, 1974, pp. xvii–xviii):

> If people's abilities and social conditions are to be improved through self-help, and if the strengths of the self-help movement are to be preserved, then it is essential that the movement itself organize and support a coordinated national effort. Such an effort could, as some project members have suggested, include a national self-help service organization. Making full use of assistance from the private and public sectors, the self-help move-

ment could, through its own service organization, play several important roles:

Public Awareness. The organization could conduct a nationwide campaign to make all segments of society aware of the potential of the self-help movement. The campaign would be a continuing effort designed to generate more interest in, and financial support for, self-help organizations.

Resource Materials. The organization could develop a resource unit to supply technical information as well as the "how to" rudiments to people seeking to learn how to improve or begin projects. Based on the data already collected, manuals and training films could be developed to provide instruction and guidance in the development of each major functional type of self-help project.

Systems Bank. Projects need counseling by both outside experts and experienced project members in such matters as how and when to incorporate, fund-raising strategies, making and marketing products, and the techniques of community organizing. A systems bank operating on a regional basis could give the projects a ready source of expertise and guidance.

Funding. A self-help service organization could effectively work for the acquisition of funds from private and public sources to further the self-help movement.

Training Seminars. Training seminars of both a general and specialized nature could be organized as an effective way of sharing and communicating ideas. Such an undertaking would not only involve self-help project members as both teachers and participants but would also be coordinated with the systems bank as needed.

This call for a national "coordinated" effort sounds necessary and reasonable, and, again, we do not doubt that it would have positive consequences. But one has to ask, "How should one think about the *process* of forming such an organization so that it maximizes meaningful resource exchange among the network of participants? Is a participant a local *unit* that stands, so to speak, between its members and the proposed national organization? What should be the structural relationship between an individual in a unit and the national center? What is meant by 'coordination,' and who is being coordinated? How does one avoid the usual outcome in which communication is far more frequent from center to local units than it is among units?" Assuming, of course, that one thinks it is desirable to avoid such an outcome. But that is the point: What outcomes does one want, and how do they determine the process of developing an appropriate structure? From the standpoint of a resource exchange network in which one seeks not only to maximize exchange but also to sustain resource redefinition to meet new opportunities and problems—constantly to keep in the forefront the universe of alternatives—the creation of a new, formal, "coordinating" organization is both an opportunity and a trap. It is an opportunity in that it can widen the horizons of individuals about themselves and their world, and it is a trap in that such organizations tend to become memoranda-dispensing centers more enamored with their viability and role than with the needs of their "outside" members. This is not a witting process but a consequence of the failure to confront the means-ends problem. In no way do we wish to derogate an informational type of network. Information is a resource and certainly helpful in the redefinition process. But more than information is required for a resource exchange network. We will be raising and discussing this issue throughout this book.

We cannot leave the discussion of *Uplift* without stating its significance in terms of the difference between thinking in terms of assets and self-dependent action, on the one hand, and disabilities and dependence on others, on the other hand. It is not possible to understand *Uplift* unless one sees it as describing actions rooted in independence and as meeting internal needs rather than responding to outside intervention. Unlike, for example, the medical-clinical model that begins with the search for an expert-layperson (independent-dependent) relationship, the *Uplift* instances represent, at least in their initial phases, a spontaneous breaking of bonds of conformity to institutional, professional, technical norms, an empowerment of people achieved by themselves, with professionals as responders rather than initiators.

The United Way

In practice, the United Way is not a resource exchange network, but because it is such a familiar agency we shall briefly use it to illustrate further the thrust of some of the questions we have raised. Historically, however, its structure and goals were very much informed by limited resources, the desire to avoid duplication of services among community agencies as well as to interrelate agencies more meaningfully, to reduce competitiveness among agencies for community monies, and to serve as a vehicle to obtain financial contributions more efficiently from individuals, business, industry, and other institutions. The name United Way was meant to convey to contributors that they were part of an organized effort to give more and better services by human services agencies that were working together; that is, there was a central, directing force dispensing money to agencies who willingly were part of a network of services. Although each agency remained basically autonomous, the very fact that it willingly became part of the effort was supposed to reflect acceptance of the need to maximize the effective use of limited resources. Furthermore, there was the assurance that those people who had the responsibility for dispensing United Way funds would do so on various bases, not the least of which was to interrelate community agencies more effectively. It would be incorrect to say that the United Way was explicitly intended to have resource exchange among agencies, except in regard to the sharing of information. Our experience over the years, however, based on discussions with agency heads and United Way administrators, leaves little doubt that, implicitly, resource exchange was a highly sought goal, less on ideological and more on financial grounds.

In the previous chapter, we discussed London's (1977) study of community agencies rendering some kind of service to mentally retarded individuals and their families. Many of these agencies were affiliated with the United Way. The reader will recall that resource exchange of any kind was remarkably minimal. And, if that was not disheartening enough, blatant hostility among some of these agencies was evident. It may be that what London found is somewhat extreme, but our experience suggests that it is not far off the mark.

The United Way is a network of agencies with the purposes we described. That is obvious enough, but how do we account for its almost complete failure to accomplish resource exchange or to avoid interagency rivalries? One part of the answer, and in marked contrast to our discussion of *Uplift*, is that *the agencies did not participate as a result of a process of redefinition of resources.* Without such a redefinition the development of a resource exchange network was precluded, despite the implicit and explicit goals of the United Way. A second part of the answer is that the structure of the network was one in which each agency related to a central node, and vice versa, and there was no incentive and reward for interagency exchanges. A third factor was that the United Way was a network of *agencies,* which meant that the bulk of the personnel of the agencies was, for all practical purposes, outsiders to the network. Essentially, it was a very re-stricted network, restricted in numbers, sources of ideas, and, there-fore, options for resource exchange. Finally, in large part because it was a network of formal organizations (each representing its own purposes, traditions, and turf), it not only made resource exchange unlikely but, no less important, it also made it unlikely that a sense of mutuality, a willingness to curb and alter one's goals for the sake of some overarching mission, would power the new vehicle. What *Uplift* (Washington Consulting Group, 1974) makes so clear is how the combination of the process of redefinition and a commitment to a "higher" value (independence *with* the sense of community) liter-ally and dramatically releases human energies exponentially. That combination was and is absent in the United Way, although it is struggling with the consequences of limited resources no less than those projects described in *Uplift*.

Our discussion of the United Way was stimulated by the sug-gestion in *Uplift* about the importance of setting up a national orga-nization to interrelate the different self-help projects and to help ini-tiate new ones. But, as the discussion of the United Way suggests, if the new organization will be comprised of agencies, it cannot avoid confronting certain serious obstacles, assuming that one of its major goals is to maximize resource exchange and to sustain the process of redefinition of resources. On an actuarial basis, one is warranted in saying that the type of coordinating organization recommended in *Uplift* tends to become an information-dispensing center more than a resource exchange vehicle. As we said before, information can be a valuable resource, but it is only one of the ingredients that make for and sustain a successful resource exchange network. Indeed, a close reading of the descriptions in *Uplift* suggests the hypothesis that *in the emergence of a resource exchange network, information becomes helpful and even crucial only after the combination of resource redefinition and a commitment to mutuality has been achieved.*

Boston Self-Help Center

We describe the Boston Self-Help Center (For People with a Handicap or Chronic Disease), or BSHC, one of many that have sprung up around the country in recent years, less because it illustrates the societal context to which it is a reaction, or the characteristics of an emerging resource exchange network, and more because it allows us to raise questions with which we shall be concerned throughout this book.[1] The people in the projects described in *Uplift* were disadvantaged because of their race, ethnic group, or economic poverty. The people in the BSHC feel no less disadvantaged because of their physical handicap. The following is from their descriptive brochure (1977, pp. 1–7):

The Boston Self-Help Center
Providing counseling, advocacy, resources, and educational services for people with a chronic disease or physical handicap.

Our History

Over thirty million Americans have some physical limitation or condition interfering with their full participation in society. In 1977, a White House Conference recognized this as a social problem and a national priority. In 1977, Section 504 of the Rehabilitation Act of 1973 was finally signed into law. This action required programs and activities receiving federal financial assistance to make their facilities physically accessible to all the population. The very newness of these events indicates the long-term inattention to the needs of a large number of Americans and the services and rights to which we are entitled. The national self-help movement, consumers who have organized to articulate demands to provide services, has risen to bridge this gap. The Boston Self-Help Center is our local response to the same need.

As with many such organizations, the spur to action was our dissatisfaction with existing services. Many were lacking altogether and others simply too specialized. We realized that there are issues and problems that cut across our differing diseases and handicaps. Being thought of as ostomates, diabetics, paraplegics, or CA's emphasized our specific physical limitations. Seeing us in terms of our deficits—our *dis*-eases, our *dis*-orders, our *dis*-abilities, our *in*-validity—interfered with our own as well as society's recognition that we were more than our handicaps. By separating us into diagnostic categories, these labels emphasized our medical dependence and blocked our awareness of the difficulties as well as strengths we share in common. Finally, we recognized that there were experiences and resources which the able-bodied population simply did not possess.

---

[1]Although the concept of networks is central to this book, no less important to us is how the concept can be used as a window through which one can get a sense of the diverse approaches people develop either to break out of confining societal contexts (that stem from institutions or the mores they represent) or to break into, or gain access to, systems from which so many are presently excluded.

Out of this perspective was born our first self-help workshop in the spring of 1974. With the financial, emotional, and physical support of Greenhouse, Inc., our first counseling group was offered. It was entitled "Living with Chronic Disease and/or Physical Handicap" and all of the members including the facilitators had chronic disability or disease.

In the succeeding three years, our groups grew in frequency and acceptance. Yet this very success forced us to see how much more activity and organization was needed. Our answer was to create, in the fall of 1977, the Boston Self-Help Center—a cooperative, nonprofit, counseling, advocacy, resource, and educational organization staffed *by* and providing services *for* people with a physical handicap or chronic disease. We are currently a core of individuals who are not only trained and experienced counselors but also have extensive organizational, research, administrative, and educational backgrounds. Two of us are now devoting full time to the development of BSHC. All of us are volunteering our time and services. We are also supported by a growing outer circle of people with specific skills. People who use our services are from all over Massachusetts though the majority are from Greater Boston. Though we have been known largely by word of mouth, increasingly people are being referred through public agencies (including the Massachusetts Rehabilitation Commission), hospitals, nursing homes and through receiving our brochures.

The Present

Our fall program is multifaceted. Our purpose is to offer a forum of communication and growth for people with a handicap or chronic disease. At present, the major channels for this are our personal growth and peer counseling training groups as well as our Personal Resource Network.

Personal growth groups consist of about ten members and two facilitators. Participants are encouraged to share their experiences in living with a disability and to use each other's resources to create alternative solutions to daily problems. In the process, we identify social conditions which hinder realization of our full potential, encourage members to initiate their own mutual support systems and to take social action. Five such workshops are currently being offered—two are general, one is for women, one is for parents of handicapped children, and one is a mastectomy support group.

Our peer counseling training groups combine theory and practice for those starting their own self-help organizations or who are either interested, or already active in counseling others with a handicap. Attention is particularly given to alternative ways (that is, physically as well as psychologically viable) of communicating bodily feelings and emotions and of learning new, or adapting old counseling methods to the specific needs and often unique abilities of a handicapped person. One introductory workshop is being offered.

The PRN (Personal Resource Network) is our answer to the need to link people—those who volunteer—to talk and be available to others with a similar disability with people requesting concrete or supportive assistance.

We offer supportive supervision to the workers in this program and accept names of people interested in receiving this service.

Our staff is also available to do individual, couples, and family counseling.

Finally, we are a consultation and resource service to organizations, institutions, and people who wish to create groups, offer services, change their physical and social environment in relation to persons with a chronic disease or physical handicap.

The Future

In addition to our present activities, we are continually assessing our own resources as well as the unmet needs of the physically handicapped and chronic disease community. Here is a sampling of programs under consideration.

1. Regular rap sessions or special occasion workshops to deal with concrete problems. We will provide the space, do the necessary organization and provide resource people.
2. Advocacy.
3. Consultation.
4. Education.
5. Social.

Organization

Participants: All those with physical handicap, chronic disease or disability are eligible for our services.

Staff: All counselors, resource people, and office staff will be people who themselves have a physical handicap, chronic disease, or disability. The tasks and jobs will be tailored to fit the talents and resources available. Should we need eight-hour-a-day office coverage, we may well use for example, people in two or three shifts for as much or as little time as will suit our time, energy, and capacity. Our answering service, for example, consists of home-bound individuals.

Location: Presently our office is at 12 Essex Street in Central Square, Cambridge, in the general building of Greenhouse, Inc. Our phone is 354-6287. Our groups are occasionally held there but more often in rented, fully accessible places. We need, though at present cannot afford, a location in the Greater Boston Area, within easy reach of all public transportation and in a building which is fully accessible.

Table of Organization:

A Board of Advisors—The Board of Advisors will meet periodically to be apprised of our activities and, where appropriate, to advise us as to future directions.

The Staff—Initially we are primarily part-time and voluntary. Eventually the organization will be self-sufficient, with staff able to earn a decent living wage. The core staff and the executive director will make the basic day-to-day decisions and administer the organization.

Town Meeting—We exist solely to serve the needs of persons with chronic illness or physical handicap. As such, we will have periodic open meetings where anyone with a chronic disease, disability, or handicap has a vote. At these meetings, we will decide basic issues and policy or at least bring before as large a public as possible the directions that the day-to-day staff is considering.

Finances: We are at present supported solely by the sliding fees paid by those who use our services and private donations. Since we, the handicapped and chronic disease community, are already overburdened by extraordinary medical and living expenses and underemployed, this is a precarious source of income at best. At present, this money pays primarily for telephone, supplies, rental fees, and so on. To fully utilize our resources (we can be a volunteer group for only a limited period of time) and to extend our services, we need more extensive underwriting through donations, grants, and contracts.

It is not necessary to elaborate on the prominence given to resource redefinition and mutuality in this brochure or on the emphasis on "advertising and exchange of needed services." But it is necessary to comment on what may appear to be a minor semantic issue but which we consider strikes at the core of the rationale of resource exchange networks. It concerns "volunteers." Ordinarily, a person who volunteers time, knowledge, and services does so out of the goodness of his or her heart. In terms of resource exchange, it is an uneven one; that is, the volunteer's reward is in satisfying a sense of obligation or altruism. Far more often than not, the volunteer's knowledge and skills (his or her personal resources, actual or potential) are only minimally increased, if at all. Indeed, one of the most common complaints about volunteers is that they lose interest and become undependable. From the standpoint of the agency, the value of the volunteers would be greatly diminished if it had to do more to sustain the interest of the volunteer. "You give, we take"—many volunteer agency exchanges have that flavor. When the BCHC uses the term *volunteer*, it may sometimes have that flavor but many times it does not and instead refers to a "swapping" or "barter" in which resource needs of both parties are explored as a basis for exchange.[2] In such an arrangement the resources (knowledge, skills) of both parties to the exchange are enhanced.

[2]The swapping and bartering of resources go beyond two-way exchanges; for example, in applying that resource of experience and expertise to battling in public arenas for rights of handicapped people and also, most

The distinction we are making is an obvious one, but what is not so obvious is the contrast it permits between a resource exchange network and the modal human services agency: The latter tends to have a relatively passive stance to recruiting volunteers and furthering their development, while the former actively scans the environment for possibilities of exchange and mutual enhancement. It is a difference that makes a difference, and in the case of a resource exchange network it becomes a kind of litmus test of consistency with the network's purposes. It is a difference that guides one in judging whether in a resource exchange network the value and process of resource definition are applied to all who are in the network. This point is also relevant to how one maps and understands the structure of a network, any network. Mapping a network so as to portray graphically its extent, types of connections, directional flows of communication, and growth pattern is no easy matter, if only because we tend to underestimate the extent of our formal and informal network connections. This is particularly the case with networks that are minimally formal, seek with vigor to cast a large net, and are relatively unconcerned with establishing boundaries; for example, the projects described in *Uplift* (Washington Consulting Group, 1974) and the BSHC. But mapping a network can, in our experience, be misleading to the extent that we blithely assume that the values that inform the network are reflected in the graphic representations. These representations may convey "resource exchange," but the acid test, of course, is what happens in practice: the strength and quality of the scanning for resource exchange, the basis for exchange, what is exchanged, and how that becomes a stimulus for other exchanges planned or not. Just as the descriptions contained in a dinner menu

---

importantly, in acting as resource service to organizations, institutions, and people who wish to create groups, offer services, or change their physical and social environments in relation to persons with chronic disease or physical handicap. This last has potential for income production. Organizations wishing to make changes for purposes of compliance or for whatever reason need experts to help them achieve their objectives, and they frequently are able to pay for the service. This puts a market value on the new resource, in no way detrimental to the people or organization that have developed the resource. On the contrary, it can be an aid to becoming self-sustaining and growth producing.

may be discrepant with how the food looks and tastes, the graphic representation of a network may be discrepant with how the network works.

As in the instances in *Uplift* and almost every other resource exchange network we know about, the BSHC sees itself as engaged in a struggle for survival requiring them constantly to seek money to stay alive and grow (pay staff, rent a central accessible location, and so on). At what price? That question has to be asked because of what we know about funding sources: They require a specific goal and plan; funding is for a limited period of time, perhaps renewable but by no means assured; and the grantee assumes a moral obligation, and sometimes it is explicitly contractual, not to deviate from the agreement. That may sound reasonable and realistic, and from many standpoints it is, but it poses potentially serious threats to a resource exchange network. For one thing, anxiety about survival may pressure the network to enter into agreements that in varying degrees are antithetical to its purposes. Less obvious, the natural history of these networks suggest that they cannot be expected to develop according to calendar time.

As we emphasized in our previous book, and as our subsequent experience confirms, there is a large element of unpredictability in when and how possibilities for exchange and growth appear. You cannot say, "In two months, we want to be at this point, and by next year we want to have this and that set of network interconnections and exchanges." Scanning the environment for possibilities of resource exchange is not like scanning a well-laid-out landscape with signs and guideposts. Assessing one's own resources and needs is one thing, but locating (and dreaming up) people who not only have what you need but who also want what you have is of a different order of complexity associated with many false starts. Precisely because the task requires scanning, freedom, and imaginativeness, it is adversely affected by time pressures and deadlines. One may know with what parties a resource exchange would be mutually productive, but when and how to bring it about may be very difficult questions to answer. In business, one may know what kind of deal one wants to make with whom, but one may also know that a lot of preliminary (not always knowable) steps will be required before the deal can even be suggested. And it is not unlike the therapeutic situation in which the therapist thinks he or she knows what is bothering the patient but is waiting for a more opportune time to say it. The grant-seeking and actual granting process almost always has the effect of increasing the sense of pressure and the need to produce. In the case of resource exchange networks, these effects can be lethal at worst and interfering at best. There is a price. And part of that price is in the short-circuiting of the process in which a widened sense of mutuality can occur as a consequence of a developing, probing, multiparty discussion during which it can emerge that you have a resource (in the context of other people's needs) that may never have occurred to you as being a resource. That kind of a multiparty discussion, characteristic in resource exchange networks, cannot be put on a time schedule.

We have been told, and the story may be apocryphal, that the Internal Revenue Service has come across instances where people of different skills provide service to each other with no money changing hands; for example, a physician who will treat his plumber and his family in exchange for the plumber's services. The Internal Revenue Service presumably ruled that each of them had to put a monetary value on their services and declare it as income. The beauty of the story is not only in forcing us to recognize how foreign the concept of resource exchange is to most of us but what a threat it can be to a money exchange society. For a resource exchange network, seeking and obtaining funding is a mixed blessing. We think we are realists, we understand well the dilemmas of the resource exchange network, and we are not advocating a stance of purity and poverty, but it would be unrealistic in the extreme to gloss over the mixed consequences of seeking and obtaining money. For anyone interested in the life history of these networks, these consequences cannot be ignored.

A final comment on the BSHC (as well as on *Uplift*) is that the stimulus for developing the network did not come from the professional community or from official community leaders but rather from a few people who were critical of the professionals and community leaders. After the emergence of the network, outside professionals may become participants. In a later chapter, we shall pursue the implications of this point, because it contains still another serious obstacle to the purpose of a resource exchange network.

Students and Resource Exchange

There is no logical relationship between the principle of resource exchange and the formation of a network. Indeed, it appears that the most frequent manifestation of the principle takes place between two people with little or no consequences for the networks of either. When the principle is combined with network formation, it is usually because people have made a commitment to the value of the combination and wish to get others to see it in their self-interest. We know little about how frequently or under what conditions an exchange between two people gets articulated in a way so as to cause one or both of them to apply it elsewhere with other people. That articulation, we suggest, is crucial if the benefits of resource exchange are to be realized, because the nature of the articulation reveals the degree of clarity attained in regard to three factors: the values that should power the exchange, what it means for an individual's diverse potentialities, and the general significances of this type of exchange for dealing with social problems. To the extent that its articulation does not address these factors the maximum benefits to be derived from resource exchange will be limited, which is not to say there will be no benefits.

These introductory comments are stimulated by numerous examples of middle and high school programs that offer students the opportunity to be of some service to individuals and agencies in their community. We refer only to examples that have the following features: They are based on the belief that students are resources and that students can render a service; the students are not put in "busywork" jobs but in those where they can acquire knowledge and skills; the settings in which the students are placed recognize the service students can perform and are prepared to give the students time and instruction; someone in the school oversees the program and has an active relationship with the students and the settings. The following is from a description of a program in the Shoreham-Wading River Central School District in Shoreham, New York (1977, pp. 1–6):

A school serves a community by educating its children. If, in addition, by serving the community in other ways it can educate its children better, then the community is doubly blessed. Shoreham-Wading River Middle School, a public school in suburban Long Island, teaches its eleven- to thirteen-year-old students by supplementing classroom instruction with responsibilities outside the school, usually for one hour each week. And, because they know their community service activities matter to everyone involved, the children live up to adult challenges of the Community Service Program.

"It makes me feel older than I really am to take over responsibilities I never had before. This is the very first time I have been able to prove what I can do," reports a child whose school experience included work at a local nursing home. Many in this same project felt repulsion or fear when they began associating with old people. Unaccustomed to wheelchairs and the smell of disinfectant, they also had to face the hostility of an elderly patient who loudly claimed, "Children don't belong in a place like this."

But kids and adults were transformed by their experience with the project; soon both old people and Middle Schoolers became comfortable with one another, developing mutual respect and even love.

"I really like her," one girl wrote of an elderly patient, "and I mean really! It's not like you're talking to a grownup. It's like you're talking to one of your best friends because she truly understands you."

Another girl outgrew her initial pity for old people through community service. She learned a new appreciation, both of old age and of her own youth: "The elderly aren't ashamed of what they are, and they aren't worried about their futures, they just want to share their pasts. The past was when they lived; now I see how crazy I was to want to grow up so fast, wishing my life away."

Others in this nursing home program developed a new social consciousness and became more introspective, learning to be critical of themselves and of staff, teachers, or family members when they seemed to neglect those in need. One parent marveled because her daughter's relationship with her grandfather noticeably improved after she began working at the nursing home. The students in the group wanted their experiences to affect many more people, so they organized their class to promote the rights of the elderly, producing a newsletter for public distribution.

These children respond so intensely to work outside the school partly because it affords them drastically new experiences: "Community service is different," one boy explains, "it's not the same as school: You don't walk into class, open your books, and study; you have fun, yet you learn a lot, especially responsibilities."

Without responsibilities outside of the classroom, most middle-class preadolescents face a very predictable daily round: off to school in the morning to spend the day with children of similar ages and socioeconomic backgrounds, home to play with the same kids or to watch television and do some homework; then to bed, with the cycle repeated the next day. The chores of home and school usually are not essential ones, and they do not require children to apply their full attention and ingenuity.

But community service offers more effective roles; a supervising teacher observes, "It gives students a 'real' experience, something which anchors their weekly schedule, that pushes them and forces them to grow." And these experiences don't easily fade; though a child may quickly forget some fact memorized for a test, years later he will remember the blind lady who finally got out of bed to hear him and his classmates sing Christmas carols.

Middle School children still have much to learn, so it's easy to overlook what they have to give. But most children this age can best develop their basic skills by applying them. That's why Shoreham-Wading River Middle School's Community Service Program includes teaching younger children among its activities. It's one thing for seventh graders to understand their arithmetic lessons, another for them to develop a number game for preschoolers, yet another when they observe the young kids' difficulties and go back to simplify the game for their level.

A supervising teacher was at first surprised, then gratified to see that the Middle School children who volunteered to teach younger students French were not her best pupils, but those who had learning difficulties themselves. Their pride and responsibility in teaching others, mixed with the confidence gained from their authority in that situation, spurred them to work harder and to develop their own skills. And their past difficulties helped them to avoid teaching pitfalls and to develop creative approaches for teaching others.

Problem solving of this type is especially helpful to Middle School children. They are at a transitional age, trying to define their identities in relation to the adult world and to understand the structure of their day-to-day experience. Children's comments after a teaching project reveal a widened perspective, for they acknowledge both that "it's going to be hard to go from being a teacher back to being a student again" *and* that "it sure is hard to be a teacher." After taking a turn as teachers, children have more patience with themselves when trying to learn, because they have seen how difficult learning can be, even for the brightest students.

Children who teach other children also learn the importance of planning and discipline; as they work with their own teachers to develop approaches to teaching, their role of dependence matures into one of cooperation. Some Middle School teachers spend considerable classroom time preparing their pupils, practically and emotionally, for their work with others. Many teachers include such considerations as part of their daily activities. After each session outside of the school, teachers and students discuss and evaluate the experience and plan for the future.

Adult teachers learn from their students' experience as well, becoming as much colleagues as authority figures. One teacher observed, "These kids can teach me a heck of a lot when it comes to dealing with people; watching them, more than once I was about to cry at just how sensitive they could be to the needs of others." And an elementary school teacher assisted by the Middle School students reported that the "experience was a very good one, not just for my kindergarteners and the Middle Schoolers, but for *me*."

As they learn to perform their community service tasks, students tend to become less competitive. "By working together and sharing their problems, the kids begin to become a real community," one teacher reports. "They learn to use each other's resources instead of striving against one another for better grades. . . ."

Of course, the difficulties of helping others can lead to some disappointments. One girl became frustrated, hurt, and angry after her initial rapport with a blind woman was abruptly ended by fits of bad temper and the patient's eventual indifference. Another boy came to think of an elderly woman he visited "as my grandmother." After she died, he wrote, "I was sad for a very long time; sometimes I think the nursing home experience has had more downs than ups with me." However, the program's philosophy accepts such experiences, preferring them to the injustice of keeping young people who are eager to mature separated and sheltered from life's realities.

Even Middle School students who are not part of a specific service project benefit from their classmates' community involvement. Almost every group the students work with—the elderly, the very young, the disabled—is brought to visit the Middle School, and students who work in the service projects are given the opportunity to exhibit their skills and to be leaders. Other students without community service experience are exposed in a positive way to people who are much younger or older than they, or who are different in some other way.

The compassion and skills developed by this type of experience are unfortunately beyond the reach not only of most children in our society but of many adults as well. In fact, the community service program assumes that a child's preparation for life requires personal and community responsibilities that are more the exception than the rule in our society. The isolation of our elderly and handicapped, placed in institutions rather than supported by caring individuals from all walks of life, makes the Middle Schoolers' contribution especially crucial. . . .

This kind of exchange strengthens the community as a whole. The children involved develop the skills and emotional attitudes required for them to become competent, active, caring adults, citizens personally concerned that every individual be developed and rewarded to his or her full capacity. . . .

When a sensitive child feels the consequences of his or her actions on another human being, what is learned is not just lessons, but also responsibilities in life. As one parent summed up his child's community service experience: "The project turned out to be more than an assignment; it became a labor of love."

Of the 600 pupils in the school, 300 participate in the program. From one standpoint, the school is part of a resource exchange network in which there are numerous community settings. That is to say, the school leadership developed the network to meet its needs as well as those of the wider community, and it appears to have paid off handsomely; that is, everyone seems to have benefited. It is an informal network, and no money changes hands. But what is the function of the students in the network? If we were to ask that question about the school personnel, we could say that they are the galvanizers and coordinators of the network, constantly scanning the community for opportunities for students. If we were to ask that question about personnel in the community agencies, we would say that they probably play a cooperative but passive role, passive in the sense that they do not initiate exchanges. To the extent that they do initiate resource exchange, it would be evident that they understand the principles of a resource exchange network.

If one of the network's purposes is to understand and act on the insight that resource exchange as a principle has far wider applicability to its members' lives and to the larger society than the school project suggests, then doubt must be expressed about realizing this purpose. When earlier we asked a question about the function of the students in the network, it was by way of asking what one wanted students to learn in addition to knowledge, skills, and the reward from being helped. There is a lot of satisfaction to be derived from the purposes and consequences of this school-community resource exchange, and it may be viewed as unreasonable to ask more of it. But the point we are raising goes beyond this particular network. What is at issue here is how one broadens people's conceptions of the possibilities of resource exchange, how one goes beyond a single, concrete focus to consider other areas to which it is applicable. In the previous chapter, we said that if you asked people what a pencil is, the answer would be predictable. But, we went on, if you asked people what are the different uses to which a pencil can conceivably be put, many people would have difficulty coming up with more than a few answers. There is a similar problem with thinking about resource exchange networks. If a network has foci A and B, it may be difficult to see that the principles of the network are no less applicable to C, D, E . . . and Z. Imagine the situation where the Shoreham-Wading River network had been developed around placing students in nursing homes. We could count on somebody in the network saying, "How come we are restricting ourselves to nursing homes? Isn't our rationale appropriate to many other settings?" And that is our point: The rationale for a community-school network can go beyond students and their community placements. It is a rationale no less usable by network participants in other spheres of their lives, but if there is not clarity about the different aspects of the rationale, the full significance and applicability of it will not be grasped.

Mention must be made here of the National Commission on Resources for Youth (NCRY), headquarters in New York City. The Shoreham-Wading River Central School District program is one of about twelve hundred programs fostered and networked by this organization. The commission has a small central staff and, located throughout the country, fifty associates of diverse backgrounds. The role of the commission is described as follows (National Commission on Resources for Youth, n.d., pp. 1–2):

> The primary role of the commission is to identify existing youth participation programs of quality, bring these to the attention of others who are potential initiators of such programs, and assist in the development of new programs.
>
> In Camarillo, California, for example, high school students do important physical therapy with children and adults in a home for the retarded. In Cornwall, New York, students operate a public museum which attracts over 22,000 visitors annually. In Appalachia, students publish a national magazine on the culture and arts of their region. These are three of the more than one thousand programs which the commission has identified as exemplary.
>
> Serving as a national clearinghouse of ideas for youth participation programs, the commission has collected, catalogued, and validated information on several thousand programs. For those that meet the standards established as essential for a good youth participation program, case studies are developed and information about them is distributed. One form of getting to the prospective consumer is the free, quarterly, eight-page newsletter, *Resources for Youth,* which describes existing quality programs and goes *by request* to 33,000 persons. The commission has provided more than 400,000 manuals, guides and films which it developed to help youth and adults establish programs. In addition, the commission has developed other "how to" materials.
>
> The commission itself has conducted demonstration programs. It initiated Youth Tutoring Youth (YTY) in 1967 in two cities. Since that time, YTY has become a nationwide program with sites established in more than 500 cities and one thousand schools. A daycare youth helper demonstration, where junior and senior high school students work in daycare centers as part of a school course in child development and parenting, was established in nineteen sites, each with a different ethnic population. The program is also being widely adopted.

As a source of assistance and training, the commission offers on-site technical assistance and training workshops to teachers and workers in how to initiate and maintain quality youth participation programs.

Since its inception in 1967, the commission has identified and brought to public attention hundreds of programs. Each year, the numbers needing the services of the commission increase as individuals, schools, and youth-serving agencies seek information and technical assistance. The commission has helped to make it known that young people can teach younger children, counsel their peers, aid in the care of the aged, the poor and the handicapped. Young people have demonstrated that they do have the motivation, perseverance, dedication, and qualities of character to carry responsibility. Above all, they have proved that they can improve the quality of their own lives through service to others.

The associates in the field, of which the principal of Shoreham-Wading River School is one, are available to assist new programs and to identify, describe, and validate exemplary programs that are then circulated by the commission. Regional meetings and workshops are arranged in response to requests. One might describe the commission as a small, formal, resource exchange network that is part of (indeed, stimulates) far-flung, loose, informal networks. By design, the relationships between the formal and informal networks occur in the field and only minimally between headquarters and the field. The commission is more than an informational network; that is, it has carried out demonstration projects, conducted first-hand evaluations of programs, renders assistance to developing programs, and seeks to initiate new ones. The NCRY has to be seen in relation to its view of our society (*Resources for Youth Newsletter*, 1975, pp. 1–2):

As we enter the final quarter of our century, we see challenges on every front. The world's economy is in upheaval, leading to worldwide energy shortages, widespread unemployment and, in some countries, starvation. In our own country, many people feel let down by the apparent deterioration of national leadership, and are pessimistic about the prospects of surmounting current problems. These views are reflected by the young people of the United States as evidenced by two national studies of American youth, one conducted by Daniel Yankelovich, entitled *The New Morality*, and another conducted by the National Association of Secondary School Principals, entitled *The Mood of American Youth*. The latter study reports that 70 percent of high school youth believe that "corruption and dishonesty are widespread at the highest levels of government." Both reports suggest that the activism of the 1960s has been replaced by conventional attitudes on the part of youth with a strong interest in personal security through paying jobs.

Despite this apparent complacency, NCRY sees this as an opportune time to promulgate the idea of youth participation. Adolescents have not changed in their desire to be needed, recognized, and valued. If there is statistical evidence of their indifference, this may merely reflect their sense of an absence of opportunities to participate in and make worthwhile contributions to their communities. Given the chance, however, as NCRY has observed in hundreds of youth participation programs across the country, young people are as eager as they have ever been to make active social commitments. . . .

One of the most refreshingly distinctive features of the NCRY is in how it redefines students as resources and in the thought it has given to what that redefinition should mean in practice (which is why it seeks to validate programs). The following excerpt illustrates this feature (National Commission on Resources for Youth, 1975, pp. 5–7).

The key ingredient in youth participation—and the one which is absent in many work experience programs—is *decision making by the adolescents.* Maturity consists largely of making decisions, first about matters affecting one's own life and then about others'. As adults, we accept the consequences of our choices and live within their confines. If young people are to move from dependent childhood to responsible adulthood, they need to practice making decisions within semiprotected settings in the company of adults who can offer guidance, support, and technical advice.

Although it is hoped that decision making will lead to successful projects and genuine community contribution, youth participation can be valuable even when projects "fail." In the company of sensitive adults, young people can learn to use failure constructively as a learning experience instead of taking it as devastating evidence of personal inadequacy. . . . Adults associated with youth participation must learn how to counsel without controlling, how to precipitate youthful decision making without dominating it. Their role is best understood as that of an advocate or facilitator who draws out of students alternative plans for action, serving more as a supportive presence than an active influence.

When students go outside the school to work with social agencies or businesses, the school must be equally careful to find supervising adults who will allow the young people maximum responsibility in their jobs. It is essential that the student be more than an observer or an obedient follower of instructions. This may necessitate some indoctrination of the receiving institution as to the goals of the program. For example, hospitals should be encouraged to teach students how to do basic kinds of physical therapy instead of expecting them to deliver linens and answer phones. If students are to work in daycare centers, the adults involved should arrange to have the young people take part in planning activities for the younger children and in supervising them.

Another essential component of youth participation involves *working relationships with adults.* Young people, including some who need to interact with a variety of responsive adults, can serve as models and informal counselors. The qualities of these adults are important. They must, for example, be able to admit the value of their own experience as adults while at the same time respecting the right of adolescents to act independently. This is a delicate balance, achieved only through sensitivity and openness. . . .

The opportunity to work with adults allows young people to see more clearly the options available to them in maturity. Often young people have a distorted view of adult life, accentuated by the artificial school culture and heavily influenced by the media. By working with adults, young people gain a detailed understanding of the requirements of various working situations. They are also exposed to habits, opinions, and life-styles different from those of their parents. Such exposure should lead both to tolerance of others and to self-exploration. . . .

Finally, youth participation should provide a situation in which the involvement of the students serves a *genuine need in the community.* In many situations, the worker needs only a minimal interest in his or her job in order to perform competently. In youth participation, young people should be drawn into situations where their caring makes things happen for the good of their community. Their decisions and their work should make a difference in the lives of the people around them. This component satisfies the deepest unmet need of contemporary adolescents; the need to be needed. As the nuclear family disintegrates and paid employment for youth becomes less likely, young people feel increasingly superfluous. The sense of uselessness and futility which arises from these circumstances can be offset by youth participation programs in which young people do something that is respected and valued by their communities. Youth participation reinforces the sense of belonging and of having obligations to the larger society. This is good not only for the individual whose self-image improves when he is valued for his contribution but also for the social fabric, which is woven out of concern and good faith among its members.

It is difficult to read about the commission and to see the tapes they have prepared—and they are by no means restricted to white, middle-class schools—without being impressed by the results.

The commission is an example of a national organization that does, as suggested in *Uplift* (Washington Consulting Group, 1974), interrelate different projects and help initiate new ones. It searches out, identifies, and describes existing programs so that each project feels the support of a new-found family while getting added impetus through its sense of value as a resource to others. The role of NCRY is thus similar to the role of the single coordinator of a resource exchange network. It is organized without acquiring the hierarchical shape or rigidities of the formal institution. From the standpoint of understanding how resource exchange networks function and what their formal and informal consequences are (how connections are made, how many people are affected in what ways, their intended and unintended numerical growth, geographical scope, and widening of foci), the Shoreham-Wading River and the NCRY networks and their relation to each other deserve intensive study. It would not be surprising if such a study showed that these networks powered by the resource exchange rationale are not as limited to a single focus as we have suggested. It might, for example, be found that a crucial factor in the degree to which the resource exchange principle is applied to new foci is a function of characteristics of those who serve as coordinators or leaders in different parts of the network. As we shall see later, the network coordinator (or coordinators) appears to be crucial in determining how varied in foci a resource exchange network becomes. We have been discussing these networks as if we are secure in feeling that we understand how they develop, grow, and change. That is not the case, and therefore we have resorted to detailed descriptions on the basis of which the questions we think need answers can be raised.

We should offer a word of caution. In none of these initial case presentations can one conclude that the effort was explicitly based on the integration of three factors: the fact of limited resources, the general applicability of the resource exchange rationale, and an articulation of a concept of networks. Aspects of these factors are suggested in each of the descriptions of these efforts, but one does get not the impression that interrelationships among these factors were formulated and served as a conceptual guide. This, obviously, is not meant as criticism but rather as a way of emphasizing that it is in the interrelationships of these factors that the potentialities of the resource exchange rationale lies. We are not partisans of labeling, because labels so often obscure as much as they illuminate. As we said in the previous chapter, the label *network* has been appended to myriad social phenomena, just as the self-help movements contains bewildering heterogeneity, and just as there are widely differing views on the nature and extent of limited natural and human resources. From our perspective, there is the danger that these unconnected factors will stay unconnected because, for example, people who are interested in networks tend not to be interested in the definition and redefinition of resources. There is no inherent interrelationship among these factors, but the emerging nature of the contemporary world requires that attempts to conceptualize these interrelationships be made.

Daphne Krause and the Minneapolis Age and Opportunity Center

To appreciate fully the significance of the Minneapolis Age and Opportunity Center (M.A.O., pronounced "Mayo") for the concept of resource exchange, the reader is urged to consult two documents: Mrs. Daphne Krause's testimony on February 22, 1978, before the U.S. House of Representatives' Select Committee on Aging, and her testimony on July 8, 1975, before the same committee. Collectively, her testimony covers 300 or more pages. Let us begin with a speech Mrs. Krause gave at a meeting in Washington in 1976 (pp. 1–13):

> Before presenting an extremely brief overview of the many programs and consortium of partners of the Minneapolis Age and Opportunity Center, Inc. (known as M.A.O.), I would like to tell you a story that illustrates graphically the callous disregard toward many of our most helpless elderly, that I believe is one of the root causes of our lack of commitment to them.
>
> It seems there was a country and a time when it was the custom to take the elderly up onto a mountain to die of exposure, when the community felt they were no longer of use. A man, carrying his father up the mountain, felt tears on his neck and asked, "Why are you crying? You know this is the law, and you have had many years to grow used to your fate." The father replied, "I am not crying for myself, my son, but for you, and what your son will do to you."
>
> There are many issues this story raises. Is it possible that in our try and our time, a neglected house, a dingy apartment, or an unnecessary nursing home, are our mountains of obliteration for our unwanted elderly? Certainly very old age is the ultimate death sentence, and I believe it is our unconscious fear of this reality that is behind our agism and neglect.
>
> We must ask ourselves, "Are all older people alike?" We will find they are not. "Are they all a burden on the community?" We will find a large percentage are comparatively or completely independent. For those who

need our assistance, we must ask, "Where does our responsibility lie? What types of services do they need, and how do we provide them? Indeed, can we even afford to do so with the increasing elderly population?" The M.A.O. experience is one answer to these vital questions.

Beginning in 1967, I met with a number of senior citizen leaders and others, to address these questions. The major priority that emerged was a need for an alternative network approach, that I called "medisupportive," for those particular seniors with multiple health and socioeconomic problems, needing various levels of medical and social supportive services to help them delay or avoid unnecessary institutionalization.

We analyzed the existing fragmented services, many of which were excellent in themselves but not sufficient to provide the full range of medical and social supportive services needed by the impaired elderly.

My first thought was to try and coordinate these existing programs and then fill in the gaps. Immediately, I ran into many problems. There were two major stumbling blocks. While most private and governmental agencies talked "coordination," it had to be within the context of their own program's funding survival and must not impinge on their "self-decided" territory. Their protective reaction was often disguised under the term "duplication of effort," when in reality you cannot duplicate services that do not exist. I also found that one of the most frequent methods of obstruction was to form endless committees, to discuss the problems, that led nowhere.

The second major obstacle was the lack of federal or local funding for a network of services, and what funding did exist was channeled through the state and local governmental agencies, which were already committed to their own programs and to already selected private institutions and agencies. Therefore, because of the limited funds available, they were reluctant to fund a new concept, and their reaction was to question why we needed to put together so many services. Why couldn't we limit our request to a few? I felt this to be wrong, because of the variable needs that had to be met, if we were to truly provide an alternative to institutionalization.

My determination was to proceed with the M.A.O. concept in several ways. First, by attempting to reassure the private agencies and institutions that we were not trying to obtain their funding, that there was room for a variety of programs, and that I would leave the door open to those who really wanted to coordinate.

Secondly, I decided to develop a consortium of partners from local resources by my analyzing their individual concerns and objectives, then designing programs that would be mutually beneficial. Some other good precepts to follow in order to gain partners are to always treat your partners as the senior partners, give them recognition first before your own agency, see that your partners get full credit for their work, don't waste time in unnecessary meetings, and always respect their autonomy. This is particularly true in your partnerships with voluntary organizations, that may fear being swallowed up by your more visible agency.

Finally, we would apply for a variety of federal funds for those services our partners could not provide.

From the beginning, some ten years ago, I knew I had to plan and develop a program that was not only humanly effective but also cost effective in every possible way. I felt this as a challenge to rethink existing methods, to take nothing for granted, and most important of all, in my planning, I never forgot the woman who told me, "I know I am going to die, but I don't want to die every day." It should also be remembered that it is impossible to be cost effective if you are not humanly effective.

The "medisupportive" concept was based on my fundamental belief that health in the future can no longer be considered medical intervention alone, however important these services are. Equally so are any social supportive services, and these services must be welded together to meet the diverse problems of the client-patient. Health is also our environmental, nutritional, and emotional well-being; really, anything that goes to make up the quality of our lives, and the most important services are always the ones based on the individual's particular needs.

I have used a quotation from Carl Sandburg, "Nothing Happens Unless First a Dream," to describe the foundation of M.A.O. It would not be an overstatement to say that many times I felt it was an impossible dream.

Finally, in 1969, M.A.O. was incorporated as a nonprofit organization. The majority of M.A.O.'s governing board are senior citizen leaders, representing major senior citizen organizations. They in turn represent literally thousands of senior members. These senior citizen governors chose others from the community to sit on the governing board, such as the mayor, a state senator, aldermen, hospitals, government agencies, businessmen, including representatives from our partners' organizations, and so on.

There are none of the usual power struggles, because the senior citizen governors retain complete control of M.A.O. through their council structure within the governing board. While the seniors' groups are divergent in the aims of their individual organizations, they are strongly together on M.A.O.'s objectives and publicly supportive of the M.A.O. programs. This is important to understand in terms of M.A.O.'s development. Also, it means that M.A.O. has direct access for information and testing the feasibility of any programs we are developing, with an enormous reservoir of knowledge and expertise to draw on.

The following litany of funding demonstrates the time-consuming difficulties of current government sources. We applied for and received various federal funding from the Administration on Aging Title III, the Office of Economic Opportunity, Model Cities, Community Development Block Grant, and Title IVA and Title XX Social Service Programs. It is impossible to convey the trauma of trying to obtain federal funds for a program you believe in. . . .

Nevertheless, it is the federal funds that enable M.A.O. to provide all its 175 social supportive services paid staff, ranging from attorneys, three levels of counselors, employment specialist, three levels of home care staff, handymen, drivers, home-delivered meals, counselors for emotional health, alcoholic and drug dependency and abuse, and so on.

I found that true and simple analogies are effective in drawing on local resources and support, by gaining community acceptance of our program. For example, one irate taxpayer called me to complain that he didn't have a car as good as the ones in which we transport our seniors. I pointed out that one senior with mobility problems that we saved from slipping and thus avoiding a serious hip fracture would more than pay for one vehicle. It is more difficult to persuade different governmental branches to look at the total picture of costs, or even to accept the notion that most human services can in the long run be cost effective. Our recording systems have become M.A.O.'s key in demonstrating this, by citing a variety of individual case histories, showing human effectiveness and comparative cost effectiveness.

M.A.O.'s current annual budget from all our federal funding is $757,000. We serve approximately 14,000 seniors with medisupportive services. Of these, we served a recorded average of 3,400 unduplicated seniors a month, with an average of 18,000 recorded services a month. About 6,100 unduplicated seniors receive medical services from our clinic with Abbott-Northwestern. Through our various voluntary action programs, we are serving a recorded 37,000 unduplicated seniors. We do not keep monthly statistics on our voluntary programs, because of their large volume; however, we do keep basic records on these seniors. All direct services given to our seniors by paid staff and volunteer staff are recorded, plus related data.

M.A.O.'s medical partner is the Abbott-Northwestern Hospital, Inc. I chose this hospital because of its proven record of delivering top-quality medical services with, as their president put it, "tender, loving care," and because of their visionary and flexible leadership, which had already pioneered new outreach programs, such as their regional organization, which provides management purchasing, consultation and so on to fifty hospitals.

As my relationship with the hospital developed, I learned about the serious financial crisis many of our hospitals face, due to a regressive cost reimbursement formula that doesn't adequately allow for capital expenditures, new technology and equipment, or even needed repairs. These problems are further compounded by the percentage of empty beds for peak loads which many hospitals carry, which drive up overhead costs. Yet, I also knew from the seniors that many of them were not seeking critically needed medical services because of their inability to pay the costs above Medicare. Therefore, I asked the hospital to subsidize the uncovered costs for inpatient and out-patient care for low- and near-poverty-income-level seniors. In return, I projected a better utilization of the hospital's resources. Not only did this prove to be true, but in the course of time, the hospital found that with increased utilization, the cost of hospital services to all Medicare patients was reduced by $4.20 per patient day. This saving, together with a rationale and methodology I wrote regarding allowable costs as collectible bad debts, with Mr. Thomas Tierney of the Bureau of Health Insurance at the national level and Mr. Jim Flavin of Blue Cross-Blue Shield of Minnesota, who have been most cooperative, has made it possible for the hospital to invest in providing jointly my medisupportive concepts.

The hospital runs the Abbott-Northwestern Hospital, Inc./Minneapolis Age and Opportunity Center, Inc., Senior Citizens Clinic, providing a nurse practitioner, visiting nurses, nurses in our clinic, plus nurses for our miniclinic centers, laboratory technicians, dietitians, a clinical pharmacist and an assistant, and provides our on-site pharmacy, where seniors can purchase prescription drugs at a substantial saving. The hospital's kitchens provide our home-delivered meals, including special diets.

Abbott-Northwestern's physicians showed their support of our program by forming the Community Medical Associates, a private medical practice which provides our five full-time physicians, and four part-time physicians. Besides staffing our joint clinic, our physicians serve M.A.O.'s patients in the hospitals, as in any private practice.

M.A.O. has its own counselors serving within the hospital, as well as in our joint clinic, to provide an unbroken service. The clinic and M.A.O. have a single intake procedure, and our social service records and medical records are kept together in one case history file to further cement the medisupportive concept to all staff viewing these records. M.A.O.'s supportive services and our joint clinic are housed together in an attractive modern building, owned, remodeled, and furnished by Abbott-Northwestern, to meet our methods of delivering network services. The space M.A.O. occupies is leased from the hospital. All services are on the ground floor. The atmosphere is warm and welcoming, reflecting the respect we have toward the people we serve. Seniors are never seen in an office atmosphere, but individually in intimate, comfortable and private "mini" sitting rooms, or modern, well-equipped examination rooms.

Besides serving seniors in our center, we bring M.A.O.'s services to their homes, and to twelve miniclinic centers scattered throughout the city, with one in the county. Some are housed in schools, churches, and other agencies' buildings. We are not charged overhead, and we do not charge for the services provided by our nurses, counselors, attorneys, or whatever other M.A.O. services are needed in that neighborhood. M.A.O. does not charge for any of its services anywhere. Seniors may make a donation if they can and wish to. It is interesting to note that while client donations are given toward direct field services, such as meals, home services, or transportation, rarely are they given for counseling, which is absolutely vital to providing a good client-patient care plan.

In designing a care plan with the senior, whether on an episodic or ongoing basis, we use what I call the "wheel" concept. The spokes of the wheel are the network of social and medical services provided by M.A.O. and our joint clinic and any other resources that our staff have developed or knows of. These spokes surround the senior and the counselor, who are in the center of the wheel. The pattern, type, and frequency of services drawn on, are based on the senior's needs as he sees it and on his acceptance of the services and without the counselor either giving, or asking for, unreal expectations. If a care plan is made that cannot be produced or the senior cannot "live up to," the senior will "drop out." I believe some of the people who need help the most are "dropouts" because medical and/or social services staff set up impossible client –patient care plans that ignore the individual's life-style and willingness or ability to participate in that plan; then on failing, the client –patient doesn't return, so he can avoid the embarrassment of professional disapproval.

The M.A.O. counselor first and always encourages the senior to be as active as possible and to do the things he can for himself, reassuring him that we will definitely come in with the services he needs if he feels tired, is ill, or if he cannot continue. Then wherever possible, the counselor involves any family and/or friends who are willing and able to provide assistance, again firmly reassuring them that M.A.O. will come in immediately, if and when they need us, or if they need a "vacation." Finally, M.A.O. provides the rest of the services needed. Rarely do we find a senior we have to do everything for. We have also found that the difference between the senior with many medical and social disabilities, who is able to stay at home with our help, and a senior, perhaps with lesser problems, who properly has to be institutionalized, is their determination and ability to participate in a sensible and reasonable care plan.

We train all our staff to ask for personal information respectfully and delicately, explaining to the senior simply and directly without professional jargonese, why, and what, we need to know in order to serve them. And we remind all our staff from time to time during regular in-service training to avoid the tendency, in interviewing a senior, of it becoming just a "routine" and forgetting that it is not so to the senior who has to bare his personal life to a stranger. Even after a relationship is established, it can break down if the staff person becomes insensitive or careless in his attitude. We ask staff to serve the seniors, as they would wish to be served, pointing out they don't know what their own old age holds for them.

Staff have volunteers attached directly to them at all levels; for example, I have a voluntary administrative assistant, and one of our three full-time attorneys is a volunteer who came on our staff after he retired. M.A.O. has around 200 volunteers in our various voluntary action programs, such as Operation Grandparents, with around 160 active every month. We train our staff to be helpful and attentive to our volunteers and not treat them as second-rate staff. Our volunteers are offered the same training opportunities and career ladder development as our paid staff. In fact, some of them eventually become paid staff of M.A.O.

Besides Abbott-Northwestern, we have several other partners, such as the Junior League of Minneapolis, who provided us with our volunteer coordinator and helped establish our free blood bank; the Minnesota Restaurant Association, for whom I wrote a program without federal funds, that provides low-cost meals in 120 restaurants during their off-peak hours.

Here again, I used the principle of better utilization of resources. Then there is the Lampert Lumber Company; Shedd-Brown, Inc.; and Young President's Organization, who are auditing our books without charge and at my request, so they can judge whether their tax dollars are spent effectively. These businesses and this organization, as well as some individuals, banks and other businesses, have made contributions to our programs, both fiscally and as volunteers, and have provided our crisis funds.

It is not possible here to relate the full story of M.A.O.'s network, its concepts, partners, programs, methods of delivering services, and training of staff. During the last few years, M.A.O. has received over 2,000 requests for consultation and training from all over America, from Canada, and other countries, and so I have just completed the foundation, which began in 1973, of the M.A.O. National Institute on Aging to share and teach M.A.O.'s programs and experiences.

I have spoken of the foundation, and this leads to the form and substance of M.A.O., which is shaped by the realities and the dream. The realities are our people's needs, the dream is how we serve those needs. Hopefully, we have taken the best of the past and dared to attempt the future. We have looked for people not afraid of human emotions, not afraid of words like *compassion, dedication,* and *service.* Our staff has joyfully entered the field of human services, because they believe in those principles. We know that emotions harnessed to knowledge and direction can be a powerful tool in helping our seniors successfully use the services we provide.

I will continue to constantly seek the advice of our seniors, accept their leadership over us, and learn from their experience. In the final analysis, my dream has one major objective, to provide seniors with the services they need, when they need them, and in the manner in which they wish to be served.

And now let us illustrate what the approach means in practice by the following case reports (Krause, 1968, pp. 27–33):

Clients: Frank and Marie B.   Case No. 413E
Ages: 74 and 71   December 1, 1971, to June 20, 1974
Income: $260/month
History:
Marie: The client's health is poor. She has diabetes, diabetic foot ulcers, diabetic neuropathy, peripheral arteriosclerosis, hyperthyroid requiring numerous thyroid medications, and anemia. Because of her diabetic condition, her circulation is very poor and results in frequent skin ulcers.

Several hospitalizations and operations through the Abbott-Northwestern/Minneapolis Age and Opportunity Center Clinic were necessary to improve circulation, such as a left lumbar sympathectomy to increase the blood flow to the skin.

The client requires custom-made shoes to decrease irritation to the back of her heels.

Frank: The client had chronic bronchitis, emphysema, recurrent abdominal pains (resulting in operations, through the Abbott-Northwestern/ Minneapolis Age and Opportunity Center Clinic, on the colon), hernia, pulmonary emphysema and fibrosis, peripheral arteriosclerosis, high blood pressure and dyspnea, and respiratory insufficiency. The client was on many medications. He was unable to care for himself, and so he needed much care by his wife, who as stated above, had her own severe health problems.

A M.A.O. counselor discussed this situation with the clients and the A-N/M.A.O. clinic doctor. Frank and Marie were determined to remain in their own home, in spite of their severe medical problems. Based on the doctor's recommendation that M.A.O. supportive services would be essential to the clients and at the clients' request, a Home Care Plan was prepared.

Action Taken/Home Care Plan

The following service plan was set up with both clients:

1. *Self Support:*
   Marie attended to as many of Frank's personal care needs as possible, her own personal care needs, and prepared a simple breakfast.
2. *Family Support:*
   The family provided grocery shopping, helped with homemaking and chores, and gave emotional support.
3. *M.A.O. Support:*
   a. A-N/M.A.O. Senior Citizens Clinic: for on-going medical care.
   b. M.A.O. Home Delivered Meals
   c. M.A.O. Homemaking services: were substituted when the family was unavailable.
   d. M.A.O. Transportation to and from medical appointments.
   e. M.A.O. Chore services as needed.

With the above service plan, Frank and Marie were able to remain in their home, according to their desire, for thirty-one months.

Costs if the Clients Had Been Institutionalized
from December 1, 1971, to June 20, 1974

	Cost
Average basic costs of nursing home care at $450/month each for above period (this is a conservative *averaged* estimate)	$ 27,900.00
Less clients' joint income of $310/month for above period (clients would have been allowed to keep $25/month each for personal needs)	− 9,610.00
Potential costs to Title XIX	$ 18,290.00

Cost of M.A.O. Services
from December 1, 1971, to June 20, 1974

Service	Number of Services	Cost
Counseling	33	$ 165.00
Home-delivered meals	2 meals a day, 7 days a week, for 31 months for both clients. Clients paid $1.00/day	3,478.00
Homemaking	41	307.50
Transportation	23	78.00
Chore	2	15.00
Total		$ 4,043.50

Cost Effectiveness

The potential costs to Title XIX of institutionalization for above period would have been approximately (after the client's income was deducted):

	$18,290.00
Less cost of M.A.O. services for above period:	− 4,043.50
Total potential "savings" to Title XIX	$ 14,246.50

Therefore, the government could pay for all of M.A.O. services and still save the taxpayer $14,246.50 for the above period as M.A.O. did.

Update
June 20, 1974, to December 31, 1977

Clients: Frank and Marie B.
Ages: 75 and 74
Income: $360/month (prior to Frank's death)
$315.80/month (after Frank's death)
History:

Frank and Marie B. continued to receive M.A.O. services as noted earlier with the exception of M.A.O. home delivered meals, until March 8, 1975, when Frank died.

Because Marie is a resourceful person, she was constantly looking for methods to compensate for her handicaps. For example, she devised a way to prepare meals from a sitting position, with her leg elevated, which allayed the doctor's concern that she avoid any lengthy periods of standing on her feet because of her pathology. With pride she demonstrated this method to her counselor. The counselor encouraged and supported her efforts, so M.A.O. home delivered meals were no longer needed.

Frank and Marie's children continued to be heavily involved with their parents, providing all the necessary grocery shopping, laundry, and small errands; their loving grandchildren visited regularly.

In late February, 1975, Frank was rushed to Abbott Hospital on an emergency basis. He was admitted with severe, chronic, obstructive pulmonary disease, bilateral pneumonitis, severe cor pulmonale, and thrombocycopenia, from which he died. Marie naturally was deeply distressed. It had meant so much to her, to be able to prepare his meals and care for the man she loved. Now, she didn't know what to do or how to go on living without him. In trying to care for him, she had been able to "overcome" some of her own severe health problems.

Her family remained at her side throughout the entire ordeal. The counselor was also supportive, including attending Frank's wake to show his respect and caring.

Marie was now alone in the house, and this concerned Marie's family. However, the family wanted to abide by Marie's wishes. The counselor, therefore, suggested that someone might be offered a room in Marie's house free of charge, perhaps, in exchange for some help around the house (M.A.O.'s live-in/live-out program.) Although the M.A.O. employment counselor was asked to find a person for this, the family was able to find someone on their own, after the counselor introduced the concept to them.

While Marie has resisted attempts or suggestions by the M.A.O. counselor to join the M.A.O. Grief Group, she has received individual therapy from the counselor, and has followed through with his suggestions to keep as busy and as involved as possible. Her continuing health problems do not make this easy. Part of that involvement led to her volunteering to be a mailing coordinator for her church. This job, which can be done in her home, involves pasting self-addressed mailing labels on envelopes. She takes great delight in this, for it is another way of showing that she still is a productive and worthwhile person, able to do something to help someone else; this is very important to Marie, now that she no longer has Frank to love and care for.

M.A.O. continues to serve her.

Action Taken/Home Care Plan

As a result, the following service plan was arranged to provide Marie with the network of services to remain in her home:
1. *Self-Support*
   Most of the time, Marie is able to prepare her own meals and attend to her own personal needs.
2. *Family Support*
   The family continued to provide grocery shopping and laundry assistance.
3. *M.A.O. Support*
   a.   A-N[Abbott-Northwestern]/M.A.O. Senior Citizens Clinic: for on-going medical care.

b. Transportation: for rides to and from medical appointments.

c. Counseling: for on-going coordination of service and support, especially during Marie's period of grief.

d. A live-in worker through employment: to live in Marie's home to ease the families' apprehension about Marie's living alone. (These services are provided without federal funds.)

e. Chores: to provide any needed handyman service around the house. (This became extremely helpful on one occasion when Marie came home from the M.A.O. clinic to find her house had been broken into. The M.A.O. handyman went out immediately and installed new locks and repaired a ripped-out screen door.)

f. Homemaking: to assist with housekeeping as a supplement to what the family can do, and what the live-in worker can do.

g. Legal: to assist with Frank's will and estate for Marie.

h. Home-delivered meals: as necessary, during periods of increased illness.

As a result, Marie continues to be in her own home. This has become extremely important to her, as it is all that she has left of her life with Frank. She thinks of him often. While Marie has resisted attempts or suggestions by the M.A.O. counselor to join the M.A.O. Grief Group, she has followed through with suggestions to keep as busy and involved as possible. Considering her health condition, this is not easy. Part of that involvement led to her volunteering to be a mailing coordinator for her church. This job includes pasting self-addressed mailing labels on envelopes, which can be done in her home. She takes great delight in this, for it is another way of showing that she still is a productive and worthwhile person, able to do something to help someone else.

Cost Effectiveness of This M.A.O. Home Care Plan Versus Institutionalization

Cost if Mr. and Mrs. B. Had Been Institutionalized from June 20, 1974, to March 8, 1975 (Prior to Frank's Death)

	Cost
Average basic cost of nursing home care at $520/month for above period (this is a conservative *averaged* estimate)	$ 9,720.00
Less clients' income of $310/month for above period (clients would have been allowed to keep $25/month each for personal needs)	− 2,790.00
Potential cost to Title XIX would have been	$ 6,930.00

Cost of M.A.O. Services from June 20, 1974, to March 8, 1975 (Prior to Frank's Death)

Service	Number of Services	Cost
Homemaking	28	$ 223.44
Transportation	17	57.80
Chore	7	55.86
Home-delivered meals as necessary (see narrative)	4 meals a day, 7 days a week (7 days). Clients paid $1.00/day	25.90
Counseling	2	13.00
Total		$ 376.00

Cost Effectiveness

The potential cost to Title XIX of institutionalization for above period would have been approximately (after the clients' income was deducted)

	$ 6,930.00
Less costs of M.A.O. services for above period	− 376.00
Total potential "savings" to Title XIX	$ 6,554.00

Cost if Mrs. B. Had Been Institutionalized from March 8, 1975, to December 31, 1977 (After Frank's Death)

	Cost
Average basic cost of nursing home care at $725/month for above period (this is a conservative *averaged* estimate)	$ 24,650.00
Less client's income of $315.80/month for above period (client would have been allowed to keep $25/month for personal needs)	− 9,547.20
Potential cost to Title XIX would have been	$ 15,102.80

Cost of M.A.O. Services from March 8, 1975, to December 31, 1977 (After Frank's Death)

Service	Number of Services	Cost
Homemaking	79	$ 886.38
Transportation	55	245.85
Chore	11	123.42
Home-delivered meals as necessary (see narrative)	2 meals a day, 7 days a week, 56 days. Client paid $1.00/day	113.12
Legal	2	26.84
Counseling	41	124.07
Employment	2	6.73
Total		$ 1,526.41

Cost Effectiveness

The potential cost to Title XIX of institutionalization for above period would have been approximately (after the client's deducted income):

	$ 15,102.80
Less cost of M.A.O. services for above period	− 1,526.41
Total potential "savings" to Title XIX	$ 13,576.39

Therefore, the government could pay for all of M.A.O. services, and still save the taxpayer $13,576.39 for the above period, as M.A.O. did.

Total Combined Cost Effectiveness for All Three Periods
(December 1, 1971 to December 31, 1977)

Potential Cost to Title XIX for above 3 periods	$ 40,322.80
Less costs of M.A.O. services for above 3 periods	− 15,945.91
Combined potential total "savings" to Title XIX for above 3 periods	$ 34,376.89

The combined potential total savings to the government after paying for all M.A.O. services from December 1, 1971, to December 31, 1977, is $34,376.89.

Human Effectiveness

The client is still at home and has avoided being institutionalized, which the client greatly prefers. Every month adds to the human and cost effectiveness of this case.

Let us now look at another typical case report (Krause, 1978, pp. 42–45).

Client: Del A.   Case No. 411E
Age: 60   October 1973 to June 20, 1974
Income: $155/month
History:
The client is a recent "widow" and a retired waitress and maitre d'hotel. She is presently sixty years old. The last time she saw a doctor was at the age of thirteen. Her husband died in May of 1973 of cancer. At this point, several problems developed:

1. She had never been married to her husband and was therefore unable to get social security benefits under his name. Having no income or assets, the client thought she might have to turn to welfare.

2. She went into depression at the thought of this and turned to alcohol as an escape from her problems.

3. She complained of frequent insomnia. She had also been experiencing abdominal pain.

Action Taken/Home Care Plan

1. A M.A.O. special health counselor was immediately assigned to the case to work with the client and find some solutions to her financial problems and to help with her depression and alcoholism.

2. A M.A.O. case counselor was put on the case to accumulate all necessary data that could be of use to the M.A.O. attorney in assisting the client.

    a. The M.A.O. attorney investigated the case and was able to prove to social security that the client came under the Minnesota Common Law statute that was in existence in the year 1941, when the client and "husband" began living together. Due to this, the client was able to apply for widow's benefits under social security.

    b. Due to the fact that Hennepin County Adult Services was pressing for commitment proceedings against this client, the client again turned to M.A.O. and its attorney to protect her civil rights. The M.A.O. attorney, counselor, and special health coordinator were able to prevent the commitment action by Hennepin County through a thorough medical and social evaluation at the Abbott-Northwestern/Minneapolis Age and Opportunity Center Clinic.

3. Because she lived in the furthest limits of Hennepin County, transportation services for the M.A.O. clinic medical examination and follow-up were needed, so M.A.O. transportation and volunteers became involved.

    The client's basic health is good. Medical examination and follow-ups showed no major problems, other than those indicated above. She is now receiving $155/month from social security and she will also be entitled to all assets of her husband; that is, the house and $1,000 insurance policy. With the help she has received from M.A.O. in relieving her financial problems, she is no longer in a state of depression, and her consumption of alcoholic beverages has diminished considerably through the further assistance of the M.A.O. counselor and his work in getting her involved with Alcoholics Anonymous. However, she will still need M.A.O. counseling to assist her and support her in independence.

    In order to show the cost effectiveness in dealing with this client's complex problems, it should be divided into two parts:

1. The costs of preventing institutionalization, or commitment, of this client.

2. The on-going support estimated to be needed in order to maintain her in independent living.

Cost Effectiveness of This M.A.O. Home Care Plan Versus Institutionalization

Cost if the Client Had Been Institutionalized from October, 1973 to June 20, 1974

	Cost
Average basic cost of institutionalization at $350/month for above period (this is a conservative *averaged* estimate)	$ 3,150.00
Less client's income of $130/month for above period (client would have been allowed to keep $25/month for personal needs)	− 1,170.00
Potential cost to Title XIX would have been	$ 1,980.00

Cost of M.A.O. Services from October 1973 to June 20, 1974

Service	*Number of Services*	*Cost*
Counseling	36	$ 360.00
Transportation	18	58.50
Volunteer	2	9.00
Total		$ 427.50

Cost to M.A.O. of Preventing Commitment of This Client

Service	*Number of Services*	*Cost*
Counseling	17	$ 170.00
Legal	15	300.00
Transportation	6	19.50
Volunteer	4	2.00
Special health counseling	3	30.00
Total		$ 521.50

Cost Effectiveness

The potential cost to Title XIX of institutionalization for above period would have been approximately (after the client's income was deducted)

	$1,980.00
Less Cost of M.A.O. services for above period	− 949.00
Total potential "savings" to Title XIX	$ 1,031.00

Therefore, the government could pay for all of M.A.O. services and still save the taxpayer $1,031.00 for the above period as M.A.O. did.

Update

Client: Del A.
Age: 63
Income: $155/month
History:
M.A.O. continued its assistance to Mrs. Del A. until May 18, 1975, supporting her in the recovery from bereavement and alcoholism by arranging a treatment program for her at her request. The M.A.O. attorney handled some carry-over complications dealing with her widow status (see original action taken, section 2-a).

Mrs. A. has been extremely successful with sobriety and has gained a sense of worth and dignity due to M.A.O.'s support. She is presently working as a counselor for chemically dependent people and has been doing so for nearly two years.

Without M.A.O.'s involvement with Mrs. A., she might have been committed to a state institution at great human as well as financial expense. For Mrs. A., M.A.O. has a special meaning, for through M.A.O. she regained her independence, dignity, and self-respect.

Cost Effectiveness of this M.A.O. Home Care Plan Versus Institutionalization

Cost if the Client Had Been Institutionalized from June 1974 to May 18, 1975

	Cost
Average basic cost of nursing home care at $725/month for above period (this is a conservative *averaged* estimate)	$ 7,975.00
Less client's income of $130/month for above period. (client would have been allowed to keep $25/month for personal needs)	− 1,430.00
Potential cost to Title XIX would have been	$ 6,545.00

Cost of M.A.O. Services from June 1974 to May 18, 1975

Service	Number of Services	Cost
Legal	10	$ 219.60
Special health	7	88.15
Transportation	2	8.94
Total		$ 316.69

Cost Effectiveness

The potential cost to Title XIX of institutionalization for above period would have been approximately (after the client's income was deducted)

	$6,545.00
Less cost of M.A.O. services for above period	− 316.69
Total potential "savings" to Title XIX	$ 6,228.31

Therefore, the government could pay for all of M.A.O. services, and still save the taxpayer $6,288.31 for the above period, as M.A.O. did.

Total Combined Cost Effectiveness
(October 1973 to May 18, 1975)

Potential cost to Title XIX for above period	$ .8,525.00
Less costs of M.A.O. services for above period	− 1,265.69
Combined potential total "savings" to Title XIX	$ 7,257.31

The combined potential total savings to the government after paying for all M.A.O. services from October 1973 to May 18, 1975, was $7,257.31.

Human Effectiveness

The client is still at home and has avoided being institutionalized, which the client greatly prefers. She has become independent of M.A.O. services and is an active member of the community who is also gainfully employed.

We do not think it necessary to do other than comment briefly on the significances of what we have quoted.

1. Mrs. Krause's thinking and actions are not fully comprehensible without focusing on the ways she has redefined people as resources: the seniors, the "volunteers," and almost every other type of individual in the network. Basically, she believes that people are capable of more than they and society say they are, and she is certainly not enamoured with job titles and educational background as a basis for judging people's potentialities. (If she has redefined people as resources, it is a process she experienced about herself in her own life.)

2. She understands that every individual is embedded in a variety of networks, parts of which can often be mobilized for purposes of support. For Mrs. Krause, resource redefinition, networks

of relationships, and "people need people" have to be seen in relationship to each other.

3. She is crystal clear about the nature and consequences of agency turfdom and competitiveness, and no less clear about the potentialities of resource exchange. For Mrs. Krause, resource exchange is not only a value or a goal but also a determinant of strategy; that is, find out what the needs of an individual or an agency are and then figure out if you have resources to meet them, so that in helping them you get something you or your agency needs. It is a form of barter.

4. M.A.O. is part of a loose, more rather than less informal, voluntary, far-flung, resource exchange network of individuals and agencies that for all practical purposes can accommodate to any idea, person, or agency as long as a mutual exchange of resources is possible. The network has aspects of the self-help rationale, but it is by no means the only principle governing exchanges. The purpose and rationale of M.A.O. is to support the determination of the clients to maintain independence, to help themselves to do this as much as their fluctuating physical capabilities allow and as their ability permits, and to call on family, friends, neighbors, and agencies for help in their efforts. The ability of a married couple to help each other is a definite part of the picture. The whole thing is based on self-help and mutual help as far as the client is concerned. Other kinds of exchange come into the picture in exchanges among the personal helping networks and M.A.O. and among supporting community institutions, where self-interest rather than self-help is the motivating factor.

5. The coordinator of the network—by self-selection and not election, by performance and not formal credentials, by force of ideas and personality and not by political power or possession of funds—is Mrs. Krause.

6. It appears that to the extent that M.A.O. and its network depend on the customs and processes of grant support (writing applications according to externally determined guidelines, having to justify one's activities according to external criteria of evaluation, the waiting period of months before one hears about a decision, the usual one-year support, the pressure to plan the application for next year shortly after one has begun this year's grant, and so on), its functioning according to its values is both helped *and* hindered. If

Mrs. Krause has balanced the positives and negatives so that the latter are less evident than the former, it is in part because her network is so large, differentiated, and supportive. She knows how to mobilize *her* networks just as she knows how to mobilize the networks of seniors in the effort to help maintain their existence in the community.

7. The implications of what Mrs. Krause has described in such detailed fashion (including the cost-accounting methods employed to determine the cost of a single instance of any service, which she was forced to do because, initially, professionals, government officials, and community agencies considered her a kind of nut or subversive who was confusing hopes with accomplishments) for public policy, funding patterns, and the age-old problems of "coordination" and the "delivery services" are yet to be adequately explored.

Many questions about M.A.O. and Mrs. Krause can be asked, but we shall restrict ourselves to those we consider most relevant to our purposes. Having said that, we must go on to say that the literature on networks is deficient in case descriptions of the development, structure, vicissitudes, and rationale of actual community networks. The reasons for this are many, and among the most important are the sheer complexities of describing an ever-changing, growing, unbounded network that intersects and overlaps with other networks. Indeed, it is probably unjustified to talk about *a* network as if it were not interrelated with other networks. One can talk about "Mrs. Krause's network"; that is, viewing her as a central node and mapping the varieties of "give-and-take" connections she has (actually, potentially, and with varying frequencies) with other people. But, if one then did that for each of these people, we would quickly see that Mrs. Krause's network is a fraction of what we could call the "M.A.O. network." That is to say, if one is interested in the resource exchanges that are taking place, or could take place, one must look at more than Mrs. Krause's network.

The problem of mapping and logging, let alone of understanding, the myriad connections and interconnections are staggering, especially because changes are always occurring. The problem cannot be avoided, because it requires us to look at the kinds of data we need to begin to answer the question "What exchanges are taking place, on what basis, and with what consequences?" If one sees oneself as part of a resource exchange network, one cannot evaluate its outcomes by looking at that network from the perspective of a single individual. So, for example, what we know about M.A.O. is largely (but not exclusively) from Mrs. Krause's perspective, and we could study the quantity and quality of resource exchanges that take place. But as soon as we do the same with another individual who is in Mrs. Krause's network, but whose own network goes beyond hers, we would probably find other resource exchanges. Mrs. Krause is under pressure to demonstrate the cost effectiveness of her rationale, and it becomes crucial to locate all resource exchanges, not only those she can see from her position in the network. This is a methodological problem in how one maps and analyzes a resource exchange network, but one that has enormous consequences for how one evaluates the activities of a network.

This brings us to a related issue. There are two "messages" that are contained in Mrs. Krause's accounts, one in the foreground and one in the background. The foreground message is that the network exists primarily, if not exclusively, to serve senior citizens. That is to say, the network stands or falls on how well it meets their needs. The method of cost accounting employed is intended to demonstrate the comparative advantages of the resource exchange approach for the welfare of senior citizens. But there is a more muted message (less mute in private discussions with Mrs. Krause): *The sense of mutuality and the benefits of resource exchange are needed no less by the "server" than by the "served." To create and sustain the conditions that enhance the well-being of others requires that those conditions exist to a discernible degree for you.* That is a conception Mrs. Krause understands and implements in an exemplary way for the "servers," and she would be the first to say there is a payoff for her that is not only derived from the knowledge that other people are being helped. And we have reason to believe it is no less true for other servers in the network. The amount and quality of resource exchange among the servers can be assumed to be considerable, although those exchanges are given little attention in Mrs. Krause's reports. As a consequence, in her effort to cost account the M.A.O. services and compare those figures with the costs of institutional care, Mrs. Krause shortchanges herself. Should one not cost account the benefits of resource exchange among the servers and compare that analysis with one for the servers in nursing homes? To anyone who knows the history of nursing homes (the scandals in the media are the tip of the iceberg) and continues to keep informed about them, the answer would be "Why waste time proving the obvious?" The point is, of course, that the obvious is precisely one of the reasons Mrs. Krause was galvanized into action (what happens to the served being another reason). But Mrs. Krause's cost accounting focus is not an oversight. She knows perfectly well that those who give funds like to see themselves as "hard-nosed" and devotees of accountability, and therefore they want "hard data" on what happens to the served. We have no quarrel with hard data and accountability except when they are in the service of denseness and memory failure. The fact is that the policy makers and funders have literally thousands of pages of testimony demonstrating that if the conditions for mutuality and resource exchange do not exist for the servers (for example, the staff and personnel in nursing homes or in M.A.O.) they are not likely to exist for the served. As earlier pages in this and the previous chapter indicated, one of the reasons resource exchange networks tend to be ambivalent about or reject the usual sources of funds (or regret having taken them) is that the funders are only interested in what happens to the served, not the servers.

Again we must ask a question, a variant of one we asked in a previous section: "However one characterizes and labels this network, how many people in it not only grasp the principle of resource exchange in relation to aged people but also see its applicability to other social problems?" Not everyone in the network is concerned in their working roles exclusively with senior citizens (for example, hospital administrators, physicians, lawyers, and so on). From the standpoint of understanding networks, as well as how and under what conditions they influence a society in whole or in part, their "spread effects" deserve the closest study. If, as we do, one judges the rationale and benefits of resource exchange networks to have desirable social consequences that provide a way to avoid some of the worst features of contemporary living, the question of how people learn the rationale and then apply it generally is a very practical one. Mrs. Krause understands this issue, but, given the pressures she is under to survive and the hostility she continues to encounter from those who are threatened by her rationale and success (for example, some nursing home businesspeople and some human services agencies), she should be forgiven if her accounts do not provide partial answers to some of our questions.

The final questions are the most obvious of all: What is the role of individual leadership (like a Mrs. Krause) in developing and sustaining a resource exchange network? In such a network, how does leadership style positively or adversely reinforce the spirit of the rationale? How do we differentiate, if we should, between the leadership and coordinating functions? And how does (or should) leadership-coordinating style change as the network expands geographically and in the number and heterogeneity of its participants? And what happens when the leader-coordinator is no longer present? In an expanding resource exchange network, does it make sense to talk of a leader-coordinator? Some of these questions can be answered empirically. Others are of the "ought and should" variety. These questions will be taken up in a later chapter. On the basis of the descriptive material we have provided, we trust that the reader agrees that these questions are of practical import.

In Chapter Two, we attempted a brief overview of the societal context out of which emerged the issue of limited resources. We say "issue" because there is no general agreement about the extent of the limitations in relation to natural resources, and hardly any attention at all has been given to possible limits on human resources. The fact is that regardless of how one views the issue there is agreement that neither natural nor human resources are used either efficiently or productively. In the present chapter, we described instances of how some individuals and groups have reconceptualized the relationships between resources and human services, attaching different labels to their new efforts, which are by no means similar in structure, development, and scope. Whatever their differences, they all explicitly or implicitly contained the principle of resource exchange and mutuality. Although not always explicit, they also reflect a concept of network and the forging of interactions with other networks. But there is another characteristic—not universal, but in our experience almost so—and that is that what we have termed *resource exchange networks* have usually been formed by a nonprofessional individual or group. Or, in the few instances where professionally trained individuals played a formative role, it was because they saw themselves in extreme disagreement with established modes of organization. This is not to say that in their network role their professional training and experience were directly relevant to the purposes of the network, because for some of them it represented a deliberate departure from their accustomed professional role and ways of relating to people. Although it should not occasion much surprise that professionals have played such a minor role in the formation of resource exchange networks and that more often than not the professional community has adopted a disdainful attitude, we shall in the next chapter look further into why professionalism has to be seen as an obstacle to such networks. This should not be taken to mean that professionalism by its nature is an inherent obstacle, but rather that in our society it has worked out that way.

4

Professionalism as
an Obstacle
to Network Development

In the abstract, most people heartily favor the principle of resource exchange. In the concrete, especially if they are asked to act on the principle, their response may not be as positive. The sources of their resistance or rejection may be quite diverse, but certainly one of the general factors these sources reflect is the way we are educated and trained to define and stay within the boundaries of our working roles. And we stay within these boundaries because it is our claim to a distinctive identity. Few developments have given as distinctive a stamp to the post-World War II world as the rise of myriad professions and the efforts to which groups have gone to legitimate their role as a professional one. Although the evidence is accumulating (Sarason, 1977; Krantz, 1978) that these rigidly defined boundaries have become personally and socially maladaptive for many people who call themselves professionals, the striving for professional status goes on unabated. Because we have come to see the ethos of professionalism as an obstacle to comprehending, let alone to acting on, a resource exchange rationale, we shall in this chapter elaborate on and criticize some of the characteristics of professionalism. Indeed, we shall be returning to these issues in later chapters when we attempt an analysis of why efforts to coordinate human services agencies and programs have been failures.

Because our position can easily be misunderstood, either by people who consider professionalism an unmixed blessing or by those who have never given the matter any thought, we shall begin by very briefly stating a few of our assumptions:

1. Within any professional group, there is significant variation in competence and even greater variation in wisdom. (There is a difference between education and training, on the one hand, and wisdom, on the other hand.)

2. There is a dynamic in the development of a profession that leads its members to see themselves as possessing knowledge and skills no one outside the profession has. Put in another way, they vastly underestimate either the knowledge of the outsider or his or her capacity to comprehend the professional's knowledge and skills. The professional is an expert to whom the nonprofessional is expected to defer. Just as, after World War II, Winston Churchill said (in regard to India) that he was not made prime minister to preside over the dissolution of the British empire, the professional, analogously, did not become a professional so that other people could tell him or her how to do his or her job.

3. Professions are sincerely concerned with standards of performance and from time to time seek to improve the quality of their members' services. As a profession "matures," however, its efforts at improvement become intertwined with elevating its status and maintaining or increasing economic benefits. This intertwining need not be consciously deliberate, although, when a new or competing profession appears on the scene, the intertwining can be quite deliberate. To the profession, an outsider is not only the lay public but also any other competing, or potentially competitive, profession.

4. Nonprofessionals, regardless of level of education, do not possess a folk wisdom superior to that of the professional. Wisdom is not differently distributed in the two populations. There has been a tendency to exalt this folk wisdom among nonprofessionals, but the justification for this is not compelling.

The Desire for Professional Status

Why has it been so attractive to be considered a professional? This begs the questions "What are the criteria for professionalism?

Extended formal education? Expertise? Specialization? Autonomy? Providing a socially needed service?" All of these criteria have a surface plausibility, but there is a self-serving aspect to them; that is, they are used as much to provide social approval and a sense of personal worth and distinctiveness as to reflect the emergence of new functions based on new knowledge. The attraction of a professional label is that it gives the holder a sign, literally and figuratively, that says to others, "I am distinctive. You should respect me for what I know and can do. I am not part of the mass. I am not interchangeable with others." Professionalism can be impersonally and "objectively" defined, but seeking to become a professional is quintessentially a quest for personal and social worth. According to census definitions and data, in 1890, 3.78 percent of people between the ages of twenty-five and sixty-four were professionals. In 1920, the figure was 4.4 percent, and in 1960 it went to 12.99 percent (Veysey, 1975). This dramatic increase has many sources, and of the more significant ones is the belief endemic in our society that attaining professional status, having a professional label, attests to one's personal and social worth. Veysey (1975, p. 420) has put it well:

> If one looks at the subject of the professions from the ground up—by perusing the pages of the United States census from 1880 forward which are devoted to categorizing and counting them—the inadequacy of the widely employed model of professionalization is apparent. All sorts of anomalies appear. Actors, for instance, are consistently termed professionals; so, nowadays, are funeral directors, yet the academicization of these groups has been relatively slight.
>
> Most key elements in widely used definitions of professionals turn out not adequately to distinguish them from other groups in the American population. The need for prolonged training is shared by artisans and craftsmen. Again, specialization is a tendency which has proceeded in many sectors of American society. Who could be more minutely narrowed in terms of function than an automobile assembly-line worker? Are the professions distinguished by a dedication to altruistic social service, as certain sociologists have claimed? Some of the most notoriously venal occupations are listed by the census bureau as professions. Even a few kinds of manual skills are rewarded with professional status—those of dentists, surgeons, and athletes, for instance. Yet businessmen are even now excluded because they deal with the buying and selling of material goods. In short, all sorts of hidden arbitrary assumptions are built into the very notion of the professions. Together they suggest that some degree of enhanced social status is the only true common denominator of the varied occupations that are given this label.

To seek and attain enhanced social status may be the true common denominator, as Veysey says. When one considers how each new profession has had to struggle for its birth and existence against the objections of older professions, of academic conservatism, and of legislative and legal tradition, it should not be surprising that issues of enhanced social status mark the history of the different professions. Professional preciousness and imperialism (as found in the guilds of another era) are social diseases that fledgling professions resist only to manifest all their symptoms once they have attained enhanced social status (a form of identification with the aggressor). From this standpoint, it is more correct to say that the common denominator among professions has two factors: first, to attain and maintain enhanced social status and, second, to make life difficult for any fledgling group the existence of which is perceived as diluting the established profession's status.

In the mass media, especially since the early 1960s and the emergence of the policy of community participation in decision making, we hear and read much about a growing antiprofessional sentiment. At the same time, as Veysey's comments suggest, the striving for some kind of professional label and status has, if anything, become stronger. We hear far less about the problems of turfdom *among* professional groups either because these conflicts are not deemed as newsworthy or because they are conducted in places and ways that escape public attention. For example, we know that much controversy surrounds the proposed national health insurance legislation, but most people are unaware that part of that controversy is like a war in that diverse professional groups, some new and some aged, are fighting to delimit which of these groups will be listed as health providers and, therefore, eligible for reimbursement for services. So, side by side with a growing distrust of professionals and credentialing grows the scramble to attain professional status. Both tendencies validly reflect societal attitudes. The major significance of the striving for professionalism—and its offspring, specialization—is that it creates a gulf between the profession and the public, and among the professions. And by "gulf" we mean, among other things, a stance that downgrades two-way exchanges of any kind and elevates *noblesse oblige* as a basis for interaction: Resources flow in one direction because the recipient is seen as devoid of relevant resources. From the standpoint of resource exchange, the most unfortunate consequence of rampant professionalism is in its narrow definition of resources and in its organizational resistance to redefinition. As we said earlier, we are not asserting that this consequence is a result of crass self-interest, or social insensitivity, or stupidity. It would be easier to deal with if it were simply a virtue-sin dichotomy. The fact is that in our society the incentives to make one want to become a professional, the rewards of status and/or money that are associated with being one, plus the organizational forms that professions develop to protect their interests, have the effect of making a virtue of clearly stated, relatively impermeable boundaries that "protect the public." Any weakening of these boundaries is tampering with the public welfare! Winston Churchill did not realize the general significance of his view of the obligations of a British prime minister.

The disease of professionalism is not in an unreasonable devotion to high standards but in the tendency to define a problem in such a way that its amelioration requires the services of certain professionals, thus rendering the problem unsolvable on manpower grounds. The definition keeps standards intact, or implies raising them, although the consequence may be (almost always is) a shortage of professionals. The profession's problem is "solved," yet society's problem still exists or is even exacerbated.

Professionalism and Participation

One of the clearest manifestations of antiprofessional sentiment is the articulation in the past two decades of the principle: Those who will be affected by the decisions of others (like public officials or professionals) have to participate in some nonritualistic way in decision making. They may be surgeons or other types of physicians, highway engineers, land planners, architects, teachers and educational administrators, social workers, researchers, psychological testers—when they make a decision that will impinge on our lives, we have a right to know, discuss, and influence it. This marked change in attitude is not wholly explainable by changes in the larger society reflecting political principles involving realignments of power. An additional factor has been the perception that the accustomed ways in which professionals make decisions frequently have unfortunate consequences. Just as the waging of war is too important to be left to the generals, our individual lives and our larger society are too important to be left to the discretion of professionals. It should occasion no surprise that this principle has not been warmly greeted by professionals. But this is less important for our purposes here than the simple fact that the process of becoming a professional always results in attitudes that make it extremely uncomfortable for the professional (and often impossible) to share decision making with others affected by his or her decisions. This is an individual psychological characteristic acquired in the process of spending years being "formed" in educational and training centers that inculcate this characteristic extraordinarily well. Malevolent and conspiratorial motivations are not involved. Through their training, professionals come to see their attitude toward decision making as natural, right, and proper.

This attitude of professionals is inimical to almost every aspect of the rationale of a resource exchange network. For one thing, in such a network there are no second-class citizens. Each member participates voluntarily and with the same "rights and obligations" of any other member. Exchanges are not determined by status or power but by the perception of mutual benefits. Significantly, although participants can vary widely in education, skills, and knowledge, each of them can be viewed, and hopefully view themselves, as having something that someone else needs. As important as what an individual can contribute is what he or she can learn to contribute regardless of titles and credentials. In a resource exchange network, the interests, needs, and abilities of participants are not defined by their titles, degrees, or any other conventional certifying characteristic. This is not to say that people have license to do whatever they want or to arrogate to themselves roles or functions but rather that' participants have diverse interests and talents that should not be overlooked *only* because they lack the relevant formal credentials. At its best, a resource exchange network is a learning network because it increases the possibilities of which a participant can become aware in relation to his or her interests and talents.

The reader will recall from some of the descriptions in the previous chapter the importance placed on self-determination in matters fateful to one's life and development. That emphasis has to be seen in terms of not only a theory of productive learning but also a reaction against the professionals' attitude that they always "know what is best" for others.[1] And the same can be said for the burgeoning self-help movement. It is not that there is an unreasoned, blind, antiprofessional bias but rather a recognition that too frequently, and with the best of intentions, the professional underestimates the importance to the individual to feel that he or she is participating on his or her own terms. The individual's right to fail is something that professionals have extraordinary difficulty comprehending. But, as those descriptions suggest, the right to fail, far from resulting in a failure, often exposes talents and strengths. This whole issue is germane to relationships in which there is inequality in authority and power. But it is no less relevant to relationships in which that inequality does not inhere in them but is projected into them.

It is debatable whether the professional attitude that is inimical to the rationale of resource exchange networks is less frequent in the general population. After all, ours is a society in which who and what you are, and the titles you possess, very much determine how (or even when or if) people will interact. However, the evidence is overwhelming that resource exchange networks tend to be developed by nonprofessionals or professionals deliberately departing from the usual professional stance. Of all the resource networks about which we have knowledge, and this includes many self-help networks, few of their participants are credentialed professionals. And if there is any doubt on that score, there can be none about the hostility some of these networks encounter from professionals as individuals or groups.

The quality of participation among people is in part determined by how people define themselves and others on a number of

[1]Mrs. Dewar's comments on this point are illuminating: "It is not just important for the individual to *feel* he is participating, he must *do* so. If he doesn't, the service, and the professional, will likely fail. He must invest himself. As a student, he must be an active learner, as a patient he must actively seek health. Professionals can't shove education and health down one's gullet. That's a fantasy. We talk about a cooperative patient or client (one who follows the professional's orders and advice), instead of talking about a cooperative professional: one who delivers the service a client wants, when he wants it, where he wants it. If we stopped talking about cooperative patients (meaning the doctor has achieved success with the patient's help), it would then make more sense to indicate that the patient had got well with the doctor's help."

bases, and one of these bases is as resources. What is distinctive about resource exchange networks, in contrast, say, to professional groups, is the understanding that people are or can be very differentiated resources and that one of the major functions of the networks is to develop and exploit that diversity. Whether it is done well or badly is, of course, important (and will be dealt with in a later chapter), but that is not the point we are emphasizing, which is that in the rationale for these networks participants as resources get defined *and* redefined.

It is so obvious that we often fail to note the interrelationships among participation, resources, and decision making. Who participates in what ways in the context of decision making already reflects a view of who has resources to contribute to decision making. In formal organizations, participation in decision making is well defined, although in almost every instance it could be demonstrated that the decision makers seek information and advice from others in the organization. And when they do not seek such information and advice one can count on nonparticipants to seek some input into the process.[2] That is to say, in practice the decision-making process is influenced by formal and informal intraorganizational networks, a clear recognition of the principle that resources relevant to decisions are possessed by people whose role, status, or title do not "entitle" them to participate. *In fact, in practice the dichotomy between decision makers and those who do not make decisions is one of the main sources of conflict and controversy in formal organizations precisely because it creates sharp differences in conception of resources relevant to decision making. Much of what is subsumed in the phrase "organizational craziness" refers not to who has responsibility for decisions, or even the substance of decisions, but rather to a process that unduly restricts the universe of alternatives from which a decision will emerge.* Few factors contribute more to this restric-

---

[2]It is part of the folklore of decision making in formal organizations that one has to look beyond administrative charts and job descriptions if one wants to understand the bases for decisions. So, for example, part of the folklore is that one should never overlook the role of secretaries in obtaining and offering information that would ordinarily not filter into the context of decision making. Aside from confirming the obvious fact of the existence of formal and informal intraorganizational networks, this folklore also speaks to the equally obvious fact that the conventional way of defining people as resources is an obstacle to be circumvented, organizational theory and rhetoric to the contrary notwithstanding.

tion than the combination of organizational hierarchy and its attendant dynamics, on the one hand, and the traditions of professional preciousness, on the other hand. It is a combination calculated in the name of efficiency and rationality to restrict participation. By way of contrast, let us listen to Cohen and Lorentz's (1977, p. 2) statement about resource exchange networks:

"People" networks are voluntary associations, in which individuals from a variety of jobs, class, and personal perspectives participate out of a sense of enlightened self-interest. Network members define other members as resources whom they can exploit in tackling a problem. The larger the number of members, the greater variety of ways in which the talents of these members can be classified, the higher the number of interconnecting links, and the more systematic the direction of the flows that connect the links—the more powerful is the potential of the network.

Networks are not groups of people with identical interests. They consist, instead, of people who can tackle a problem in common from different vantage points, who can exchange different points of view, and who can find strength in a certain amount of challenge and opposition. A network is a group, then, that finds ways of pulling together, deriving strength from overcoming forces that tend to pull the group apart.

Because the network should consist of dissimilar people searching to attain a common objective, it must be continuously open to the entry of new members, as well as initially open to diverse persons. If a group's membership is fully defined and closed off in advance, it is not likely to be receptive to the introduction of new resources and energies, especially those that appear to threaten and challenge the status quo.

What so often leads groups to develop an "insider-outsider" dichotomy, and therefore to become parochial, is an overriding concern with hierarchy. No group is ever completely devoid of hierarchy. The question for networks is whether the hierarchy is rigid or flexible. For people networks to work, the structure must encourage flexible hierarchy. On any given issue to which the network addresses itself, it should be possible to change the hierarchical structure to take advantage of individual resources and talents. Flexible hierarchy also facilitates shifts in topics and issues.

Networks are functional systems, dealing with matters of actual or potential need. By being able to adopt new missions and objectives more easily than organizations, which tend to become ends unto themselves, networks avoid becoming "relict" systems. Because these networks are functionally directed, continuously adopting new tasks, they may seem to be unstable as individual interests change and the roles of individuals shift within the hierarchy. Such short-term instabilities are overcome, however, by the common interests of the members in focusing on the flow and interchange of ideas and activities, and on the emphasis on the qualities of the individual as resource. Under these conditions, network members can tolerate delayed gratification. They are able to grin and bear a particular problem of relatively little interest to them, for they know that their interests and worth will eventually be tapped by the network's shifting its action focus. Thus, any short-term instability is really an element that makes for long-term, dynamic equilibrium.

This statement implies several assumptions. First, diversity among participants is an antidote to parochialism if only because it increases the alternative ways a problem can be posed and attacked. This, of course, does not guarantee that the quality of decisions will be better, only that more of the universe of alternatives may get on the table. But more is implied than the correlation between diversity among participants and the range of alternatives that can surface. Diversity among participants is a prerequisite for developing interconnections with other networks, thereby increasing further the resources that are potentially available to everyone. It also can act both as a corrective against the tendency to see only differences among individuals and groups with different labels and roles and as stimulus to perceive communalities and complementarities of interests among people with widely differing labels and roles. Diversity is not, of course, an inherently "good thing," but in the development and elaboration of a resource exchange network the attitude toward and the achievement of diversity are crucial. In everyday living, we glibly accept the maxim that everything is related to everything, at the same time we find ourselves railing against the lack of connectedness in our worlds. The resource exchange rationale is a way whereby we can begin to exert some control over blind interconnectedness and self-defeating disconnectedness. Second, the informal resource exchange network permits quicker response to emerging possibilities because there are no ironclad rules about who can raise problems and participate in discussion, decisions, or exchanges. Third, roles and functions of participants can and are expected to change, as much because of self-interest as because of a need to satisfy the sense of belongingness. One might sum up by saying that in a resource exchange network, participation is seen as a right, a control against parochialism, and a condition for individual change and development—all of these being either antithetical or a source of problem to professionalism. Professionalism is based on an exclusionary principle; a resource exchange network is explicitly based on an inclusionary one.

It might appear from this discussion that the traditions of professionalism have adverse consequences only for those the professional considers lay or outsiders. Such a conclusion cannot be justified on empirical or cultural grounds. We have emphasized how in recent decades the principle of participation (those who will be affected by a decision have a right to participate nonritualistically in that decision) has been articulated and given legislative sanction. If these developments have not been greeted with applause by the professional community, it should not lead us to overlook one of the momentous changes in the status and power of professionals: Like everybody else, most professionals are now part of or directly affected by large formal organizations. The hallmark of the professional, and one that in the past accounted for the attraction of professional status, has long been autonomy; that is, the right and the obligation to determine the conditions under which the professional will dispense services. More often than not, in the past autonomy was associated with solo practice. That is far less the case today when professionals find themselves "slotted" in large, formal organizations composed of diverse professionals and nonprofessionals.[3] The result has been that these professionals now complain about not having a voice in decisions that very much affect their lives as well as those of the clients they were trained to serve.

One health professional put it thus: "As professionals, our primary allegiance is to our clients, but as members of the organization our allegiance *in practice* is expected to be to the organization. But that dilemma is nothing compared to trying to get a voice in decisions about how services will be rendered. Make no mistake about it, we are functionaries and after a time you give up trying to influence what is going on. Sure, it's a pain in the neck to let the public participate in policy matters, and I confess I would rather it were otherwise. What the public does not know is that we have the same problem they do: having something to say about what affects our

---

[3] Anyone who has any doubts on this score would find it instructive to study (among others) the modern hospital, the Veterans Administration, some of our large industrial organizations, and our universities. In relation to the negative professional response to the principle of participation and to the adverse effects on professionals of their increasing embeddedness in large, formal organizations, the reader is referred to Sarason (1977) and Bledstein (1976).

lives." This professional was refreshingly candid. Most profession-als, however sensitive to encroachments on their autonomy and right to participate, fail to see that the principle of participation is no less a right of "the public" than it is of any professional group. They prefer the game to be governed by the rule "Heads I win, tails you lose." We do not say this unkindly but simply as a way of emphasizing how the process of becoming a professional instills attitudes that di-vide the world between "us" and "them," between "our" rights and "their" rights. (Professionals, of course, begin to understand and to react against the thrust of irritating professionalism when they are in the role of layperson; for example, a physician who sees his or her child's teacher or principal as insensitive, arrogant, controlling, and status conscious, or the educator with a sick parent trying to deal with imperious medical personnel.) This way of dividing the world is, of course, not peculiar to professionals, and if human history is re-plete with examples of this tendency it helps explain the presence of the compelling tendency to seek to gain more parity in human rela-tionships. If we have concentrated our attention on professionals, it is because the cult of the professional is one of the distinguishing characteristics of the modern era, and even though one of its sources is the sincere desire to improve the public welfare this is no warrant to overlook its status as a mixed blessing, especially for those people who put a high value on participation and who see the definition and uses of human resources as a bedrock problem in contemporary society.

An Illustrative "Case"

A couple of officials of a state social service agency had long been aware of the usual fractionation of services within state govern-ment and between state government and voluntary social agencies. They knew that, despite their rhetoric, and that of others, about an emerging network of services, the realities were otherwise. As one of the officials said, "When we go before a legislative committee, we make our pitch about more effective cooperation and how our goal is an effective network of services among all relevant agencies. And, as you have seen, we have charts to 'prove' it! But, really, nothing has changed. Sitting here in the capital, we are little more than conduits for distributing money from the state and federal government."

Their concern was being transformed into anxiety because there would be no increase in state appropriations, which meant that because of inflation there would be less money to go around. They decided to hold meetings around the state to which they would invite representatives of state and voluntary agencies to discuss the possibility of a new effort at coordination. There would be twenty to twenty-five people at each one-day meeting. Hopefully, they thought, some kind of resource network might emerge. One of the officials had read our book, *Human Services and Resource Networks* (Sarason and others, 1977) and contacted one of us (Lorentz) about making a presentation at one of the meetings. And how can you say no to a request from someone who has read, and even liked, your book?

Before describing the meeting, something must be said about how two of the officials saw the problem. There was no doubt they wanted to improve the quantity and quality of services rendered to citizens. But no less important to them were the feelings of isolation and discouragement they encountered in the staff of social agencies. They attributed these feelings to two factors: The state was moderately large, and, except for a few metropolitan areas, it was primarily rural, so that many agencies were far from sources of professional stimulation; all agencies were struggling with inadequate resources to deal with long lists of clients.

What was distinctive in this assessment was the belief that, even if resources were dramatically increased, the lack of intellectual stimulation among staff members would be a barrier to improvement of present services as well as to conceiving of innovations in existing programs. In our experience, policy makers, at best, are only dimly aware that the needs of the served have to be seen in relation to the needs of the servers. These two officials were poignantly sensitive to the isolation and low morale of many staff members, and they hoped that some kind of network could be developed that would dilute the consequences of these feelings. They had only a vague conception of how this network could develop and be sustained. They knew that one cannot legislate "togetherness" and that a one-day meeting of people who did not know each other (and most had never met the two key state officials) could be pleasant, even interesting, but nonproductive in its consequences. It could also be a boring disaster, which is near par for this kind of course. There are networks, and there are networks. They are not of a piece. It is not difficult to describe what a particular kind of network should accomplish, but it is no easy matter to choose among the different steps and strategies that will take one from point A to point B to point C, and so forth.

For example, if one wants to develop a network based on some principle of resource exchange, on what basis does one start with a one-day meeting of twenty or more people who may not know each other, and, in this particular instance, who did not know the hidden agenda (a term used here nonpejoratively)? Is the problem one of numbers or of determining by individual discussion people's readiness to discuss resource exchange seriously? How do you use your existing network to locate key individuals who, if they participate, will open new possibilities for network growth and diversity of resource exchange?

We shall deal in a later chapter with these and related questions, but we introduce them at this point because they point to the questions, "What do you mean by participation? How do you create the conditions consistent with that meaning?" How you inform people about a meeting; how you exchange views with them; how you emphasize the voluntary aspect of participation; how sincerely you convey that there are not, nor should there be, predetermined "solutions," how you clarify the possible relationships between self-interest and mutuality—the nature of these actions defines in practice what you mean by participation. To the extent that you, with the best of intentions, assume a superiority of knowledge, values, and direction, to the extent that you are insensitive to the internal and external constraints people may experience in regard to resource exchange, to the extent that you have a timetable to which you want others to accommodate, to the extent you underestimate the myriad bases on which resource exchange can occur—to these extents, you may be arrogating to yourself rights and responsibilities that are no less those of other participants.

We will have much more to say about these matters later, but it is important to note here that if participation (as a political principle) is part of your rationale, you have taken on the thorny task of how to remain vigilant to the consistency between your actions and that principle. Professionals—and that is what the participants and the state officials were—are certainly not the only people who ignore or gloss over this problem, but their training and outlook are no aid to becoming sensitive to the issue, even in relation to other professionals. From the standpoint of resource exchange, participation is not a slogan, rallying point, maudlin abstraction—or mushy, spongy, semantic play—but the concrete practice of theory controlled by the knowledge of the mine fields that one traverses in the effort to make practice consistent with theory. At best, one only partially succeeds in traversing the field without injury (inconsistency). At worst, one is not aware there is a mine field, and one's efforts are aborted by a mine that appeared harmless.

The meeting was to begin with the usual introductory remarks leading up to a presentation by Lorentz, followed by a question-and-answer period. There would then be a break, after which the participants would form into three small groups to discuss networks and resources. Lorentz would circulate among the groups to play a "facilitating" role. The organizers of the meeting expressed doubts about the structure of the meeting, although it was not clear what the sources of these doubts were. Lorentz had doubts, but did not feel it was her place to express them. However, when the organizers verbalized their doubts to her, she made the following suggestion. As soon as the meeting was called to order, each participant would be asked to write down the two or three major needs they had in their work that were not being met. The needs could be in the form of information, skills, and so on. The papers on which these needs were written were then to be posted on a wall. Then the participants would be asked to spend about fifteen or twenty minutes reading these statements of needs. Behind this procedure was an assumption and a hope. The assumption was that the participants, at least some of them, would see that there were others in the group who conceivably could be helpful to them. One could count on their perceiving similarity in needs, but one could only hope that the needs would be stated in ways that would also reveal the resources people possessed. Lady Luck was obviously on Lorentz's side that day, because most participants spontaneously saw that there were people in the room who could help meet their needs and vice versa.

Lorentz then made a short presentation emphasizing the significance of what had just occurred, as well as the importance of social agencies learning to exchange resources with each other on a basis that did not require a money exchange. During the question-and-answer period, a few of the participants rather strongly said the following (paraphrased): "I agree with what you are saying, but what you are not taking into account is that if my superiors found out that I was actively engaged in some kind of resource exchange with other agencies, I would be called on the carpet and told to devote all my energies to agency business, of which I have more than I can handle." Frankly, this struck Lorentz as strange. If only one person had expressed this view, one might be tempted to interpret it as that person's basic disagreement with the idea of "bartering" for resources. But it was a view expressed by several people, and none of the other participants dissented. Although we do not see ourselves as babes in the woods in matters of bureaucracy and organizational craziness, the fact is that Lorentz had trouble giving credence to what was being said. She asked: "Do you mean that if you could demonstrate that by exchanging resources with other agencies you could do more and better for your clients your superiors would not listen and agree?" The answer was, "They might listen but would not agree."

There was a coffee break after which three small groups were formed. We shall restrict this report to the first group with which Lorentz met, because her experience in it was not markedly different from that with the other two groups. The members of this first group did not know each other, and in the first few minutes awkward silences alternated with small chit-chat. Lorentz suggested that each individual identify the agency in which they worked and something about what they did. There were three people from visiting nurses associations, a university person whose research interest was in self-help groups, one person from the state agency on alcoholism and drug abuse, and another one from juvenile corrections. Initially, the discussion centered around feelings of being overwhelmed coping with the disparity between large and difficult caseloads, on the one hand, and limited resources, on the other hand. And then Lorentz turned to the nurses and asked, "Could you tell us in what ways and to what extent alcoholism is a problem in the homes you go into?" The answers were not ambiguous: Although they do not go into homes to deal with alcoholics, the problem for the nurses is real and frequent, particularly in rural areas. After the nurses had recounted their experiences, the participant from the agency on alcoholism and drug abuse expressed surprise, and even consternation, about his not being aware of the nurses' experiences and how much overlap there was between his and their problems. He then said that at the end of the meeting he wanted to arrange for a time when he could get together with them, because they could be of help to one another. Lorentz then turned again to the nurses and asked, "Given the variety of problems you encounter in homes, to what extent are you dealing with issues around self-help; for example, with diabetics, physically impaired people, senior citizens?" As the nurses were answering the question, the university professor whose research interest was in self-help broke in to express her surprise at her lack of knowledge about what visiting nurses experience. The nurses were in turn surprised to learn how research on self-help had burgeoned in recent years.

The most obvious thing one can say about the meeting was it confirmed again (not that it needed reconfirmation) that the left hand does not know what the right hand is doing. However appropriate as a description, it is too facile as an explanation. Certainly, part of the explanation is in the consequences of the interaction between rigid agency boundaries and the competition for limited resources. But another part of an explanation lies in the nature of professional training, which leads people uncritically to assume that, if people have different professional labels, they must be doing very different things and possess nonoverlapping skills. Professional training emphasizes differences from rather than communalities with other groups. So, at the beginning of the meeting the participants saw each other as strangers not only in a personal sense but also in terms of being different kinds of professionals. We do not wish to blow out of all proportions what happened as this one-day meeting progressed, because it would be erroneous to conclude that barriers evaporated and enthusiasm reigned. But, in the meaningful sense of the term, participation, to the extent that it occurred, came only after the perception of communality of interests and needs. Indeed, despite this, one came away from the meeting mightily impressed with how hard it is for professionals to participate in such a meeting without protection from the stance of professional preciousness and uniqueness. It is a stance that pervades all aspects of their work. *And yet, in one important respect almost every one of the participants was hypersensitive to the political principle of participation, and that was in their own agencies where they felt that regardless of their knowledge, skills, and accomplishments they were not participants in decisions that affected them.* In their roles in their own agencies, they understood well the wastefulness of attitudes and practices that restricted participation on the basis of status, titles, and "objective" credentials.

What would require explanation would be if professionals as a group developed resource exchange networks, or if more than a few of them participated in them, or if such networks did not arouse in them suspicion or even hostility. As we said earlier, it is not fortuitous that so many of the networks based on a serious commitment to the principle of resource exchange were developed by nonprofessionals and in part were a reaction to the adverse aspects of professionalism.

But why have we singled out professionalism as a barrier to resource exchange networks when so many other individuals and groups share identical attitudes? After all, professionalism could not have become as general as it has if it did not have strong societal support. It's like television crime programs and cigarette smoking: A lot of people want them. Our answer is that the entire arena of human resources is now densely populated and essentially controlled by myriad professionals, with the major consequence that resources have become more limited; and, even more fateful for the future, there is little recognition and discussion of the possibility that human resources are no less limited than natural resources. It really makes little difference if one believes that human resources are unlimited in relation to needs if at the same time one recognizes the glaring discrepancy between how we define needs and the resources relevant to deal with them. How do you reduce that discrepancy when in the foreseeable future there is no reason to believe that resources, as we customarily define them, will discernibly increase, if only for economic and political reasons? And those who would argue that it is necessary to transform our society so that it becomes based on new political, economic, and moral grounds will have trouble pointing to other national systems that have "solved" the problem. If anything, the evidence seems to be that, regardless of the political and economic system, the trend to professionalism, specialization, and bureaucratic organization is remarkably similar. What will be required is a radical redefinition of what we mean by human resources, and we have tried to indicate not only what the redefinition may be but also the barriers that it will encounter. And those barriers are many and strong, not the least of them being those assimilated, unverbalized perceptions of what is right, natural, and proper—perceptions that confuse what is with what could be.

Finally, there is a feature of professionalism that is subtle, pervasive, and adverse in many of its consequences, especially in the area of human services. It is not a feature unique to professionalism, but, because of the way professional thinking and practice dominate the human services, it has to be given special comment. We refer to the marked tendency of professionals to rivet on the defects of people, on their disabilities, on what people cannot do. As a group, professionals do not know how to look for strengths and assets, let alone how to use them to help people build on their strengths. Professionals, precisely because they look at, or "treat," or help *individuals*, cannot grasp and act on the fact that strengths or deficits are not in or on individuals but are characteristics of *social contexts;* that is, they derive from the *transaction* between individual and context, and the influences flow from both directions (Sarason and Doris, 1979). As we shall see in a later chapter, the failure to grasp this simple fact in large measure accounts for the harm caused by the assumptions about old people that resulted in the initial Medicare legislation. Only within the past couple of years have there been belated attempts to remedy the situation. In any event, the focus on deficits is a polar opposite to the concentration on strengths and contexts that one finds in the resource exchange network. The emphasis is on what people can do and on what exists in their environment that can serve to reinforce strengths. These are such contrasting mental sets that it is no wonder that professionals have played practically no role in the development or implementation of a resource exchange rationale.

It could be argued that we are too hard on or unfair to professionals. After all, the argument would run, the professional is not different from other people, and, in fact, the adverse features of professionalism could not have developed without a societal "compliance" factor. That is to say, the professional did not foist professionalism on a recalcitrant society. There was something in the culture that made for a positive response to the cult of professionalism, just as in recent decades there has emerged a negative response (Sarason, 1978a). Besides, professionalism may be based on exclusionary principles, but professions are not. It is not technical needs that leads to turfdom and *noblesse oblige* but fear, greed, and insecurity; and professionals are by no means distinctive in these respects. No less than other people, professionals have dual need for networks: One in their professions and one in their several lay roles in which they have to deal with other kinds of professionals as well as with other laypersons. Besides, the argument runs, must one not avoid adopting the stance that the nonprofessional has a kind of folk wisdom the professional lacks, a stance no less invalid than the one that says the professional knows best? And, finally, are there no professionals, increasing in numbers in recent years, who have either spearheaded or participated in arrangements that try to avoid or remedy the negative aspects of professionalism?

We agree with these arguments. If we have given special attention to the professional, it is not because he or she is unique in attitude or action but because the professional has been given and has taken status and power (personal and political) that are mammoth obstacles both to the process of redefining resources and to new social arrangements that emphasize what people can do rather than what they cannot do. In the final analysis, social change comes about through alterations in attitudes toward power that lead to the altered distribution of power. And in respect to power the professional cannot be treated as if he or she is like everybody else. There are signs that those alterations may be beginning to take place in professional communities, but this chapter was written on the assumption that these alterations are in their earliest stages, and their future course is very problematic.

In this and the previous chapters, there were two themes that we make little effort to interrelate, even though on the surface it might appear they were antithetical to each other. One of these themes concerned the quality of participation in a resource exchange network, and the other concerned the role and goals of the network leader or coordinator. It is beyond the scope of this book to examine leader-participant relationships in different types of networks. We assume that in different networks these relationships take different forms and direction and are not problematic in similar ways. That is to say, the rationales place different obligations on, and give varying degrees of authority to, the leader, thus determining in explicit ways the characteristics of network participants. And the problem becomes even more complicated because, regardless of type of network, we assume it makes a big difference if the network is an informal one of individuals, or is embedded in a formal organization, or is a network of formal organizations.

In the case of a resource exchange network, the relationship between participants and leader (or coordinators) requires the closest scrutiny, because it is a kind of litmus test not only of the quality of the *exchange* process but also the "spread effect"—the degree to which exchanges lead to more and new kinds of exchanges. But there is another reason for close scrutiny, and that has to do with the mixed emotions associated with the role of leadership. The word *coordinator* appears with greater frequency in the network literature than does the word *leader*. This is especially true for descriptions of resource exchange networks. The term *coordinator* is a much more neutral word that is used to convey consistency with that aspect of the rationale emphasizing parity in participation. As we shall see in the next chapter, the virtues of neutrality should not lead us to confuse appearance with reality. Too much is at stake to allow labels to direct us from recognizing some age-old human dilemmas. In World War I, we called sauerkraut *liberty cabbage*, a harmless kind of word play. And when funeral directors preferred the designation *mortician*, or barbers became *hairstylists*, or liquor stores became *package stores*, there is a part of us that knows nothing has changed (however much we may recognize that these changes say something about changes in the culture). What differences are intended, and in practice what differences are there, in the title *coordinator* and *leader*? It is to this and related questions that we turn in the next chapter.

5

Issues of Leadership
and Coordination

In the previous chapter, we quoted
at some length from a statement by Cohen and Lorentz (1977) on
"people" networks. One purpose in doing so was to underline differences in the rationale for participation in a voluntary, informal, resource exchange network of individuals, on the one hand, and the
organizational craziness that in practice stems from the rationale for
large, formal organizations, on the other hand. Another purpose
was to suggest that people networks have a more sprawling, loose,
ambiguous structure than do networks of formal organizations. It is
reasonable to assume that these differences already inhere in the origins and developmental vicissitudes of these two broadly defined
types of networks (each of which can be broken into subtypes, depending on one's purposes). This is but another way of saying that
more important for our purposes than arriving at a typology of networks is the task of better understanding their origins and development. It is our belief that such an initial focus will ultimately provide
a basis for description and categorization that does not do undue violence to the distinction between phenotype and genotype. The
flight into typologies, like the flight into health, can be quite mischievous in its consequences. No one can quarrel with the effort to cate-
gorize as a way, so to speak, of separating apples and oranges. We

have always known that apples and oranges looked and tasted differently and used that knowledge in practical but limited ways. But it was not until relatively recently that we were able to go beyond the phenotypical dissimilarities to genotypical similarities, as a result of which the uses to which fruit are put is far beyond those of earlier times. Analogously, we know there are different kinds of networks, and we can give labels to them that are not empty of meaning, but it is our belief that at this stage of our knowledge we should stay loose and not be imprisoned in typologies. And to illustrate what we mean we quote again from Cohen and Lorentz (1977, p. 1), who remind us how little we know about "the planning and designing of people networks."

Much of what gets done in life is accomplished through loose, informal arrangements that exploit sets of connections among people. In effect, ideas and actions circulate within and among networks of people. They are energized, supported, evaluated, and modified, in making their way from inception to implementation. Sometimes people networks are very close-knit, defined by class, profession or economic status—for example, college alumni or Wall Street lawyers. At other times, networks are wide open, based upon individuals and groups from varying backgrounds who develop relationships out of a common experience—for example, the Civil Rights or anti-Vietnam War movements. Networks are used to get someone a job, to start a business, to find a house and to organize a political campaign.

Most networks that involve people just happen—through accident of birth, educational setting, or through job tracks. They are rarely planned and engineered. On the other hand, networks involving "things"—from transportation to telecommunications—are made from scratch. They are planned and engineered. These engineered networks are closed systems. Every node and link has a function designed to meet an overall objective. Opening a machine to the unexpected, the unknown or the unassimilable can cause the system to grind to a halt—for example, sand in an automobile carburetor, or a blown fuse in a spacecraft.

Even those people networks which seek to be closed to outsiders can never be hermetically sealed. When such networks approach the state of being closed systems, they tend to lose energy and momentum. Shut off from the influx of new people and new ideas, they are likely to wither on the vine and die. The most successful and long-lived people networks (like the most successful civilizations) are the ones that remain open to newcomers. These kinds of networks provide multiple pathways along which individuals can establish links with one another and to third parties and beyond.

The planning and designing of people networks is still in its infancy. While sociologists and social anthropologists have recognized the importance of social networks and have analyzed their modes of operation, the attempts to engineer such networks have been relatively few. Yet it seems to us that the deliberate creation of people networks represents a major opportunity for advancing a wide variety of national objectives.[1]

It would be more correct to say that only in recent years have we become aware of how little we know about the deliberate development of people networks, but that such deliberate efforts have long been a feature of human societies. That statement may be no less applicable to other types of networks, raising the interesting question, "Do different types of deliberately fashioned networks have different contexts of origins?" However, what is seminal in Cohen and Lorentz's concluding paragraph is contained in the connotations of such words as *deliberate, planning*, and *designing: Who* deliberates, plans, and designs?

We said earlier that networks exist, they are not created, and by that we meant that whenever we identify a network, and however we define it, it is an outgrowth of, overlaps with, and continues to be embedded in existing networks. The fact that an observer may see a "new" network, or that a few of its participants may feel that something new is emerging, should not obscure its connectedness with existing relationships. Indeed, as we shall see later, the degree to which those who are trying to forge a new network (that is, to reassort existing network relationships and to seek new participants) are sensitive to this continuity is fateful for the network's future, regardless of its formal or informal characteristics. But in all that Sarason and Cohen and Lorentz have said is the assumption that

[1]This suggests that a major emphasis in research should be to experience and study the creation of networks. Put in another way, we have to understand better the phenomenology of those who develop networks, if only to see why some networks live and die. The researcher ordinarily will not know about new networks until after their beginning phases and after the death of some efforts. Our suggestion would be that researchers on networks should seriously consider experiencing and developing a network, because that experience would enrich their understanding of the networks of others they ordinarily study as outsiders. On May 23, 1978, the National Institute of Education (NIE) issued "Request for Proposals [RFP]: Research on Social Networks in Education." On the first page are the following sentences, which they italicized. *"NIE is not interested in receiving proposals whose aim is to establish or operate a network. Such proposals will be considered inconsistent with the purpose of this RFP."* Such a policy about the relationship between knowledge and action, between basic and applied research, ignores and is at variance with significant aspects of the scientific endeavor (Garner, 1972).

there are times when an individual, or a few individuals, take on the task of deliberately changing their existing networks for some new purpose. Literally, they seek to lead others in new directions. They see themselves as "here" and others as "there," and their task is to bring these others to their psychological "here." We say *psychological* because in the case of networks physical proximity may not be possible, desirable, or necessary.

In Chapter Three, we reported in some detail instances of the development of informal and formal resource exchange vehicles. In the case of *Uplift* (Washington Consulting Group, 1974), we presented 2 of the 100 instances it contained. The descriptions in that book are too brief to permit us to come to definite conclusions, but it is hard to avoid gaining the impression that in the overwhelming number of instances an individual "designed and planned." By any definition, the individual was the leader in forging a network informed by (among other things) the principle of resource exchange. In the case of the Shoreham-Wading River narrative, we were able to determine that it was the school's principal (Dr. Dennis Littky) who was the leader. As for the Minneapolis Age and Opportunity Center, it is gratuitous to say that Daphne Krause was the "creator," and the same holds for Mrs. Dewar of the Essex Network. Not only do we know more about M.A.O. and the Essex cases and, therefore, we are more secure about our conclusions on these cases, but they are also the most clear and developed instances of the concepts of networks and resource exchange. Insofar as the forging of resource exchange networks is concerned, we shall assume there is a key person, a leader. The role of that person may change as the network develops in numbers, scope, and geography, but the quality of that development has to be seen in terms of the initial leader.

By our use of the word *leader,* it is obvious that we are differentiating, as we suggested at the end of the previous chapter, between leadership and coordination. That the leader of a resource exchange network also performs a coordinating function goes without saying, but unless one confronts the leadership function one will not understand why some resource exchange networks flourish while others remain static or wither away and why the development and sustenance of these networks may be remarkably different depending on whether they are informal ("people's" networks) or formal. The rationale for resource exchange networks confronts the leaders with some enduring, thorny, and, perhaps, some unresolvable dilemmas. The reader will recall that in Chapter One we discussed our lack of complete satisfaction about the term *leader-coordinator* and discussed Mrs. Dewar's misgivings that the term would inaccurately convey an activist role. Neither we nor she could come up with a better term. We urge the reader to pay more attention to our description than to the shorthand labels.

Leadership and the Emergence of the Network

Reconstructing the emergence of a resource exchange network is no easy affair. Even when there are written descriptions to go on, they are almost always reconstructions, by one or two individuals, that are not meant to be comprehensive, and, of course, their objectivity is subject to different sources of distortion. As we know from the field of history, there is a big difference between the facts and the truth and at different times a particular event or process is seen in new lights. And, depending on one's focus, one can emphasize the role of individuals (their personalities, status, background), or institutions, or "the times." Each of these foci can be illuminating at the same time that it distorts the overall picture. All of the methodological problems of historiography confront the person who tries to write the history of any resource exchange network. The fact is that nobody has taken on this task, if only because these networks are not yet seen as important social phenomena posing worthy conceptual issues. Our task here is not one of historiography but rather of trying to discern the outlines of some questions based on our experiences and observations; that is, questions that when clarified (and reclarified) can serve as guides to productive historical reconstruction. The task is complicated by the paucity of written materials, and we are forced, therefore, to use our experiences and observations, hoping that it will encourage others to go beyond us.

But why begin with leadership? Our answer is implicitly contained in the contents of the previous chapters. In recent decades, many people have become aware of the fact and consequences of limited resources; many people have experienced the insensitivities of large, formal bureaucracies; many people have become disillusioned with what they see as failures to solve social problems; many people have become wary of experts and professionals; and many people no longer see a positive correlation between public expenditures and the public welfare. And, crucially, some people have tried to think and act in new ways both to increase resources (or use them more effectively) and to alter the meanings they give to their lives. In short, the times were right, so to speak, for the age-old idea of resource exchange to reappear as a way of dealing with individual and social problems. The idea occurred to many people, fewer people tried to do something about, and even fewer were able to implement and sustain the idea in action. How do we account for those networks that have been sustained, those that have disappeared, and those that have been so altered that their original purposes are no longer apparent?[2] Leadership is certainly not an unimportant part of the answer.

Stated most briefly, the leader of an emerging resource exchange network has to have arrived at a point where he or she believes that resource exchange is the major avenue by which the needs of people in their different societal roles can be better met. That is to say, different people have different talents, information, and needs that they could "exchange" to mutual advantage without money becoming a barrier. That is stating the principle abstractly. In actuality, an individual experiences the principle quite concretely in terms of certain people in certain kinds of settings, and what grips the individual is that he or she can or should seek to implement the principle. Some individuals have no doubts about "should," but they do about "can"; others feel they should and they can—and they do. At some point, the individual talks to others, seeks their thoughts and advice, and enlists their participation. This is not done in random fashion, because the person's thinking and action are embedded in his or her existing networks. Whatever this emerging leader does (for example, choice of the first, second, third person he or she talks

[2]These questions are identical to those which have been studied in regard to utopian communities, which, not incidentally, were always in part based on the principle of resource exchange. For the most part, these communities were usually exclusive in terms of participation and deliberately geographically isolated from the rest of society. The varying fates of these communities were determined, among other things, by the initial leaders. The present chapter, as we shall see later, is based on considerations contained in Sarason's *The Creation of Settings and the Future Societies* (1972) and our previous book *Human Services and Resource Networks* (Sarason and others, 1977).

to) says something not only about the leader's existing networks but also about his perception of how he would like to see those networks extended.

Put in another way, in the leader's mind the principle of resource exchange has become tied to a strategy for action, and how this connection is formulated is crucial indeed, because the principle does not tell you how to proceed, the alternative ways one might consider, the pitfalls one should expect to encounter, the time perspective you should adopt, and many other procedural considerations. Even if you are aware of these considerations in the abstract, you still have to make them concrete in terms of your situation.

Success or failure at this early point is determined in large part by the leader's adherence to the logic of participation, because these issues of tactics and strategy should not be decided by the leader alone. The leader is an imperfect being, and one of the sources of imperfection inheres in his or her sense of mission, a very mixed blessing. It is as much to exercise some control over the leader's imperfections as it is recognition that others have something to contribute that these issues of tactics and strategy should not be decided by the leader alone. *Wrapped up in the principle of participation is the principle of resource exchange, and both principles must be seen in relation to each other.* In this early stage, it is usually only the leader who sees this relationship, and it is one of the leader's most important tasks to articulate this relationship and to be a model of it in action. One might say that the growth of the network is the growth of a constituency informed by the principles of participation and resource exchange. This does not mean that the leader is like a public opinion pollster who wants to find out what the electorate wants so that a political candidate will then be able to say what the public wants to hear. But it does mean that, from the very beginning, the leader, no less than other participants, has a voice in all matters. If in this early stage the leader has the most influence, because of the interaction of force of personality and ideas (the leader is self-selected), it has its positive and potentially negative effects: positive because it gets the process going and potentially negative because, in the longer run, it can constrict the range of the network's substantive foci as well as changes in participants' roles. In this initial stage, the leader is a kind of teacher, vigilant to how easy it is for him or her to manipulate others so that they willingly do what the teacher wants at the expense of learning the nature, consequences, and dilemmas of self-determination. The reader may recall that in the quote from the National Commission on Resources for Youth (Chapter Three) emphasis was placed on the student's right to fail in a supervised, self-chosen work activity. It is not that one wants the student to fail but that if failure occurs it is under conditions from which the student can learn; that is, he or she literally can capitalize on the experience so that the investment gives a return.

The leader is or should be always walking a tightrope, trying to avoid falling off the side that enmeshes him or her in the net of a labeled ego trip (a felicitously brief phrase) or off the side that lands him or her in the net of directionless passivity. Leadership is an opportunity, but it is also a trap. Leadership in action is never only in the realm of ideas; it is always entangled with personal motives, assets, and liabilities (Sarason, 1972). The leader of a resource exchange network has committed him- or herself to certain principles, but virtuous principles like love are not enough. How to be consistent with those principles, how to remain vigilant to what contributes to inconsistency is sufficiently difficult so that one does not have to look far to find here one of the major contributors to failure. As we shall see later, there are other contributors waiting in the wings.

It is strange how leaders of resource exchange networks do not like to be perceived as leaders. When they are asked to explain their role in the emergence of the network, they rather guiltily admit that they once played a leading role (although some will resist calling it *leadership*) but that such is no longer the case. In every instance of a resource exchange network that has endured over several years and about which there is a fair amount of description, the leader of the early stage is still a leader, although other leaders have emerged. And it is the emergence of new leaders that belies the deceptive modesty of the initial leader, because one of his or her goals has been, particularly if the network has become extended, to facilitate the emergence of new leaders.

For example, in the case of the Essex Network it is an unassailable fact that Mrs. Dewar, a private citizen, was the leader, the moving force. As the network began to mushroom, she realized that if the future was like the recent past, she would be unable to give network activities the attention they required. "We will need," she said, "another coordinator." She resisted using the term *leader* and began to cast around for someone sympathetic to a resource exchange rationale and the coordinating function. This is not to say that at that time there were no network members capable of performing such a role. Some members were either already playing that role in relation to their particular substantive focus (that is, extending their network around a particular focus), or they simply did not have the time. What Mrs. Dewar sought was someone who had or could develop a grasp of the overall picture, not someone committed to one or two foci, but someone capable of seeing new opportunities for broadening the network's substantive scope—not someone who would be in charge of a switchboard, so to speak, but someone who could take the initiative to alter and enlarge the circuitry. Mrs. Dewar wanted another Mrs. Dewar. And if she saw and called herself a *coordinator*, and sought another one, it was another instance of how labels can be misleading when in the service of undue modesty. Mrs. Dewar did get another "coordinator," and for a year or more he largely functioned as a coordinator under her tutelage. What bothered Mrs. Dewar was that the coordinator did not seem to be taking initiatives; that is, he did not seem to be *leading* and coordinating. Not being a person who easily circumvents issues dear to her ideas and beliefs, she openly raised, discussed, and helped him with what was at stake. What she had underestimated, according to the coordinator, was how long it takes to become familiar and to act in accord with the rationale in a growing, geographically far-flung network.[3]

What was remarkable about meetings as time went on was that, although Mrs. Dewar was there, it was the "coordinator" who largely orchestrated and directed the score. The network, in effect, had two overall leaders: each involved with different and overlapping parts of the network, both working hand-in-glove with each other so that both had more knowledge than anyone else of the network's wide-ranging activities.

In this section, we have been emphasizing a single point: Although coordination is central to the rationale of a resource ex-

---

[3]Mrs. Dewar and the coordinator differ in many ways: sex, age, social status, education, and so on. They are very different kinds of people. Mrs. Dewar had forged her ideas over years in various human services settings where (by virtue of status and personality) she always had a leadership role or was in some relationship to setting leaders. If she underestimated what it takes for a young person "to take hold" in unfamiliar surroundings and from the standpoint of a rationale easy to grasp but difficult to put into action, it is understandable at the same time that it talks to the thorny issue: Who can be a network leader, and how can he or she be prepared for the role?

change network, the individual who develops the network must also be a leader. The ability to lead *and* coordinate is essential; however, that ability may be manifest in strikingly different ways in different people. When we think of leadership, what ordinarily gets conjured up in our minds is a forceful, assertive individual for whom the making of decisions is a "natural" activity stemming from the combination of role and temperament. More often than not, when we think of leaders it is in terms of individuals in formal organizations; that is, individuals who have been selected and elected to lead a part or the whole of a bounded, formal organization. But that imagery is not appropriate to the leadership-coordinating role in an informal, voluntary, unbounded network like the Essex one or like some of the others described in Chapter Three. Decisions are not made by a leader. Leaders are not elected—they emerge. Of the many leaders encouraged and coached by the Essex Network, most have jobs in institutions where either the vantage point or the content of the job made networking, once experienced, seem a logical process to adopt. The question then emerged: "Can a resource exchange network develop and be sustained *within* a formal, bureaucratic organization?" We shall return to this question in a later chapter, but for our present purpose to clarify the leadership issue we shall briefly discuss two instances where that question can be answered in the affirmative.

The first instance is Mrs. Daphne Krause, also described in Chapter Three, who is head of the Minneapolis group. That Mrs. Krause is the leader of a formal organization interconnected with many other large organizations goes without saying. That she has implemented the resource exchange rationale to an impressive degree illustrates what can be accomplished when personal characteristics and ideas are so well fitted for each other. There is, however, one fact that has to be introduced: Mrs. Krause *created* the formal organization and built the resource exchange rationale into it from the very beginning. It was not a matter of introducing the rationale into an *existing* formal organization but rather one where the rationale was a determining force shaping the organization. In this respect, one must be wary of using this instance as a basis for a generalization about the viability of the rationale in formal organizations.

The second instance is Dr. William Fibkins, whose efforts we described in our previous book (Sarason and others, 1977). In a mid-

dle school on Long Island, he developed a teacher center based
explicitly on (among other things) two related considerations: (1) resource exchange among teachers and (2) resource exchange between teachers and the surrounding communities.[4] That teacher
center is one of the most interesting we have knowledge of, and the
role it plays in the lives of the teachers is best indicated by the fact
that they contribute personal funds to meet some of its costs. But
what is no less atypically significant is that the principal, superintendent, and board of education essentially have permitted Dr.
Fibkins the time and latitude required to "coordinate" the center-
community network. For example, Dr. Fibkins has become part of
the Essex Network, has attended several of its smaller meetings (in
New York City, New Haven, and Essex), is a connecting node between the two networks, and has arranged for different kinds of
exchanges.

We know of several instances where an individual in a school
tried to develop a teacher center and failed, primarily because of two
factors: (1) the failure to use and develop informally the intraschool
and school-community network before raising the question of
formal recognition and status and (2) the usual reluctance of school
administrators to depart from past policy. The prepotent tendency
to organize early in a formal way before one has used existing networks to develop a rationale and a constituency is not a failure simply of leadership but rather of leadership not informed by an understanding of the nature and use of networks for action. This, of
course, does not mean that if there is such understanding success is
assured, but it does mean that if one seeks to introduce an innovation
into a formal, bureaucratic organization (especially if it is one with
long-standing traditions) one's strategy must be based on a sophisticated view of the size and strength of existing informal and formal
networks, on the one hand, and their interrelationships, on the
other hand. As has been said elsewhere (Sarason, 1976a, p. 325):

---

[4]Dr. Fibkins' manuscript on the creation of the center and network is
entitled *Teacher Centers and Professional Burn-Out* and is in the process of being completed for publication. Like Mrs. Dewar and Mrs. Krause, he came
to the resource exchange rationale after many disappointments and failures
with more traditional ways of changing and improving the quality of education. And, as with them, the rationale impelled him to action.

What individuals or groups will be directly affected by the proposed program? What issues of territoriality will it raise for which agencies, professions, and other interest groups? Who can be counted on to put obstacles in the way of the proposed program? Who has the power, actual or potential, to prematurely terminate the program? When you try systematically to answer these and related questions—and these questions refer to one's own organization as well as to external ones—you will find that what you propose to do impinges on networks radiating far into the community; that is, that what you propose to do will become related to quite an array of existing relationships. Indeed, performing this exercise is instructive in giving one a healthy appreciation of the myriads of interlocking networks that exist in a community. Unfortunately, an appreciation of this has always come *after* the program has failed, or has been aborted, or has fallen far short of the mark, or has been so transformed that its original goals are no longer in the picture. But even that is a too charitable assessment, because in many instances the major "lesson" articulated is that there are a lot of stupid, selfish, power-hungry people in the community who feed on well-intentioned, health-giving professionals.

In this section, attention has been centered on the role of leadership in the emergence of a resource exchange network; not leadership in the abstract but in its peculiar character and dilemmas in the effort to be consistent with that rationale and its implications. Later in this book we shall return to the issue of leadership and the viability of resource exchange networks in formal organizations. Let it suffice for the moment to add that in these days—when the concept of network has become quite fashionable and deliberate efforts "to develop new and to coordinate" existing resource networks reflect public policy—the nature of leadership-coordination (in informal and formal settings) is not an issue that can be avoided, although that is precisely what people are trying to do. We shall now turn to other facets of the problem.

Scanning, Time, and Imagination

In the previous section, we indicated the special problems of the leader of an emerging resource exchange network. The qualities that a leader needs—any kind of leader—are not inherent in him or her but are determined by the interaction between the person and the situational task. We may say that two people are indubitably leaders but after a moment's reflection say that one would be far more adequate than the other in dealing with a specific situational task or context. For example, one leader may be far more adequate in building an organization (or developing a network), while the other is far better in sustaining what has already been developed. One of them may excel in periods of sustained crisis, while the other would be adversely affected. What a situational task requires of a leader is no less important than the qualities of the leader. Because they are concretely embodied in a person, the abstraction "leadership qualities" tells us nothing about adequacy. Indeed, when we use that abstraction without qualifying it in terms of specific task and context, the consequences can be unfortunate, because it implies that a leader is adequate to any or all circumstances. This is like the burden placed on the classroom teacher who is supposed to be equally adequate with each pupil. Not only is he or she supposed to like them equally, but he or she is also supposed to manage each of them equally well. Reality, of course, lends absolutely no support to such an expectation. Faced with an "unruly" class, some teachers are far more adequate than others, just as some teachers are far better than others in dealing with parents. And this in principle is no less true than the school's leader: the principal. In the 1960s, few things were as clear as the differences among principals confronting student and parental unrest.

Although empirical studies are lacking, our experience strongly suggests that most efforts to develop a resource exchange network abort for two major reasons. The first is that the self-appointed leader does not have (among other things) those personal qualities that attract and persuade others to participate, qualities that excite the sense of mission and community in others. These are qualities crucial to the creation of a setting.[5] The second major reason, and we consider it more lethal than the first, is either the lack of clarity about the resource exchange rationale or the *relative* lack of some cognitive traits required by the rationale, or both. Let us now examine the peculiar relationship between rationale and cognitive traits. Some aspects of these relationships are peculiar to the

---

[5]In *The Creation of Settings and the Future Societies* (1972), Sarason defines a setting as when two or more people get together in new and sustained relationships to accomplish stated goals. The smallest instance would be marriage, and the largest would be to overthrow an old and create a new society. A setting need not be tied to a particular, bounded space. The development of any network can be viewed as the creation of a setting, and therefore the problems of leadership have to be seen in terms of the early context of development.

emerging phases of network development. Others hold for any point in the development of the network.

It is one thing for a leader to accept the principle of resource exchange, it is another thing to ferret out the basis on which people differing widely in status, job label, age (and a host of other variables) have something to give to and get from each other. So, for example, if you know that a researcher needs to secure a certain kind of population to study, your task is not only to help him or her secure that population but also to ask yourself, "What individuals or groups could be helpful in carrying out the research at the same time that their educational needs will be met?" In *Human Services and Resource Networks* (Sarason and others, 1977), we describe how a network leader arranged for a researcher to train high school seniors to collect, analyze, and present the data the researcher needed. That was in all respects a highly successful experience for everyone, so much so that as a matter of principle this kind of barter or exchange has to be met if any researcher desires access to schools where a member of the Essex Network is a gatekeeper. Subsequent instances leave no doubt that a mutually beneficial exchange is possible if one is aware of the different needs of different groups and if one is not prisoner of conventional stereotypes and their limiting connotations.

Not surprisingly, researchers who approach the network leader-coordinator (or are "referred" to him or her by a network member) are initially taken aback by the requirement of some sort of meaningful exchange. Researchers, and they are not alone, are used to formulating *their* needs and seeking others to accommodate *them*. Faced with the requirement of exchange, they can come up with all kinds of reasons why the research has to be done in precisely the manner they propose and why to let other considerations enter into the process is tantamount to vitiating the entire effort. It takes a while for the researcher to understand that there is no intent to transform or to subvert the research problem and that there need be no inherent incompatibility between meeting his or her needs and those of different individuals or groups in the setting. Two things are at issue: (1) the "moral" stance that if one expects "to get" one should be prepared "to give" and (2) the cognitive task to figure out who could benefit from an exchange. To do justice to the cognitive task requires that the leader-coordinator be a person who is continually scanning the environment for "matches." We are all familiar from literature with the scanning mind of the marital matchmaker who catalogues people's needs and characteristics and, computer style, comes up with possible matches. Our experience, observations, and reading of the available literature lends force to the conclusion that the most successful, sustained resource exchange networks have had leader-coordinators who possessed this scanning ability to a very high degree. Conversely, less successful or aborted networks have tended to have leaders having this ability in limited degree.

To meet or work with a network leader-coordinator possessing this scanning ability is an experience. And it can be mystifying or upsetting to somebody who does not think in these ways. Someone once described such a leader-coordinator in these ways: "It is as if her mind is always *racing*. You can almost hear those mental clicks. It's a radar type of mind that sees things and connections in the social fog that most people cannot. I get lost trying to follow the connections she comes up with." To people used to perceiving others in terms of labels, job descriptions, and institutional affiliations, or who (like most of us) uncritically assume that because agencies and institutions have different names and stated purposes they do not have common needs and features, scanning for purposes of resource exchange occurs, if at all, within very narrow limits. In truth, the analogy to radar is inaccurate, because the scanning we are describing involves more than noting presence and direction of individuals and settings; it penetrates beyond surface appearance. It would be nearer the mark to say that we are dealing with a mixture of a restless curiosity and scanning, and both are in the service of possible instances of resource exchange. This cognitive mixture is only understandable in terms of a commitment, a passionate commitment, to resource exchange as a basic value by which lives are mutually enhanced.[6]

[6]Mrs. Dewar's response to the above is instructive: "I think that 'scanning ability' is not enough for a coordinator. He must have the associational habit. This is one trait I really worked at in training Richard Sussman, and he now is a master at it. I would say to him 'whom does that person or idea make you think of?' For ages he would look blank, and I would tell him. Gradually he got the idea, then the habit, which then becomes a reflex. Another element of training is to stop the instinct to do things yourself. I had not only to keep Richard from doing things, I also had to stop members from expecting him to do things. When there was something that needed to be done I had to keep saying 'your job is *not* to *do* things, your job is to think: Whom do we know or whom can we think of who would profit from doing this? For whom is this an opportunity?' "

The three leader-coordinators we have known well (Mrs. Dewar, Mrs. Krause, Dr. Fibkins) share one other cognitive characteristic. We are indifferent as to whether one calls it "imaginativeness" or "the capacity to generalize." It is the characteristic that has allowed each of them to apply the principle of resource exchange far beyond their agency or geographical area. They have not been confined by an initial substantive focus (such as old people or schools), if only because they recognize that to do justice to that focus will require resources found in relation to other foci. There is a centripetal feature to their thinking that permits them to see "connections."

These network leader-coordinators were not "born that way." In point of fact, each of them came to the principle of resource exchange relatively late in their lives, but once they grasped the principle there was, so to speak, no stopping them. The principle served not only to *re*organize their thinking but their perception of their world as well, and when that interacted with an activist proclivity they began to change the external world. We know many people in the community who can be described as network leaders in that they can stimulate and organize other people around a problem or goal and can get them to contribute their resources or to secure them elsewhere. They, too, are activists and leaders. They are doers, and they accomplish much. In sense and depth of purpose as well as in brightness and imaginativeness, they are like the network leaders we have described. But, unlike them, they are usually oriented to a single task or focus, they see their role as getting others to contribute to remedial action, and they are content to stay within the boundaries they have set for themselves or others have set for them. By virtue of what they accomplish in regard to one task, they may be asked to concentrate on another problem, and, crucially, they almost always do not see connections between the two tasks. Many of them have the cognitive capacities of Dewar, Krause, and Fibkins, but these capacities are not in the service of or organized by the principle of resource exchange.

We do not wish to convey the impression that the three people we have described are "special" or "superior" as *people* (whatever that may mean) or that they are "smarter" in a cognitive sense. Their distinctiveness lies not in intellectual or personal characteristics but in arriving at and grasping (a most apt metaphor) a principle that reordered these characteristics in a new way. They were changed as people and thinkers, and they proceeded to change the world around them. Nor do we wish to convey the impression that their numbers are as miniscule as the frequency of three would suggest. These are three people we have come to know well. We have met and heard of many more, but our knowledge of them is too scant to come to any secure conclusion. As we pointed out in an earlier chapter, these people usually do not write for publication, and their activities have had little significance for social scientists who do.

When a resource exchange network has been developed and sustained over a period of years, participants surface who seem to possess the cognitive and motivational characteristics of a leader-coordinator.[7] A developmental process then begins, because grasping the rationale and acting consistently on it is not like "solving" an arithmetic problem: Having solved the problem, you do not have to solve it again. What needs to be learned is a way of thinking and acting in relation to a constantly changing scene, cast of characters, and opportunities. Rarely, if ever, is one dealing with *an* opportunity for exchange, the nature and future of which is very unpredictable. Indeed, one of the most difficult things to learn in pondering a particular possibility of exchange between two people is how to see that exchange in terms of the needs of other participants. That is to say, how can that exchange be facilitated and enlarged, because its thrust has implications for the needs and resources of others? For example, if you know that a principal of an elementary school is seeking tutors to work with pupils with academic problems and that the principal of a high school is seeking opportunities for high school seniors to engage in educationally meaningful projects, the possibility for a mutually beneficial arrangement is clear. And if another network member is working with senior citizens and seeks ways of meeting their need to feel needed and helpful, how can this be entered into the equation so that it is fruitful for the elementary school pupils, the

[7]What keeps a network coordinator going? Let us listen again to Mrs. Dewar: "When I explain my role to people, they often say, 'You must have a ball!' The answer to that is, yes, she does. And so do other coordinators. The sensation felt by them when a match they have brought about works and takes off on its own momentum is that of a real high. The explanation seems to be that outward integrations achieved have inner reverberations. There is a kick in 'getting it together,' for everyone concerned but especially for the coordinator. He has taken the risk and has, added to the feeling of integration, the vindication of a studied gamble."

high school students, and the senior citizens? And what if other network members have expertise in regard to learning problems; for example, if they teach in a college or university and have students who conceivably can give and get something of value? What started out as *a* possible exchange has become one of several possible exchanges, and learning to let one's mind operate in this free-wheeling and yet highly organized way is not easy.

Most of us spend our lives in restricted or boundaried settings unaware of how this constricts our knowledge and resourcefulness in regard to locating and utilizing resources. To break out of this narrowness requires more than the right mix of cognitive and motivational characteristics; that is, a mix that is a necessary but not sufficient condition to do justice to the rationale. Dewar, Krause, and Fibkins did not learn it overnight. It required a difficult developmental process, as they have attested, and what they learned they have had (and will have) to learn again and again. They were not dealing with a process or substantive problems that permit formulas that merely have to be applied to new problems to get the desired results. So, when an individual with the potentials for being a network leader emerges—a process of self-selection—it is the network leader who can be of most help in the person's development.[8] Equally important are network meetings during which one's way of thinking is reacted to by others, sharpening one's awareness of how easy it is either to be inconsistent with or to underutilize the resource exchange rationale.

Another characteristic of these people is less a cognitive one (in the narrow sense) than it is the set to redefine "problems," to "reassort" and to "enlarge" the kinds of people to be encompassed in possible actions. Take, for example, the following excerpt from a statement of Mrs. Dewar written, somewhat despairingly, in reaction to the tendency of people to think in terms of deficits rather than strengths:

---

[8]That our use of the label *leader* is appropriate is seen in two ways: (1) the way the network leader (for example, Mrs. Dewar) will seek to develop a closer relation with the "potential" leader and (2) the way the latter will seek out the former. The Essex Network, the reader will recall, is not a formal or incorporated collection of people. It has no "constitution" or hierarchy of roles.

Self-help groups remain isolated, with boundaries reminiscent of other human service agencies—no interaction with professionals other than those connected with the disability around which the self-help is organized (and little, enough often, with them) and none with other parts of the community.

While the self-help group is centered around one disability or deficit, human service agencies encompass multiple calamities in their concerns. Human service professionals are trained to deal with all these different kinds of social pathologies and lack any kind of expertise in what to do about strengths. (Social workers were originally supposed to look for and build on strengths, but the medical model has long triumphed over the other.) The mission of the agency is expressed in terms of the kinds of disabilities that will be encompassed. Small wonder that professionals view their agencies and each other in the same terms, deficits, and problems. Not enough money, time, space, too many or too few clients, too much intra- and interagency friction and competitive maneuvers. Boundaries are seen not as clarifications and delineations of areas of competence and activities (what the agency has to give) but as barricades determining who may come in and who must stay out, what and who is ours and what is theirs.

Fastening attention on what ails everybody and what everybody lacks, clients, agencies, professionals, make one think in terms of getting, not giving. Members of a teacher center said, after hearing about network rationale, "We just can't do that. *We lack so much.* If the community wants to help us, fine. But we can't *give* in return!"

That teachers fail to see strengths in themselves that would be bound to come out in an interchange makes one wonder what they see in their students. The fact that they could not conceive of almost any opportunity for service from community members in ways that would benefit the server as well as the school makes one wonder about teacher training. The helper principle has evidently eluded them, that you learn through teaching, that you get help by helping, that school tutors improve more than their tutees is still a secret. When Johnny can't read, Johnny is said to need help, never mind how many times Johnny has learned to read better, faster, if he helps someone else to read. Listing people and programs under disability classifications puts service agencies and schools in the same position as self-help groups. The common denominator of the groups is the deficit. You can only deal with that group in terms of that deficit. If you try to deal with strengths, each person must be dealt with individually. Talented children are dealt with as if they presented another type of abnormality and are segregated accordingly and with many of the same results. What happens when groupings are made according to strengths: interests, areas of helping competencies, elective studies, community projects? Enthusiasm for the project and for learning around it propels students into self-help and mutual help to overcome any deficit that stands in the way of group accomplishment. The release of positive energies in staff as well as students is notable. But these programs are looked on as alternatives for bright or recalcitrant students, the exception, not the rule. That's not the way teachers are taught to teach. That's not what school's about.

We do not pretend that in this section we have done more than to raise and briefly discuss two facets of the relationship between network development and the resource exchange rationale. The first facet reflected the ways in which the logic and nature of the resource exchange rationale require that the leader-coordinator possess certain cognitive characteristics. When a rationale serves as the basis of action, not all people are able to act appropriately on it. One can have a good grasp of psychoanalytic theory (or any other personality theory from which a therapy is derived) but not be a good clinical analyst. One can have a deep understanding of the principles of democratic action and organization and yet in practice act inconsistently with that understanding. And one can be highly sophisticated about a theory of learning and still be unable in action to create the conditions within which the desired learning will occur. The ability to wed any theory with practice so that it does not appear to be more a divorce than a wedding is not frequent. The resource exchange rationale is not a theory but a principle stating that people have far more to give and get from each other than appearances suggest or our thinking allows.[9] It makes no difference whether it is a principle or a theory. If it serves as a stimulus for action, people will vary widely in the degree to which they possess the characteristics implicitly or explicitly suggested as necessary for consistent action.

The second facet is similar to the first in that, although the leader-coordinator has to be aware of a myriad possibilities of exchange, he or she at the same time has to be sensitive to "good and bad," practical and impractical exchanges. Being able to imagine a productive exchange does not mean that the appropriate conditions exist for it to occur. Indeed, how to use the network to bring about

---

[9]We assume that from descriptions in previous chapters the reader has not gained the impression that "exchanges" take place in an ambience characterized by transiency and an interpersonal superficiality—much like the imagery that gets conjured up by the term *market economy*. The word *exchange* is shorthand for a sustained process in which people become part of each other's social and intellectual environment, not in the sense of maudlin togetherness but in the sense of each enlarging the other's knowledge as well as possibilities for action.

the appropriate conditions (much in the fashion of the marital matchmaker) is one of the leader-coordinator's most important facilitating functions.

In one respect, our discussion may convey a distorted picture of the leader-coordinator if only because the word *leader* conjures up images of people with authority and power inhering in their formal role. We must remind the reader that our description and analysis are based on our knowledge of several resource network leaders who, with one exception, were part of an informal, voluntary network and whose leadership role was silently acknowledged, involving, as that assent did, no formal obligations of any kind to the leader-coordinator. These leader-coordinators want to be, can be, and are perceived as being helpful individuals, and therein lies their influence. They take initiatives without being directive, and they respond to the initiatives of others in similar fashion. And few things give them more satisfaction than to see and support the emergence of a new network leader-coordinator.

Network leader-coordinators emerge as a result of self-selection. That has always been the case where the resource exchange network is informal, voluntary, and unbounded (or where an exclusionary principle is absent). That has also been true in the few instances where such a network is in or related to a formal organization although, as we have stressed, this happened in very atypical circumstances. What happens when as a matter of policy a formal organization (we shall restrict ourselves to those in the public sector) decides that it needs a network leader-coordinator? Given the concerns about efficiency in the use of existing resources and the recognized need for "better coordination," plus the increasing popularity of the network concept, this question is of more than theoretical interest. We have had the opportunity to observe a few instances where agency policy makers came to understand the resource exchange rationale and *selected* a coordinator, with predictable results. For one thing, their choice was far more determined by what they thought were desirable personality rather than the cognitive characteristics of the person. Some of these people had in fact demonstrated leadership qualities, but in regard to tasks and rationales unrelated to the resource exchange rationale. Although the policy makers were very sensitive to existing barriers to coordination and the relationship of these barriers to past efforts to achieve coordination, they were amazingly insensitive to what this would mean to the new resource coordinator. Finally, and crucially, although they were attracted to the resource exchange rationale and thought they understood what this meant for action, the fact is that they had no understanding of one of the most important features of the development of a resource exchange network: *It cannot be programmed according to a predetermined time schedule*. No less important than any of the other leader-coordinator's cognitive characteristics is how he or she conceptualizes and utilizes time as a variable.

Time as a Variable

When we say that a resource exchange network is informal and voluntary, we are emphasizing the absence of written or explicit rules governing behavior, attendance, or even substantive focus. When a person says he or she is a member of such a network, it does not mean the same thing when that person says, "I am a teacher in school X." As a teacher in that school, the person has a role that defines his or her obligations and tasks, requires him or her to relate to people in other roles, and subjects his or her performance to a process of evaluation by others. The teacher's days, months, and years are scheduled: What he or she does and when are very much influenced by time considerations over which the teacher has little or no control. So, in the culture of the school (or other formal organizations) we hear of "the page 72 syndrome"; for example, "by October 1, my class must be on page 72 of the book." It is quite otherwise in an informal resource exchange network.

The difference is no less clear from the standpoint of the leader-coordinator. The principal of a school, no less than the teachers, lives by a schedule. Indeed, one of the complaints of principals is that they spend too much of their time developing schedules in which time is a built-in factor. And it is the same with leaders of other types of formal organizations. To them, time is a precious commodity, because the system of which they are part is based on considerations of time. We are told that when you get behind the rhetoric of any formal organization "the bottom line is green." But bottom lines are not calculated every day, but only at certain predetermined times. Of all the factors one must pay attention to in describing and understanding a formal organization, clocks and calendars are among the most important. The leader-coordinator of an informal resource exchange network is not under such externally imposed constraints (and neither are the members). For one thing, the leader-coordinator has no power to develop any schedule to which members must or are expected to adhere. The network does not have a self-imposed task that must be accomplished by a certain time. The leader-coordinator cannot tell anyone what to do and when. On the contrary, the leader-coordinator has to be acutely sensitive to the voluntary nature of participation, which can only be achieved when an individual perceives no conflict between self-interest and exchange. When and how this perception occurs varies tremendously and can be very unpredictable, but one thing is certain: It cannot be programmed. This is a lesson all leader-coordinators learn the hard way and for reasons illuminating of the differences between informal and formal networks. When a person initially grasps the principle and potentialities of resource exchange and starts to act on it, there is a sense of mission, enthusiasm, and excitement that propels the person "to get things going." *There is an internally determined time pressure, experienced in much the same way as people in formal organizations react to externally determined time pressures.* This need to act usually has the consequence that the person is frustrated by the unwillingness of others to share the enthusiasm and the seeming inability of some people to grasp the principle.

In the book (Sarason and others, 1977) devoted to the development of the Essex Network, we discuss why it took a year before the network could be said to have emerged. The false starts that marked that year were productive only in illustrating that telling people about the principle, talking about it in the abstract, and not learning in concrete detail what were the resource needs and capabilities of people, were unproductive. One does not "announce" or "proclaim" a network, and one does not bring people to a meeting in the hope that at the meeting people will get and desire to act on the message. The network leader-coordinator has a lot of homework to do before approaching an individual, let alone a group. And part of that homework requires scanning and using his or her existing networks to figure out how, when, and on what basis a person may be approached or a meeting convened. At the same time that the leader-coordinator must be aware of the traps in actions impelled by time pressures, he or she must have or develop a *sense of timing*: that sense that says that the conditions for resource exchange between two or more individuals exist. In practice, what we call the "sense of timing" is based on knowledge gathered from and discussed with network members. The leader-coordinator does not act alone on some isolated perch of social isolation but rather through and with other members. The credibility and usefulness of the leader-coordinator inheres in large part in the degree to which his or her interaction with others is consistent with the principle of exchange and the political principle of participation.

If resource exchange networks cannot be developed according to a time schedule and if a network leader-coordinator must not feel under the pressure of time to act, it is obvious what the sources of incompatibility are between network rationale and the rationale of a formal organization. As we pointed out earlier, the two instances where that incompatibility was in large measure surmounted were atypical, in that the leader-coordinator was relatively free from time pressures. Dr. Fibkins was "granted" the time; Daphne Krause had it by virtue of being the initial leader of the formal organization. But even here, as both attest, being in a formal organization sets definite and interfering limits to exploiting the resource exchange rationale. By virtue of being a member of a middle school, there are some constraints on Dr. Fibkins as to range of foci and geographical area. And in the case of Daphne Krause the need to keep her agency afloat (to write and obtain funding grants), to hire and oversee personnel, and to anticipate and react to interagency competitiveness and criticism, clearly interfere with how much time she has to exploit the potentialities of the resource exchange rationale. That both of these individuals have been able to implement the rationale to the degree they have says as much about the cognitive clarity with which they grasped the rationale, and the compatibility between their personal characteristics and the rationale, as it does about the strength of their motivation.

6

Definine a Resource
Exchange Network

U p to this point, we have been
concentrating on resource exchange and redefinition of resources.
This we have justified on two grounds. First, they are concepts and
processes that help illuminate the nature of our society and the ways
in which its culture and traditions shape our thinking. But a more
practical and pressing reason is that national and international developments have put the problem of resources on the agenda of social action. Obviously, there are many perspectives from which to
view resource exchange and redefinition of resources, and the one
we chose emphasizes that the two should be seen in relationship to
each other. If what is socially needed is to increase resources, resource exchange without resource redefinition is a limited approach. The major disadvantage of our position is that bringing the
two together exposes and therefore forces one to deal with obstacles
arising from the very nature of our traditions and culture. And they
are obstacles the strength of which cannot be overestimated. Professionalism, the nature of formal organizations, and the characteristics of bureaucratic structures work against recognizing, let alone
acting on, the potentialities of resource exchange and redefinition.

In our discussion of these concepts, it was clear that we saw
them in relation to the network concept, but we never dealt directly

with that relationship; that is, we did not define our use of the concept of network. Indeed, we used that concept loosely, and deliberately so. To some readers, it may have appeared that we were no less guilty than others in using the network concept as a sign of virtuous intent, with the result that it confused rather than clarified matters. If we postponed dealing directly with the concept of networks, it was because of several considerations. For one thing, resource exchange and redefinition contain issues, theoretical and practical, that can and should be understood apart from other considerations, if only because the obstacles to recognizing them as issues are so formidable.

Secondly, resource exchange and redefinition refer to values and processes. That is to say, it is one thing to think of them as ongoing or potential activities, and it is another thing to make the judgment that they are necessary and desirable and that such a value judgment should lead to action: to start or build on the process. Put in another way, resource exchange and redefinition contain values that should inform action. Unless you are clear about the values that are justifying your actions, you lack the basis or criterion by which you or others can judge the appropriateness of your efforts. So, the decision to concentrate on resource exchange and redefinition was to persuade the reader that they were desirable for the following reasons: They should increase the resources an individual can use to accomplish his or her purposes; they should expand an individual's awareness of his or her environment, interests, and potentialities; they should foster the sense of mutuality and community; they should, over time, influence the larger society and its institutions. These "shoulds" are not unique to resource exchange and redefinition, but they are "shoulds" very infrequently realized in living in our society. Resource exchange and redefinition are powered by the belief, and what "data" we have confirm it, that they will give more expression to these "shoulds." They are not panaceas. Far from it. They simply have more promise than the concepts that undergird so many of the activities in the societal institutions of which we are inevitably a part.

What, then, are or should be the relationships between these values and concepts, on the one hand, and that of networks, on the other hand? There is no logical relationship between them, in the sense that one is necessarily derived from the other. Their relationship is that between theory and practice or, more correctly, between values and action. One can get agreement among people about a theory or a set of values, but as soon as that theory or values serve as a basis for action it quickly becomes apparent that there is far less agreement about which actions are consistent with theory or values or about how to make decisions among the range of seemingly consistent actions. The concept of networks provides one of the ways to think about implementing resource exchange and redefinition, and if one goes that route a number of questions arise: "What is a network? What are the characteristics of a resource exchange network? How can such a network be developed and maintained? What are the obstacles to development and continuation?"

The final reason we postponed dealing with these questions is that we thought discussion would be more productive if it followed one about the role and characteristics of the leader-coordinator. The definition of a network is not independent of who defines it. The definition will vary depending on whether it is seen from the perspective of the leader-coordinator, a participating member, or an outside observer.

What Is a Network?

The form of the question is potentially misleading, because it suggests that a network has the characteristics of a "thing," as in the question "What is a pencil?" For example, what do we mean when we say that a family is a network of people? An initial answer might be that we mean they are biologically related, although in that sense we quickly realize that the mother and father may or may not be biologically related or that each of their children may have been adopted.

A second answer might be that we mean that they interact with each other in apparently predictable ways, and our predictions will be fairly accurate, even though we know nothing directly about their feelings and motivations. That is to say, if we could systematically observe their overt behaviors we could discern regularities in their interrelationships. From this standpoint, one could say that the family is a network in that their relationships among themselves have some degree of regularity or pattern. We do not think of a married couple as a family or network, but as soon as they have a child we say there is now a family, implying that from that point on there will be an alteration in the behavioral regularities between husband and wife because of the new regularities each will establish with their child. Intuitively, we know that the imagery of a network is appropriate to the family and not to the husband-wife relationship.[1] But when we say "intuitively" it is because each of us has experienced being in a family and therefore knows that by limiting our attention to the overt behaviors of a family we cannot comprehend how complexly interrelated the members of a family are. Psychologically, we know we are part of a web, a network. It is not only a matter of personal identity but also of the knowledge that what you do can have a "spread effect" in the family and that what any other member does can have a similar effect. And it can all happen at the same time. Psychologically, the family is not static but a changing, evolving complexity. The family *is*, but not like a pencil *is*.

Members of a family will say just that: "I am a member of this family." They will not say, "I am a member of this network called a *family*." Why use the fancy-sounding concept of networks instead of the familiar one of family? The family member might say, "It makes no difference if I say *family* or *network*. I know what *my* family *is*." One does not have to do new studies to assert that if you interviewed each member of a family in depth, you would not get the same description of that family. Furthermore, some members would be unaware of aspects of familial interrelationships: their occurrence and basis. The family member has nothing to gain by using the concept of networks unless he or she wants to exercise control over the tendency to see only part of the picture of family interrelationships. It is the rare family member who will want to do that, although he or she will be required to do that by some family therapists. It is the outsider (such as researchers or novelists) who will employ a concept of networks in order to see as many interrelationships as possible and to capture their different facets. *How you define a network is largely determined by whether you are an "outsider or insider" and by the basis for action it is intended to provide.*

[1]This is only true if we arbitrarily restrict ourselves, as we have done above, to an artificial, socially isolated husband-wife relation. Even without a child, the husband and wife are part of a variety of networks, each has more or less stable relationships with others, that were and will continue to be fateful in shaping their relationship with each other. Not infrequently, of course, when a couple has a child their relationship is not only altered but exposes the degree to which their past relationship were shaped by membership in preexisting family networks.

Anthropologists have long been interested in describing kinship networks, and that literature contains some staggeringly complex interrelationships (graphically or verbally portrayed), which few readers are willing or able to take the time to grasp, and few (if any) in the kinship network comprehend in its quantitative and qualitative ramifications. The anthropologist is an outsider who does not seek to change kinship networks. As he or she proceeds, the anthropologist will use what is learned to deepen understanding and to protect against incomplete description. That is quite a different role from that of a family therapist such as Bowen (1965), who is also interested in kinship networks but from the standpoint of altering them. And, precisely because he has taken on the obligation to help a troubled individual (the patient), Bowen and the anthropologist are not using the same concept of networks. There is overlap in meaning in their concepts of networks, but their different agendas for action explain the limits of that overlap. It also would explain why, if Bowen worked therapeutically with an individual who was in a kinship network studied by an anthropologist, we would have to conclude that the concept of network is an invention (as all concepts are) that can be employed in differently productive ways. All of them would start in agreement about the core features of the network concept: *Any individual has varying degrees of connectedness with many other people; the basis of this connectedness will vary; these other people may or may not be connected with each other but those connections are potentially possible through the individual; in the same way, through these other people the individual's connections can be increased; the individual's knowledge of the scope or his or her connections is less (and usually a good deal less) than that of an "outsider" mapping the individual's connections.*

There may be agreement about these core features, but depending on one's purposes different features may be stressed and related to nonnetwork variables (such as personality, race, region, or social class), or some or all of these features may be used either for planning social action or for helping an individual. Politicians, fund raisers, journalists and reporters, leaders of organized crime, operatives of intelligence agencies, some family therapists, and people in each of the social sciences employ the network concept, albeit for different purposes and with varying degrees of completeness and clarity.

Given our interest in resource exchange and redefinition, as well as in implementing these concepts, the concept of networks was, so to speak, a "natural" because it could provide a guide for action, not only in the development of the Essex Network (Sarason and others, 1977) but also in viewing the efforts of others with similar goals. It was a guide in the sense that it required us to keep in mind two things: (1) our tendency to underestimate the scope of our own networks and the resources they contained and (2) helping others see that that was true for them as well. To maximize the quantity and quality of resource exchange would require sustained vigilant scanning of the people we knew or through whom we could come to know because of the potential "match" between what we and they needed and could exchange.

What Is a Resource Exchange Network?

All that we have said about the previous question ("What is a network?") is no less applicable to the present one. For example, let us imagine that a researcher wants to study the Essex Network for the purpose of determining its membership, how it works, and the degree to which it accomplishes its purposes. And he decides to start with the membership, because that would appear to be a relatively simple question and, also, the answer to that question is necessary for his other purposes. The first obstacle he would encounter would immediately tell him one of this network's characteristics: It is informal. There is no membership list. So, being resourceful, he finds out that Mrs. Dewar was the key person in the development of the network, and he meets with her. After not too many minutes, his head would be reeling by her listing of members: numbers, heterogeneity, and geographical dispersion. After the interview, the researcher would begin getting phone calls from Mrs. Dewar because she forgot to mention this, that, and the other person who is in the network. This may be upsetting to the researcher, because such forgetting introduces "error" in his descriptions. (By the time he is through with the study, he will have found out that this "error" is probably characteristic of all his interviewees.) If he should happen to meet Mrs. Dewar a few weeks later, he would be given more members whom Mrs. Dewar feels have "joined" the network. Whatever a resource network *is,* it is from Mrs. Dewar's perspective a constantly changing affair, much like the difference between seeing a movie and any one (or even several) of the thousands of frames of which it is comprised. But Mrs. Dewar is not a collector of lists and does not equate quantity with quality. What the researcher would learn, if he asked the right questions, is that for each member of the list Mrs. Dewar knows (or tries to know) his or her multiple interests and roles, because it is that knowledge, combined with the scanning-associational cognitive characteristics, that permits her to raise and creatively answer the question, "For whom is this particular instance an opportunity?" What Mrs. Dewar knows about a member is not contained in a listing, and it is this qualitative knowledge, together with her "matching skills," that bring about a quantitative increase in the size of the network.

Then the researcher begins to interview some of the people on Mrs. Dewar's list, and he learns that the membership lists they provide can vary considerably from each other, and none of them come close to the size of the list given by Mrs. Dewar. Furthermore, if he showed each member Mrs. Dewar's list, he would frequently be told, "I never heard of or met *this* person. *That* name I know is a network member, because she has been mentioned in discussion, but I have never met her." Finally, the researcher interviews Richard Sussman, the other leader-coordinator, and finds that he is familiar with almost every name on Mrs. Dewar's list although he has not personally met them all. The researcher then finds out from him that, although Mrs. Dewar knows about almost every person on his membership list, she has not met them all.

The researcher concludes that the Essex Network literally does not have the same meaning for anybody. And yet each of them says he or she is in varying degrees a part of it. From the standpoint of Mrs. Dewar and Mr. Sussman, the Essex Network is a geographically far-flung, densely populated "thing" in which each member has three characteristics: what his or her activity in the network has been or is, what it potentially could be, and the fact that each member is embedded in other networks containing resources exchangeable with those of present network members. This scanning perspective from which they view and define the Essex Network is different from that of members who tend to identify with a smaller part of the network, as well as in one other very significant respect: the ease with which they use their network relations to explore resource exchange. Mrs. Dewar and Mr. Sussman not only are radarlike scanners for people as resources but they also pursue people. Other members of the network vary in this regard, ranging from a few members who are embryonic Dewars and Sussmans to those who are more passive in initiating action.

The Essex Network is not comprehensible (and, therefore, definable) except as a composite of the differing perspectives of the members. That composite is not easily arrived at. One does not really "arrive at" a network, because a network is always "arriving" and changing. For example, during the first three years of the Essex Network the members tended to see it as Mrs. Dewar's network: It was, so to speak, her baby, and the members had become part of her family. Activities revolved around her and her ideas and initiatives. At the end of the fifth year, that is far less the case. Some members now see Mr. Sussman as the center, while others see Mrs. Dewar that way. That change was subtle and continuous, and today new leader-coordinators are emerging, so that the Essex Network consists of several parts, each of which has a different leader-coordinator. You might say that it is decentralized, with Mrs. Dewar and Mr. Sussman continuing to discharge the responsibility of seeing the larger picture.

The researcher may conclude that the Essex Network has the features of a crazy quilt, but a crazy quilt has a very definite function that it performs well. One may be hard put to verbally describe the quilt's pattern, regardless of whether it is pleasing to the eye, and different eyes will see it differently. To the creator of the pattern, there is no craziness, and some beholders will agree, even though the basis of their agreement will not always be the same. Some beholders will have little interest in the pattern and are only concerned with the degree of warmth the quilt provides. The researcher may decide, like a person who is buying a crazy quilt, that trying to describe the Essex Network, verbally or graphically, is interesting and difficult but not as important as how well it performs its function. Its function is resource exchange and redefinition. In relation to what? And in trying to answer that question the researcher is told that in the Essex Network information gets exchanged as well as time and services on a *quid pro quo* basis. The researcher persists and asks, "What kind of information gets exchanged and around what problems and tasks are new working relationships formed?" The answer he gets is, "There are no stated limits, no prescribed foci." Information and exchange can be about alternative schools, engaging high school students in research, teacher centers, citizen groups concerned with water quality, transportation for elderly and handicapped people, parenting groups, preretirement programs, daycare centers, and so on. Some members are interested in this and others in that. Some members may be interested in several things, although in terms of exchange one interest predominates. If the researcher could attend the minimeetings that go on between the general meetings, he would find that they have different foci. The agenda for a minimeeting is less heterogeneous, but each general meeting tends to have a different organizing theme. The researcher is likely to conclude that the Essex Network has diverse foci. He would be only partially correct because if he talked with Mrs. Dewar and Mr. Sussman he would see that, although they recognize there are these different foci, they also see that on the level of action these foci can be related to each other in terms of resource exchange. That is to say, these foci are substantively different from each other, but when one seeks to increase resources to deal with a focus, one must look at other foci in terms of their needs and available resources. So, to these leader-coordinators there are actual and potential interrelationships among the foci. This is less true for most network members, although over time more members see and act on the principle.

We have emphasized that there are at least two ways of defining a resource exchange network: from the standpoint of the leader-coordinators and from that of network members. And we have suggested that both ways have to be integrated. There is a third perspective: that of the researcher as if he or she was naive about networks. In real life, the researcher would be knowledgeable about network concepts and aware of the different sources of error (in himself and his interviewees) to which his data would be subject. He would certainly not ignore the perspectives of his interviewees, but just as certainly he would not accept their reports as completely valid. He is an outsider trying to understand insiders, a role that is a mixed blessing because, at the same time that he values objectivity and critical analysis, he knows (or should know) that understanding the thinking and actions of others is, to say the least, beset with difficulties. In any event, he would end up with his description and definition of the Essex Network, and it would differ in some respects from the pictures of those he studied. In what respects, we cannot say. In the literature on networks (see Sarason and others, 1977), there has been a good deal of theorizing about network concepts, numerous attempts to develop a typology of networks, but few systematic studies of the development and maintenance of networks (resource exchange or any other type, formal or informal). If the concept of networks has become popular, it is a popularity not reflected in the research literature. To be sure, the research literature on networks has grown rapidly in recent decades but nowhere near the point at which one is justified in saying it has become a fashionable research area. And this rapid growth has its drawbacks precisely because of the tendency to study them from one perspective: that of the researcher at *one* given point in time. This lessens the difficulties of definition by oversimplifying the nature of the activities under study.

We strongly believe that it is not until we have more and better descriptions of network formation, activities, and vicissitudes that we will better understand their actual and potential roles in society. We are not opposed to definitions and typologies, but we are aware that more often than not, and especially in regard to new research areas, definitions and typologies obscure more than they illuminate. Let us illustrate what we mean by discussing a provisional definition of the Essex Network:

> The Essex Network is an instance of a loose, informal, voluntary association of individuals whose interrelationships (their frequency and substance) depend on a few self-selected individuals seeking to make resource exchange a basis for existing and new interrelationships so that membership expands, interrelationships are reshuffled, new clusters are formed around new self-selected individuals who will serve a role similar to that of those who brought them into the association. There are no geographical, substantive, educational, or status criteria for membership; no formal rules; and no time- or calendar-determined tasks. Members may or may not know each other, although each knows self-selected individuals and some members. They have access to each other; the most frequent way this access initially takes place is through the self-selected individuals; over time, access takes place more directly.

To determine whether something is an instance of a class of things requires that we look at as many instances as possible, permitting us to factor out features that are common, accidental, or unique. This, unfortunately, we cannot do, because descriptions of what might be appropriate instances do not exist. How would one decide what would be an appropriate instance? Take, for example, the two descriptions from *Uplift* (Washington Consulting Group, 1974) in Chapter Three. From the very brief descriptions of the early phase of these projects, one might intuit (one does not really know) similarities to the Essex Network: self-selected leaders, informality, voluntary, resource exchange. However, in contrast to the Essex Network, there was from the very beginning a single, time-influenced task or focus that would require formal structure and roles and would, therefore, change the basis for interrelationships. There would be rules and obligations, if only because survival and success depended on earning more money than was spent.

But, someone could ask, why compare the Essex Network to *Uplift*, where every one of the hundred instances was consciously a self-help effort? There are several answers. One could legitimately say that the Essex Network is also a self-help effort, just as one can say that both contain the theme of resource exchange. Also, because one calls the *Uplift* examples "self-help" does not mean that they are not complex networks, aspects of which may be similar to the Essex Network. One should not prejudge possible similarities and contrasts by labels. And yet, despite some similarities, we are left with the feeling that their comparability is like that of apples and oranges: Both are fruit, but our experiences of them are quite different. Depending on one's purposes, the fact that they are fruit may be more important than the different experience they provide and the functions they can serve for us. Likewise, to other people the fact that they are both fruit is of not practical significance. We are suggesting that this is a problem not in esthetics but rather one of purpose and goals. If, as in our case, the purpose is how to think about a resource exchange network so that it will lead to involving increasing numbers of people, without restricting the basis or foci of exchange, without limiting their freedom of choice, at the same that the sense of community is strengthened, the differences between the Essex Network and *Uplift* are of very practical significance. If, as in the case of every *Uplift* instance, disadvantaged individuals band together to help each other and to form an organization that will facilitate securing public or private funds, it is understandable and laudable, especially when they succeed in purchasing needed resources. However, from the standpoint of resource exchange not based on money but rather on resource redefinition and exchange, one can ask if, in the transition from an informal self-help group (in which resource redefinition and exchange are frequent and the norm) to a formal organization, seeking funds does not reduce the frequency and quality of resource exchange. That is to say, at the same time that more resources can be purchased for money, the "barter type" of exchange occurs less.

In no way are we suggesting that these groups should not seek to gain more resources in all possible ways. What we are suggesting is that if resource redefinition and exchange were equal with any other purpose and if they were the basis for network development, it is conceivable (we would say likely) that more resources would have become available than by only going the route of the formal organization. But that suggestion assumes that something akin to the Essex Network can exist in a formal organization. We will examine that assumption in a later chapter. Suffice it to say here that to whatever extent a formal organization can develop or become part of an Essex-type network it will have gained more resources.

A caveat is in order here. It could be argued that it is both unfair and incorrect to say that the *Uplift* (Washington Consulting Group, 1974) instances are competing for funds. That is to say, they are not competing, in that the members, after banding together cooperatively, have access to rebates and reduced prices that are part of the economic process that advantaged people have regular access to. It pays the sellers to sell in bulk, hence the reduced prices and rebates. In competition, someone loses, and this is not the case in these instances. Our earlier comments, however, were directed to the consequences of seeking public (or private or foundation) monies, where one is competing for limited resources and where there are externally determined constraints on how funds can be used. There is funding that produces an economic plus, by economizing where more money ordinarily would have been spent (Daphne Krause and M.A.O. being a good example). There is funding that produces economic good by enabling people to change from consumers of human and financial resources to producers and creators of them. Unfortunately, the more frequent consequences of receiving public support, aside from reinforcing dependence rather than independence, and focusing on people's deficits rather than assets, are several: The organization becomes increasingly concerned with internal matters, boundaries among organizations become stronger, and resource definition as a value and process becomes less central as the need for organizational survival and continued financial support takes center stage.

We do not have a ritualistic abhorrence of funding, but we have seen too many instances where seeking and obtaining public funds—a process in which one is aware (or is made aware) that one is competing for funds and that one must conform (or appear to conform!) to externally determined guidelines and criteria—have had disastrous consequences, especially for those groups committed to some kind of resource exchange rationale. This does not mean that these groups disappear. Many of them survive, in an organizational sense, but there is an obvious discrepancy between what they wanted to do and what they are in fact doing. Given the rationale of the resource exchange network, it should be apparent that the sources of and conditions for funding have to be given the most searching examination. In regard to the *Uplift* examples, our comments reflect a fear derived from the experience of countless people: You can win the battle of funding and yet lose the war of purpose and goals.

Let us take another example described in Chapter Three: The Shoreham-Wading River report about how pupils in a middle school spend time each week in a community setting, not doing busy work but performing human service functions that are both necessary and educationally meaningful. There are again several points of similarity to the Essex-type network, the most obvious one being the theme of resource redefinition and exchange: These young students can be helpful to less fortunate people, and the students need these experiences for their educational and personal development. What is also involved is a change in a school's perception of a variety of other community agencies and, in turn, a change in the latter's perception of the former. Another point of similarity is the voluntary basis of participation by students and agencies. A third point of similarity is the wide range of possibilities by which exchanges can occur.

Beyond these points, the similarities cease. Granted that resource exchange is a major goal, we are not dealing with an Essex-type network. To be sure, a network was formed, but its characteristics are not those of the Essex one. For example, one can say that the network is composed of students, some school personnel, directors of community agencies, and people with varying handicaps. The relationships between students and handicapped people are determined by school and agency personnel. It is not a goal of this network to facilitate resource exchange relationships among agencies, among handicapped people, or among students. Furthermore, if a major purpose is educational in the broadest sense (that is, to expand the student's understanding of self in relation to environment), one can ask, "What is the student learning about the principle of resource exchange in society?" From the descriptions of the program, it appears that its success as an educational venture is judged by what students learn about themselves and others in the helping process—not, in addition, by what they have learned about their community. We can assume that school personnel and agency heads have grasped the idea of resource exchange but not its general potential or implications.

Here, again, we are not being critical. If more schools and community agencies engaged in such efforts, our educational system would be discernibly better than it is. Our comments are intended to underline two points: First, *resource exchange can be embedded in different types of networks* and, second, *for a network to exploit the potentials of resource exchange, resource exchange must be equal with any other purpose, and, therefore, must make it possible that interrelationships can be formed between any two people in the network.*

It could be argued that we are too quickly passing over the fact that a school's major responsibility is to students, and, although it can and should be part of a community network, there are limits of time, personnel, and responsibility to what a school can do. Put in another way, by virtue of being a formal organization with a legally based mandate, one should not judge a school by the degree to which it exploits a principle, such as resource exchange, that certainly is not clear in its mandate. This argument suggests that a formal and traditional organization such as a school is not conducive to the development of an Essex-type network.[2] We shall discuss this

---

[2]Suffice it to say here, when we say "Essex-type network" we are not asserting that the Essex Network is all it should or could be, but we are suggesting that the potentials in its rationale are of great practical significance. If formal organizations turn out not to be hospitable to the rationale, the question is why this is so and to what extent the rationale is absorbable.

suggestion in a later chapter. But this is precisely the kind of argument that for so long was a massive obstacle to redefining what a school is or could be and, therefore, ill prepared the school for dealing with the impact of social change on it. The Shoreham-Wading River School, others like it, and the efforts of the National Commission for Resources on Youth (see Chapter Two) are all instances of resource redefinition and exchange in response to changes in society. They are also instances of redefinition of school-community relationships. So, when we suggest that schools may be able to become part of a community network in which resource exchange is a dominant feature (far more than it is now), it is not for the purpose of transforming them into Essex-type networks but to suggest that if they examined more closely the possible relationships between the resource exchange rationale and network development they would gain more for themselves and give more to others. What is instructive about the Essex Network is that its form is not related by chance to its function. It should be obvious by now that a resource exchange rationale can be expressed in different types of networks, but that does not mean that in any one instance the form of the network does justice to the rationale.

It could be argued, as we shall see in later chapters, that precisely because a school is a formal organization—embedded in a larger organization and having an ideology and structure reflecting a long history and traditions—it should not be asked to pursue the networking developments to which we have referred. More correctly, of the different vehicles through which these developments can occur, the formal organization should not be put high on the priority list. Within, between, and among organizations, there are individuals who, formally or informally, perform a networking function. Indeed, the Essex Network consists almost exclusively of such individuals: Each is a member of a formal organization seeking ways in which the needs of some of its constituents can be matched with the needs of constituents in other community settings. In short, these members (like the Essex Network itself) are *intermediaries*.

What we are suggesting is that intermediary individuals and vehicles can develop the resource exchange rationale more effectively and consistently than the formal organization as organization. This suggestion, which stems from our own experience, receives abundant, independent confirmation from the detailed descriptions of Friend, Power, and Yewlett (1974) we present in Chapter Eight. And the empirical basis for this suggestion is what led us to the role of the "resource exchange ombudsman" we propose in Chapter Nine. As we shall see in Chapter Seven, the formal organization's capacity to subvert the resource exchange rationale is, unfortunately but inevitably, extraordinarily high, but that should not blind us to the possibilities of intermediary individuals and vehicles for accomplishing the goals of the resource exchange rationale. The "reticulist" (network maker) in formal organizations that Friend, Power, and Yewlett (1974) describe so beautifully and the functions of the resource exchange ombudsman, modeled after the functions of the Scandinavian ombudsman as "citizen protector" (Gellhorn, 1967), are realistic approaches to dealing with the characteristics of the formal organization.

To anyone seeking to develop a resource exchange network, the thorny question is, "What would the network have to look like to make each person in it more accessible to every other person in it for the purposes of resource exchange and expanding the numbers and variety of people (resources) in it?" Not "anyone" seeks to develop a resource exchange network, but rather self-selected people with a mission (and we do not use that word in any pejorative sense). This factor, as we pointed out in the previous chapter, is necessary but far from sufficient either for getting the effort off the ground or for successfully helping to maintain it. No less important is the individual's understanding of the fact that, although the resource exchange rationale can be implemented through different network forms, these forms can vary considerably in the degree to which they maximize both the frequency of resource exchange, their variety, and the numbers of people that can be involved. Wedding a network to a rationale is not an esthetic but a conceptual problem that has yet to receive serious discussion permitting those who undertake the venture to have some idea of the advantages and disadvantages of the different alternatives for action and some idea of the traps into which they may fall.

For example, from the earliest beginnings of the Essex Network Mrs. Dewar realized that for a network to take advantage of a resource exchange rationale, especially if the network would contain different substantive foci, there could not be only one or two leader-coordinators. How to locate, attract, or nurture leader-coordinators

was one of her self-appointed tasks. She knew that as long as she remained the prime mover and the center of things the frequency and
scope of resource exchange would be unduly limited. In her imagery, the Essex Network should become an interconnected and
changing network of mininetworks, each of which would have its
own foci and dynamic. Indeed, one of the ways in which the Essex
Network differs from all those we have described in earlier chapters
is in the emergence of new leader-coordinators, so that it is no longer
accurate to describe the network as Mrs. Dewar's, which is how many
people labeled it in the first two years. To her, the concept of networks opened up possibilities, and her task was to figure out which of
them was most appropriate to the resource exchange rationale. The
point here is not how she conceptualized the relationship between
the resource exchange rationale and a type of network, but rather
that she knew there was a conceptual problem; that is, the rationale
did not tell her how to proceed, or how many different ways she
could proceed, and with what expectations. That understanding is
unusual and it is in part explainable by another distinctive feature:
The Essex Network did not have to be developed under the pressure
of time. If we know anything about behavior under time pressure, it
is that it constricts the possibilities of which one will be aware and
makes a virtue of necessity even though the virtue may be transient.

How Does a Resource Exchange Network Come to Be?

In addressing the question "What is a resource exchange network?" and in trying to see similarities and differences among instances of them, we were comparing them from a cross-sectional, not
a longitudinal, perspective. Each of them was at a different point in
time in its history. Consequently, we cannot say that their current
forms and functioning have characterized them in the past and will
characterize them in the future. So, when we talk about different
types of resource exchange networks, we cannot assume that their
differences were somehow inherent in their beginnings. For example, most of what we know about organizations (their structure,
administrative style, internal dynamics, and interorganizational relationships) come from studies done long after these organizations
were formed. As has been discussed in detail elsewhere (Sarason,
1972), we know very little about the context out of which organiza-

tions emerge and develop. Why do some organizations never grow up; that is, why do they go bankrupt? Why do so many organizations seem to be functioning inconsistently with their stated purposes? Why does it seem that "organizational craziness" has become the norm?

In suggesting that these questions should be described and analyzed from a developmental perspective, with special emphasis on the prehistory and earliest phases of a setting, Sarason was not suggesting that the chronologically mature organization could be explained by knowledge of its gestation, birth, and infancy—just as some used to argue that adult personality was largely if not wholly explainable by early child-parent relationships. Sarason's argument had several parts. First, living as we are in an era in which the rate of creation of new settings is the highest in human history, we needed to focus on their earliest phases of settings in the hope of learning how they can develop to be more consistent with their stated purposes. Second, the new setting (like the new human organism) experiences a rate of change and transformation that will be greater than any time in its future. Third, creating a new setting is an inordinately complex process, because it involves commitment, forging new relationships, garnering resources appropriate in quantity and quality, and dealing with interorganizational connections. Fourth, it is a process that generates changes in the leader that make it increasingly difficult for him or her to steer a course between the Scylla of indulging his or her personal needs and the Charybdis of conformity to externally generated pressures. Fifth, the tendency is both subtle and strong to protect the new setting by sharpening boundaries with other settings as well as among individuals and groups within the new setting. These are the major features of a new setting, Sarason maintains, to which one must look if one is to understand why new settings abort and disappear, or become so transformed that their initial rationale is hardly apparent, or change but consistently with their rationale. Explicit in his argument is the thesis that the differences one finds among chronologically mature settings obscures the recognition of the possibility that in the process of their creation they had many features in common and that the developmental transformations that occurred reflect an interaction between the demands of the process of creating a setting and characteristics of the larger society.

Sarason's conceptualization and description of the creation of settings are applicable to how resource exchange networks come to be. In fact, in his emphasis on the context out of which new settings emerge (the "prehistory" and the "before the beginning" stages), the new setting is seen as the resultant of the interaction among many types of networks, and by its very emergence it alters these interactions and initiates new ones. He emphasizes that the too frequent failure of those in the new settings to understand and deal with these network interactions, past and present, always has adverse effects. And in the emphasis on the significance of the leader, especially in regard to sensitivity to the universe of action alternatives appropriate to the setting's rationale, we see another key aspect for understanding how resource exchange networks come to be. It is not our purpose here to demonstrate, as we could, that how resource exchange networks come to be can be put in terms of the creation of settings.[3] Our purpose has been to emphasize first, that, just as the frequency of setting creation requires that we understand the process better, so should the increasing popularity of the network stimulate efforts to describe and understand how networks come to be. Second, just as in the creation of settings the fact of limited resources is so poorly predicted and confronted, it is likely that one of the factors limiting the scope of resource exchange networks is in the looseness of the conceptual tie between their rationale and the fact of limited resources. Third, by focusing on how resource networks came to be we would, as in the case of the creation of settings, see more clearly

---

[3]From the standpoint of the creation of settings, the development of a resource exchange raises some interesting questions. For example, in Sarason's (1972) descriptions there is *a* leader, and Sarason discusses the ways in which the "socialization" of that person affects and is affected by processes and events internal and external to the setting. In the development of a resource exchange network, there is also a leader but, if he or she is consistent with the rationale, he or she actively supports the emergence of other leader-coordinators. In that respect, Sarason's description is not appropriate to the development of a resource exchange. But the difference is more apparent than real, because Sarason emphasizes the obligations of the leader to support others in ways that further their development as leaders, which is in marked contrast to the more usual attitude of leaders who, rhetoric aside, are threatened by leadership characteristics of those in their core group. This attitude toward leadership explains a good deal about why so many new settings are inconsistent with their original purposes. It is an attitude that is the polar opposite to that of the network leader-coordinator.

how our individual ways of thinking, acting, and goal setting reflect our culture at the same time that that same culture is the major source of obstacles. And, fourth, by adopting a longitudinal approach to resource exchange networks we are less likely to be satisfied with static typologies and definitions, which, whatever their value, are poor guides for action.

In short, how resource exchange networks come to be will in our opinion turn out to be a more productive question than what a resource exchange network is. The second question is, of course, subsumed in the first, but the advantage of the first question is that it focuses attention on the connections between theory and practice: the natural history of, and the vicissitudes that occur in, the relationship between a resource exchange rationale and network formation and how this illuminates the fact that there are different types of resource exchange networks and, no less important, that many of these networks never develop because they die an early death. Any theory of resource exchange networks has to explain why some networks live and others die. The question "What is a resource exchange network?" is not likely to come up with an explanation.

It is noteworthy that in the twentieth century the people who have contributed most to our understanding of individual behavior had a developmental approach. Freud, Gesell, Piaget, and Erickson are examples that come to mind. Binet should also be on the list, because he was quintessentially the clinical developmentalist, less enamored with typologies than with how individual differences come about (Sarason, 1976b; Wolf, 1973). When people, especially in the United States, used his scales and developed typologies (*idiot, imbecile, moron,* and so forth), they were doing violence to Binet's developmental way of thinking and researching. The developmental approach to networks in general and resource exchange networks in particular holds the most promise for our understanding of ourselves and our society.

What Is Exchanged?

We have used the term *barter economy* to characterize the theme of a resource exchange network. One connotation of that term refers to the fact that money is not exchanged, although each partner in the transaction puts a value on what he or she gives and gets. That value may take into account time, services, information, or ideas but in our experience a person enters into an exchange with relatively little "cost accounting" of what is being given and gotten. Far more often than not, the person is motivated by a strongly felt need and is predisposed to give a lot if that need can be met, which is precisely what the person who meets that need also frequently feels. To an outsider interested in cost accounting, it will appear many times that one person is "paying more" than the other, although, phenomenologically speaking, both people in no way feel cheated or used. In large part, this is because the person knows not only what he or she needs but also that he or she does not have the money to get it. In such a situation, most people will not think about the resources they possess that others who can fill their need may want.

For example, on the very day this section was being written one of the authors (Sarason) received a call from a stranger who was a school principal. The principal was in the process of formulating his doctoral dissertation, which would focus on some issues raised in one of Sarason's earlier books. Sarason immediately knew that he was going to be asked to give time to this person, and he was prepared to say he would see him one time.[4] But before Sarason could reply the principal went on to say that he hoped that the thesis could be formulated in a way so that if there were data of special importance to Sarason, Sarason could obtain and use them. The level of Sarason's interest quickly rose. He was prepared to see the school principal more than once! Whatever the motivations of the school principal, he knew that if he stood a chance of getting Sarason's sustained interest and help, he had to figure out something that was in Sarason's interest. This principal's forthright approach is unusual, especially in light of his perception that he was bartering with someone of higher status.

_____

[4]A personal note of explanation. I will see anybody who wants to see me. This rule may have once had something to do with altruism and a sense of _noblesse oblige,_ but it was not long before I learned that it was a rule for my narrow self-interest because some of these meetings turned out to be enormously helpful to me in terms of ideas, entry into new networks, and so on. If someone cost accounted how much time I have given to these requests, it would appear that by whatever reasonable price one put on my time, I have paid quite a price. Phenomenologically, it has been on balance an even exchange (Sarason).

In societies with barter economies (fast disappearing from this earth), each instance of barter between two people is ordinarily independent of all subsequent ones between them. In each instance, each individual wants to get at least an even exchange. Our experience with resource exchange networks gives a different picture, in that members frequently and knowingly give more than they get because of their expectation that when the time comes when they need more than they can give they will not be rebuffed. Someone once said that money had to be invented as a basis for exchange among strangers. Implied in that saying is the knowledge that there are features to exchanges among friends that are absent among strangers. One is willing to give more to a friend than to a stranger, the expectation being that there will be times when the friend will give more to you than he or she will get. In other words, any one instance of exchange is not seen as independent of past and future exchanges, and this is what characterizes what we have seen in resource exchange networks. When a person initially becomes a part of a network, there is a wariness about the evenness of exchanges that tends to lessen over time.

The development of resource exchange networks can be justified (as we have largely done) in terms of people's narrow self-interests. Or, again as we have done, they can be justified in terms of the larger society grappling with social problems and the fact of limited resources. Or, as we have suggested, they can be justified for their potential to enlarge a person's knowledge of his or her world, interests, and capacities. These are all legitimate justifications for developing resource exchange networks, but they are probably insufficient for sustaining and enlarging them, if only because narrow self-interests may be quickly met, or not quickly enough met, and there is then little reason to continue to be active in the network. The outsider who rivets only on what gets exchanged among members of an ongoing network will not easily discover the glue that binds the members together and helps explain evenness *and* unevenness of exchanges. In a successful resource exchange network, members come to view each instance of exchange in terms of past and future exchanges. That is to say, there is a desire to be helpful stemming from the satisfactions, personal and intellectual, derived from participating in network affairs. In the case of the Essex Network there is no doubt that the general and minimeetings are important personal and intellectual occasions for its members. They are occasions to which members look forward, occasions that contribute to a sense of belonging.

In an earlier chapter, we pointed out that the relatively recent popularity of the network concept, as well as that of self-help, has to be seen in the context of a widespread discontent with working in or dealing with large bureaucratic organizations themselves enmeshed in a bewildering federal, state, and local complex (Sarason, 1977). The terms *alienation, anomie, isolation, loneliness,* and *fragmented lives* have become standard fare in descriptions of contemporary life. Although some would argue, justifiably, that there is nothing new in these descriptions, that they describe feelings and attitudes that have long characterized people in our society, there are grounds for asserting that since World War II people have given public expression to these feelings to a greater degree than ever before. And these expressions have been associated with exploration of new life-styles and social groupings calculated to increase the sense of worthiness and community. At the same time that there has been a heightened awareness of and need for individuality (its expression and requirements), there has been a striving to forge a more satisfying basis for social and group interaction. The appeal of the network concept, however superficial that appeal and the response to it may be, must be seen in this larger social context. This is especially important for any network committed to any degree to a resource exchange rationale. In our experience, those resource exchange networks that have wittingly or unwittingly capitalized on people's need for a sense of community have the glue that will help sustain them. What gets exchanged is more than ideas, information, or services, and that "more" is in the unverbalized but quite potent message that people, need and want each other.

In the next chapter, we turn to a set of issues that we have stated but skirted. To what extent can the potentialities of the resource exchange rationale be realized in a formal organization? What are the obstacles to resource exchange when the survival of an organization depends on money? In the public sector, particularly in regard to human services, can one alter incentives and rewards so that agencies as agencies will be more disposed to make exchanges with each other? If the potentialities of the resource exchange rationale are better realized in an informal network of individuals rather than one of formal agencies, can a public funding policy be devised that is not self-defeating?

7

Coordination and Resource Exchange Among Formal Organizations

A resource exchange network is a voluntary, loose association of heterogeneous individuals willing to consider ways whereby each is willing to give and to get needed resources from others, to seek to increase the number and diversity of participants, to place no restrictions on the substance of foci of exchanges, and to resist putting considerations of exchange and planning under the pressures of funding and the calendar. That description, of course, represents an "ideal type," and we know of no resource exchange network that meets all of these characteristics. From what we have said in previous chapters, the reader may have concluded that we regarded informality as a crucial characteristic of these networks and that their potential for increasing resources within the structure, traditions, and ambience of the formal organization was minimal or nonexistent. If we have communicated that bias, our doing so stems from a number of considerations.

First, the many resource exchange networks we have come to know were not only informal but also deliberately conceived alternatives to the perceived failures of formal organizations. Second, the two formal organizations we have studied that were implementing a resource exchange rationale were *created* by individuals committed to the rationale, despite which these organizations suffer restrictions because of their single foci (such as old people or teachers in *a* school), funding pressures, and time constraints. Third, there are many organizations whose prehistory (their informal stage) contained many of the features of a resource exchange network that disappeared or became diluted as they became transformed into formal organizations. Fourth, attempts to introduce a resource exchange rationale into *existing* organizations (that is, created on the basis of a very different rationale) have been marked by failure, giving rise to the belief in the minds of most people that formal organizations in the human services are self-serving, deliberately uncoordinated, destructively competitive entities impermeable to change and fit objects for change only by those people with fathomless reservoirs of unfulfilled masochism.

It could be legitimately argued that one must not confuse past failures with future possibilities or underestimate the powerful forces for change impinging on all organizations in the public sector. Therefore, to say that formal organizations are lethal soil for the resource exchange rationale may be both premature and unduly cynical. But, if such a stance of openness and optimism is to be justified, it cannot be by assertion or wish-fulfilling fantasies or a belief that reason and necessity will invade the minds of people and bring about the desired change. On the contrary, we have to try to understand why the formal organization in the human services area has been markedly successful in avoiding recognizing and acting on a resource exchange rationale. In an earlier chapter, we identified the dynamics of guildism as one of those obstacles, but that raises the chicken-and-egg question, "Did the rise of professionalism and specialization foster the growth of discrete, bounded, independent, distinction-seeking agencies, or did these agencies arise as an attempt to deal with social turmoil and disorganization (in ever burgeoning urban areas) in the course of which the dynamics of professionalism based on arguments for specialized knowledge and skills provided these agencies a philosophy of efficiency that gave them greater claim to public support? We put the question in historical terms not because history directly provides answers for today's issues but because it may sensitize us to the fact that human services agencies as we know them today have a long past that cannot be ignored by those who wish to alter them in the present. The evidence is compelling that, whether one is talking about the public school system or the myriad social agencies, their origins were largely the result of efforts of affluent middle- and upper-class *citizens,* many of them women, confronting from different vantage points and in different ways the consequences of wave after wave of immigrants pouring into cities, perceiving them either as a threat to the established order or as pathetic victims of an impersonal, exploiting society. In short, these agencies, far from having their origins in professionalism, were a melange of formal and informal efforts of "concerned citizens." The interested reader should consult Levine and Levine's (1970) *A Social History of Helping Services* and Sarason and Doris' (1978) account of the public school system. The professionalization of helping and educational services really began to take hold at the beginning of this century, a process facilitated by the snowballing adverse consequences of unprecedented population growth and the emergence of social work as a profession.

When Henry Ford became a legend in his own time for the means he developed to mass produce automobiles, combining the principle of the division of labor with the benefits of and need for efficiency, it said as much about the culture as it did about Henry Ford. Specialized knowledge and function, and the importance of organizing them for the purposes of efficiency, were proudly considered part of the American "genius," and that was no less valued in organizing a human service or a school system than in producing an automobile. Once the human service agencies came under professional domination, specialization of function, within and among agencies, became an unquestioned "good." Waiting off stage, however, was a question the human service agencies (including education) would have to confront and that Henry Ford earlier had successfully "solved": "How do you put the pieces together?" And when that question was put on the social agenda after World War II, it was couched in terms that spotlighted how congenial the Henry Ford-engineering mentality was to agencies and the helping professions. The phrase "coordination and delivery of services" became a rallying point. Faced with a galaxy of specialized human services agencies, seeming inexorably increasing demands on society's fiscal and human resources, with no compelling evidence of a high correlation between expenditures and desired effects, and with shorter intervals between exposures of scandalous conditions and of insensitive services, it seemed obvious to some people that the problem was a technical one: how to put the pieces together in an efficient manner.

Not surprisingly, new specialties arose to deal with these "system" problems by conceptualizing the relationships among the pieces so that the system could "deliver" precisely the product (services) that people needed. If the pieces were awesomely diverse and uncoordinated, they became rationally and functionally related in the awesomely complex system charts that resembled the inventions that Rube Goldberg so hilariously portrayed in his zany cartoons, except, of course, without the satire. Almost overnight, the pieces were proclaimed a system or network, conjuring up the images of the wondrous efficiency of the broadcasting networks and the telephone companies. The truth was and is that these efforts produced regulation, not coordination or resource exchange. Human service agencies and helping professionals became caught in a web of regulations that threatened their autonomy and turf and tested their ingenuity to continue doing what they had been doing. Far from redefining themselves in relation to other agencies, they competed more strenuously than before for their piece of the pie. What the systems and network planners did not understand, despite the fact that many of them had spent years in human services agencies or had taught generations of agency personnel, was that each of these agencies viewed itself as special, even unique, and that to expect that it would graciously and willingly redefine itself and its relations to other agencies was ridiculous, on the face of it. But it was not the first time in human history that theories, schemes, and inventions had little or no relationship to social reality, if only because they did not comprehend the cultural context for which they were considered appropriate.

What we have said about the role of specialization and professionalism in reinforcing the preciousness with which agencies view themselves is being said clearly by many people in leadership positions in diverse human services areas. The following are excerpts of an address by Bertram Beck (1977, pp. 1–3, 4–6, and 12–13) general director of New York's Community Service Society:

As we approach the end of the seventies, those of us with a concern for the human services must acknowledge a growing sense of dissatisfaction that the promise of the sixties has not been fulfilled. During the sixties, in response to a variety of pressures, we witnessed a significant expansion of government funds flowing into social programs. As we reach the end of the seventies, we find much skepticism concerning the value of the programs launched in the sixties, pervasive doubt that governmental programs can solve social problems, and a growing lack of respect for professions including social work.

The response of the social work profession to this threat is to try harder to make progress on the road professions have traditionally traveled to gain economic security for their members. Legal and administrative measures are sought that favor the fully credentialed. This is always done, of course, under the banner of public interest, not self-interest. That road, if pursued as a major avenue, leads to disaster not because it is self-serving but because it is out of tune with the times and ignores the sense of direction derived from the experiences of the last two decades.

One such experience is the demonstration that, while it is difficult to prove that increased social expenditures result in a commensurate decrease in human misery, we can with certainty prove that they result in a vast multiplication of public and voluntary agencies on a federal, state, and local level, each concerned with different aspects of the human condition.

Congress tends to act on the basis of perceived needs or problems. Therefore, during times of welfare expansion programs are established to deal with persons of a particular age; or to deal with a particular social problem such as mental retardation, juvenile delinquency, child abuse, alcoholism, drug addiction; or to make social provision for mental health, public health, education, and the like. Each time the President signs such bills into law, a new federal bureaucracy is established which then has its counterpart on the regional, state, city, and often neighborhood level.

Once congressional action establishes public bureaucracies and sends dollars flowing into the nonprofit sector, or sometimes the proprietary sector, everybody who holds a job becomes a partisan of the particular program. In that fashion, program maintenance rather than customer service achieves dominance. Medicare and Medicaid are prime examples of the way in which reimbursement to providers for care determines the nature of the care given and its intensity—not patient welfare. Coming closer to home, it seems likely that the incidence with which foster care is provided has a higher correlation to the availability of funds for providing foster care than to fluctuations in family function. Where providers lead, consumers may follow so that there can be created alliances between persons who benefit from daycare or nutrition programs and persons whose jobs and livelihood depend on the existence of such programs. Most who advocate for social measures have a need to see themselves as concerned not with their personal welfare but with the general welfare. However beguiling such notions may be, it is well that we at least recognize the possibility that self-interest is an important motive force in our behavior as it is in the behavior of others. . . .

Although budgetary constraints and ignorance concerning the relationship of education to quality practice are the major factors in downgrading requirements for social work jobs, there are other elements. Not only is there the aftermath of the new careers movement but there is a restlessness with structural impediments to participation that are historically related to the civil rights movement. Increasingly, persons of diverse physical capacities, sexual orientation, ethnicity, and the like proclaim their right to participate. This makes supine acceptance of the legal barriers to employment less likely than was the case in past decades. The human potential movement with its focus on various avenues of self- and group exploration to the goal of self-actualization is another development which deemphasizes professional credentials. Also there is the retardation of our economic growth and our decline as a world power. Edging toward a less expansive economy, there may be diminished interest in aggressive economic competition and heightened interest in finding satisfying work in the service of others. . . .

Striving to gain mastery over the sprawling service system, federal, state, and local governments have turned to management experts who introduced regulatory controls more suited for the assembly line than for human services. The regulatory control mechanisms introduced by such experts seek "to control costs and benefits indirectly by encouraging the use of means which are presumed to be efficient and effective. In practical terms, accountability is to one or more regulatory agencies which determine when an expenditure of public funds is (or is not) legitimate. The accountability is in terms of adherence to regulations with respect to the eligibility of clients, or the nature of means . . . employed in the operation and the like." Agencies which best conform to the regulation will be looked on with favor by the funding sources.

Social workers personally involved in giving humane human services realize that there is a fatal flaw in these regulatory control mechanisms and the management technology used to institutionalize them. They are created within the context of duplicative chaotic service delivery and are based on the assumption that if the organization behaves in a certain way in respect to certain people, beneficial results will accrue. There is, in fact, no measure of the actual impact, only of the means. Fundamentally, the whole apparatus is irrelevant to accountability to clients. The nub of the matter is lost. Sometimes, in fact, accountability to clients cannot be achieved because of adherence to regulations. . . .

And here are excerpts from an address by Sanford Kravitz (1978, pp. 4–5, 12 and 19) of the School of Social Welfare at SUNY (State University of New York) in Stony Brook, New York:

Witness the growth of pressure within the profession for clinical practice and the increasing pressure by our students for psychiatric clinical training. Growing numbers of students who enter our schools of social work are demanding that we prepare them for the most narrow parameters of practice. As many will now attest, this is an issue of increasing concern to large numbers of graduate schools. There are also increasing numbers of our practicing colleagues and our students who are hell bent on either replacing psychiatrists or deriving their professional satisfaction from basking in the reflected glow and warm comfort that focusing on unconscious behavior apparently provides. All this despite the failure of this branch of medical practice to address the fundamental human problems of our society. The growth of private practice and its focus of attention on those able to pay for services has contributed to a serious decline in the pressure for broadly based universally available services for those families in desperate need for such services. While I support licensing in terms of its professional recognition factors, I question the fundamental motivation of many of the social work groups supporting licensing. Bert Beck ably stated this argument at the recent NASW [National Association of Social Workers] symposium.

I wish to make clear that I am not intent on painting our entire profession with a broad brush of criticism; I am expressing a deep concern for substantial movement backward that I think is of serious portent. . . .

The term "community development" has come into international usage to connote the processes by which the efforts of the people themselves are united with those of governmental authorities to improve the economic, social, and cultural conditions of communities, to integrate these communities into the life of the nation, and to enable them to contribute fully to national progress. This complex of processes is then made up of two essential elements: the participation of the people themselves in efforts to improve their level of living with as much reliance as possible on their own initiative; and the provisions of technical, and other services, in ways which encourage initiative, self-help, and mutual help and make these more effective.

This frame of reference, like the family, is not new to social work, but it has been absent or neglected in recent years as practice interests, partially in response to funding interests, have changed and as clinical practice has remained focused on individual behavior. . . .

Turner said in 1968 that we were at a crossroads. My view of the past ten years is that we may have paused at the crossroads, but we moved down the road. I believe we may have taken the wrong direction. Large numbers of us are primarily engaged in defining human ills as the product of individual failure and are seeking legislative sanction to probe the unconscious. And yet there is sufficient concern to keep wondering if that is where we belong—as allied health personnel—waiting for the physician to sign the prescription for the Valium or urging more support for the expansion of private practice.

The reader may have noticed that both Beck and Kravitz have a marked ambivalence about the trend toward individual private practice. (Many social workers are leaving agencies for private practice, and many incoming social worker students seek preparation for private practice.) We agree with their explanations but they are incomplete. What needs to be added is the fact that many social workers, and it is by no means peculiar to them as a group, find working in agencies a stifling, parochial, frustrating experience in which the sense of autonomy and growth gets extinguished (Sarason, 1977). Ironically, the long social and historical process that spawned the fantastic growth of discrete, unrelated, special-function, competing human services agencies—and to say they are systems or networks is to play loose with logic and language—has, to recast the title of Beck's address, dehumanized the professional servers no less than those they serve. Walled off in their enclaves, possessed by the need to feel special in their functions, perceiving themselves as buffeted and unappreciated, constantly aware that they do not and will not have the resources they feel they need and deserve, it is no wonder so many of them flee the scene or have no intention of entering it. In one's private office, true to the spirit of professionalism, you own the turf, set the rules, and are in control. The scene has changed; the spirit of professionalism and specialization has not.

Let us be careful not to scapegoat the spirit of professionalism and specialization in the human services area. It is a spirit that has been nourished in countless ways in all spheres of our society. For example, one might ask, "Where did personnel in the human services area become imbued with the spirit of professionalism and specialization?" To answer that question, let us turn to a recent article by White (1978, p. 40) on the university. It has the title "Minds in a Groove," with the subtitle "Too Often, Professionalism Is Synonymous with Parochialism."

In recent decades, the university has come to occupy a central place in society, but despite all its influence and talent it is failing to meet some of its most important social obligations. It has been unable to solve the closely related problems of increasing specialization of studies, the growing isolation of professional education, and the cleavage between professional programs and the humanities.

Because of those failures, university people—both the teachers and the taught—are highly trained in limited areas of knowledge but lack an understanding of how that knowledge relates to humanity.

That, of course, is not a new problem in American higher education. For a hundred years or more before World War II, the predominant academic debate centered on the antithesis between science and humanism. Such twentieth-century philosophers as José Ortega y Gasset, Alfred North Whitehead, and John Dewey wrote at length on the subject. Ortega warned of "learned ignoramuses," and Whitehead feared that specialized education would produce "minds in a groove." . . .

We face momentous decisions on such matters as the underutilization of human resources, the quality of the environment, our use of natural resources, population control, food production and distribution, genetic manipulation, and even the creation of life through "artificial" means.

For those of us in higher education, the fundamental question of the times is how to instill in our students not only professional capabilities but also what Whitehead called the "energies of mind" that can steer technological and social development along humane paths. It is this latter function that we are not now performing. . . .

Alfred North Whitehead's half-century-old prediction about the result of specialization appears to have been an underestimate. Not only our minds are in a groove, but our academic institutions as well. Educators in the professions are not aware of the limitations of their knowledge or of the great influence they now have on the course of events, while their colleagues in the humanities are unable to adjust to change. Each sees the other's disciplines as being out of step with the world, while the real problem may be that neither has an accurate perception of the world. One is reminded of Frost: "We dance around the ring and suppose,/ But the secret sits in the middle and knows."

Perhaps the best way for us to begin to establish a shared perception of the world is to reestablish a commonality in the undergraduate program. We need to redefine the meaning of undergraduate general education, scrap the present cafeteria-style approach, and develop a common core of essential learning. If we can achieve the understanding necessary for this task, we will be better able to deal with those parts of the problem relating to graduate study, interdisciplinary work, and overcoming spatial and organizational obstacles.

If the university is to merit its important place in society, teachers and administrators ought to be working toward a stronger union of professional and liberal learning. We owe such an effort to the students so that their lives and careers may be more fruitful, and we owe it to society so that life may be richer for everyone. The final test of the value of higher education is not how good we are as professionals or as humanists, but how competent we are in improving the human condition.

White, Beck, and Kravitz are recent additions to a long list of people who understood that the rationale for professionalism and specialization—whether it was applied in education, human services agencies, and the health fields generally—guaranteed that the structure of functions and relationships within and among formal organizations would be recalcitrant to mutuality and exchange at the same time that this structure contained the seeds of self-defeat. Although this simple point has long been recognized, the fact remains that efforts to change this state of affairs have not acted seriously on this recognition, by which we mean devising incentives and rewards that would make it more in the self-interest of formal agencies to confront their limited resources, to redefine their relationships with each other, and to get out of the personal and intellectual straitjacket of undue specialization. The fact is that efforts at change have utilized incentives and rewards, carrots and sticks, that have perpetuated or made worse the very conditions they were intended to remedy. When Beck, reluctantly and plaintively, suggests that we may be too far down the road, too enmeshed in a trap of our own making, he is acknowledging the total failure of past efforts at change because they did not deal with, they contained no new ways of thinking about, some of the most important factors that shaped and continue to shape the parochialism of the formal agency.

An Attempt at the Holistic Delivery of Human Services:
Analysis and Implications

The title of this section is that of an unpublished report prepared by a member (Perkins, 1977, pp. 3–6) of a Department of Health, Education, and Welfare (HEW) task force investigating alternative means of integrating health, education, and social services. Perkins' report centers on a specific case of attempted integration of services: the Bunker Hill Health Center.

The Bunker Hill Health Center was originally intended as a "Life Services Center," designed to serve Charlestown, Massachusetts, residents by providing them access to comprehensive services, including health, education, manpower, legal, cultural and leisure time, and social service facilities. (Figure 1 depicts the organization design as initially envisioned.)
As originally defined, the aims of the Bunker Hill Life Services Center were

1. "To provide family-centered health care with comprehensive coordinated and continuous services which are acceptable, accessible, and available

Figure 1. Bunker Hill Life Services Center Resource Relationships

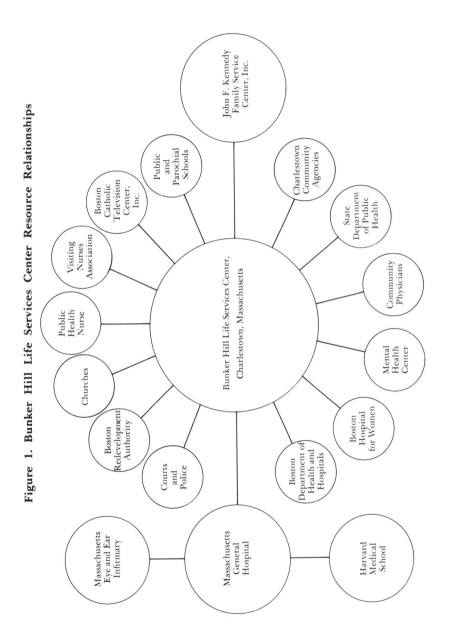

2. "To generate new opportunities for physical and mental well-being and productive contribution to the community
3. "To utilize technology to the fullest and most realistic extent in the solution of individual and community problems
4. "To train professionals, preprofessionals, and nonprofessionals for community service
5. "To evolve a new system of live services which is replicable in other urban and semiurban communities"

In spite of top-level support and encouragement, however, the attempt to obtain federal support for this ambitious program failed. While the sequence of events cannot be precisely known, a general outline can be drawn. The Bunker Hill experience, which seemed to typify that of other attempts at integrated service delivery, is as follows.

First, a promise of support was made by a high-level HEW official, a deputy assistant secretary for health and medical care. Second, a dollar figure was established which represented the needed financial support, and the proposal was referred to federal agency programs representing potential funding sources. This second step was accomplished through conferences, meetings with federal program officers, and so forth. The Bunker Hill project involved conferences among federal officials at the agency head level: the Office of Education, Social and Rehabilitation Services, and the National Institute of Mental Health.

In the third phase, project sponsors were confronted with a plethora of reasons—both legitimate and concocted—that explained why the project could not be federally funded. Common defenses were the previous obligation of program funds and "moral" commitments which could not be broken. Lack of a distinct "health entity," for example, was given by one federal program director as a reason why health funds could not be used to support the Life Services Center.

Finally, the meetings and confrontations persisted—one envisions a bureaucratic arm-wrestling contest—until the project sponsors surrendered. Unlike the "Mississippi Delta" project, which ended successfully after thirty-five conferences, the Bunker Hill sponsors were unable to form the alliance needed to support a life services concept, and its initiators were left to dissect the proposal along categorical lines.

One does not need much imagination to conjure up what went on as representatives of formal federal agencies met (and met, and met, and met) to find out if there was some way in which they could justify pooling some of their resources that would allow the Bunker Hill Center to implement its plan. Apparently, there was complete agreement that the proposal for the center had an acceptable rationale. The problem was, "How could autonomous federal agencies, each with different but overlapping concerns and missions, each with a sense of specialness, each represented by a professional obligated to protect the agency's interests, find it in their *self-interest* to pool resources?" (The federal agencies do not provide direct human services, but they are led and populated by professionals who have had experience in human services agencies.) We italicized *self-interest* because each of the federal agencies had to be able to justify (to itself and higher officialdom) that it was not only giving resources but in some fashion would be getting "rewards" compatible with its mission; that is, by giving it would be getting. They could not find such a justification. Based on his interviews with the federal participants, Perkins (1977, p. 6) identifies three primary causes for the failure.

First, "There were few rewards, and therefore was little motivation, for federal program officers to meld resources in the joint funding venture. In fact, their support would have resulted in some loss of identity, perhaps offending "pure" constituent and special-interest groups." In these few sentences, Perkins has succinctly identified what we regard as the major obstacle to the consideration, development, and maintenance of a resource exchange rationale within and among human services agencies. *"There were few rewards, and therefore was little motivation, for federal program officers to meld resources in the joint funding venture."* Put in another way, the existing incentives and rewards work for the maintenance of interagency boundaries, for the avoidance of risk taking, for the status quo.

Second, "joint funding by federal agencies represented a change in the status quo which was threatening to those whose experience lay in the more familiar categorical review system." And, third, "Joint funding was simply more trouble than categorical funding, and the mechanisms for handling such projects were quite cumbersome. This is not to say that it was impossible to fund the project, rather that it was too difficult in light of the preceding two constraints" (Perkins, 1977, p. 6).

And what was true for the federal agencies was also true for the local human services agencies. "In retrospect, it can be said that HEW lacked the orientation, incentive structure, and organizational machinery to respond effectively to the Bunker Hill proposal. *And there was little evidence that local planners were significantly better prepared to implement the concept of integrated services*" (italics ours). Perkins' conclusions are identical to our own in connection with our discussion of a section of a federal agency that wanted to support the development of networks "out there" but was not aware that the section was asking others to do what it could not do in its own ball park.

Let us listen further to some of the things Perkins says under the heading "Constraints to Integrated Service Delivery." What follows are conclusions Perkins (1977, pp. 11–13) came to from interviews with individuals from the local human services agencies.

Professional Specialization. Many sincere individuals with whom we spoke seemed to be afflicted with a "professional myopia" that prevented them from seeing the interdependent nature of human problems. Through training and tradition, they were critical of efforts at coordination, while at the same time lamenting the failure of "the system." Others were able to see a need for coordination, but each felt that his profession was uniquely qualified to captain the service delivery team.

Risk Aversion. We continually encountered complaints about the "risk-averse" stance of HEW personnel whom local planners encountered. An unwillingness to take risks, if as extreme as alleged, might more directly affect innovation than services integration. However, it appears that most integrative efforts are—almost by definition—innovative in their approach to the delivery of services, and are therefore hindered by such attitudes.

Perceptions of the System. An attitudinal problem, which we observed to be both pervasive and intractable, seemed to emanate from the way community service providers viewed the total system. While our study focused on the HEW role, those we interviewed at the local level spoke from another perspective. Almost invariably, they described what appeared to be an incredible mosaic—or miasma—of complex, confusing and often contradictory programs. While HEW was generally an important part of the system, it was by no means preeminent. Local and state governments, other federal agencies, and a myriad of specialized organizations all affected those attempting to provide integrated services.

Given the limited availability of time, knowledge of funding sources, and psychic energy, this very complexity creates a disincentive to cross organizational boundaries. And, since the rationalization of HEW alone would still leave major components of the funding mechanisms in confusing disorder, it seems clear that an integrative effort cannot be restricted to the boundaries of a single component of the provider system.

Shortage of Qualified Generalists. The difficulty in coordinating services provided by disparate professional groups is compounded by a dearth of individuals who might be termed "credentialed generalists": those who have the vision to understand the multipartite nature of human problems and who hold the respect of specialists engaged in providing services. At present, only those who have first distinguished themselves through specialization are seen as acceptable directors of interdisciplinary efforts. And the problem is, of course, that this is a difficult and time-consuming way to become credentialed.

The other side of this issue is the lack of respected interdisciplinary educational programs which are able to produce individuals with the needed expertise. However, until roles exist for generalists who can exercise genuine decision-making authority, the independent expansion of educational programs is unlikely to have significant impact.

Perkins must be congratulated for the insight, remarkably underemphasized by many people but obvious once it is stated, that the current state of affairs is not caused only by the structure and traditions of human services agencies—as if in some platonic sense they are inherently walled off enclaves of parochialism—but by our centers of higher education, which turn out antigeneralists (precisely the complaint of White, whom we quoted earlier in this chapter). It could be argued that these centers of education and training turn out the kinds of specialists agencies want, but the historical record suggests that these centers have been and still are far from passive in their emphasis on specialization. The historical record aside, today these centers and the human services agencies employ incentives and rewards that inculcate in students and staff the most narrow of orientations.

We are for "qualified generalists," and it is gratuitous to acknowledge they are in very short supply, but we would challenge Perkins' suggestion that "until roles exist for generalists who can exercise genuine decision-making authority, the independent expansion of educational programs is unlikely to have significant impact." Certainly there should be roles for generalists, but as soon as the generalist depends on his or her decision-making *authority* in a formal organization the dynamics of resistance, controversy, and subversion take over. From the standpoint of the resource exchange rationale we have discussed earlier, the task of the generalist would be to create those conditions in which the incentives and rewards work to stimulate people to redefine their conception of self-interest and limited resources so that they come to see that they have something to gain by exchanging resources. The generalist may see the larger picture, he or she may know about more of the pieces than anyone else, but to expect that by having authority those pieces can be "integrated"—Thou shalt integrate, Thou shalt cooperate—is to fly in the face of all past efforts to "integrate the delivery of human services," to reform agencies and their interrelationships. Unless the generalist has a firm grasp of the resource exchange rationale—its dependence on voluntary, informal processes powered by self-interests, its undermining by calendar-determined decisions—his or her actions very likely will result in instances of "The more things change, the more they remain the same." *The generalist in the formal organization, like the leader-coordinator in a resource exchange network, must depend on informal processes.* Whether it is possible for a generalist to act like a network leader-coordinator will depend as much on special circumstances as it will on the interaction between his or her cognitive and personality characteristics and grasp of the resource exchange rationale. Even when these criteria are met, it is an open question how much of the resource exchange rationale can be exploited, knowing as we do the existing characteristics of human services agencies.

Why did the agencies that would comprise the Bunker Hill Center go to the federal government for support? That may seem like a silly question because the answer seems so obvious: money. Without denying that more money than these agencies possessed would be required, it is valid to suggest, in light of Perkins' account, that the many agencies involved in the proposal never seriously considered to what extent they could be helpful to each other with their existing resources. In our experience, and that of many other people, the knowledge that there are funding sources short-circuits any attempt to explore resource exchange. The tendency to define resources as those which one pays for and, therefore, controls has four major consequences: It works against resource exchange among agencies, puts the agencies on the grant-getting and grant-maintaining treadmill, increases competition among agencies, and puts the agencies in a stance of undue dependence on funding agencies. It also tends to escalate the size of the funding request, and what gets obscured by all of these consequences is the extent to which fiscal and human resources are limited. The issue, as we have said, is not whether the Bunker Hill Center would need more money but rather whether it needed the amount it asked for. From the perspective of the agencies, they needed the money. From our perspective, they probably needed far less than asked for. One's conception of need is not independent of how one defines resources and their limits.

We cannot suppress this question: "Would the story have been different if a Mrs. Dewar or Mrs. Daphne Krause had been on the scene?" Mrs. Krause has demonstrated that one can create a multipurpose formal agency (and it is amazingly multi) that over time develops resource exchange relationships with other formal agencies, and she has done this, deliberately, without direct federal funding. In fact, given the scope of her agency's activities, and the number of people in her and other agencies providing truly integrated services to a very large number of senior citizens, her budget is, by conventional standards, very low. But, as we have stressed, Mrs. Krause was one of Perkins' generalists who understood the potentials both of the resource exchange rationale and, no less important, informal support networks. And what if Mrs. Dewar had been on the scene? That question assumes that human services agencies would have been aware of her existence or that they would have been responsive to attempts on her part to become part of their effort. After all, Mrs. Dewar is a private citizen, with no formal credentials, with very decided ideas about resources and linkages, and someone who has become part of a series of far-flung informal networks with little or no visibility. In order for formal agencies to become *responsively* aware of her existence, her ideas, and the potential resources she could bring to bear on a problem, it would have signified that they had begun to overcome the worst fears of professionalism, specialization, and credentialism. They would have been on the road to redefining their conception of themselves and resources. As we shall see later, there is reason to believe that in the informal structures of our communities there are people similar to Mrs. Krause and Mrs. Dewar. If they are unrecognized and underutilized, it is not because of their lack of generalist or leader-coordinator capacities.

The Experimental Schools Program and the Bay Shore Experience

In marked contrast to the previous illustrative case, the Experimental Schools Program represented a federal initiative to make it possible for selected school systems to overcome their internal fragmentation and unrelatedness to their communities.[1] Up until this program, different parts of a school system could be receiving support from different parts of the Office of Education, thus reinforcing rather than overcoming fragmentation and markedly constricting the spread of hoped for benefits. After two decades of piecemeal support to schools, it was apparent that the capacity of school systems to integrate their programs and services had not been strengthened and that community participation in the affairs of school systems was still a slogan and not a reality. So, with great fanfare, including a special message to Congress by President Nixon, the Experimental Schools Program (E.S.P.) was announced. The program became operational in 1971 when eight urban sites were awarded planning grants. By 1973, eighteen sites, eight urban and ten rural, were being funded.

The following quote is from Cowden and Cohen (in press, pp. 1–3):

The Experimental Schools Program was based on the policy notion of comprehensive change. This notion remains a familiar one to the federal practice of social policy but at the time of E.S.P. it offered a novel approach to federal reform efforts in education. Throughout the sixties, a number of efforts in education, including Title I, Head Start, and Teacher Training, had attempted to change local schooling by focusing on a particular population or aspect of a school system. For example, Title I focused on the use of school resources for disadvantaged students; Head Start provided a preschool experience as a means of better preparing students for school life; Teacher Training focused on the provision of instruction for teachers in new curricula and pedagogies.

Federal reformers were inevitably disappointed with these efforts and began to see the limited effect of their efforts as a function of their focus on a single aspect of the school system. Inevitably, the existing constraints of those parts of the school system not included in their reform efforts were seen as eventually usurping or supplanting what change was planned or

[1] We are indebted to Peter Cowden and David Cohen for allowing us to see and quote from an early draft of their forthcoming book on the E.S.P. Their book will be an important contribution to our understanding of the seemingly intractable problem of the coordination of resources in human services agencies as well as in school systems. The reader may not regard school systems as human services agencies, but, from the standpoint of fragmentation, definition of resources, and effective use of resources, they present identical problems. And, let us not forget, one of the distinguishing features of school systems since World War II is their ever increasing relationships with human services agencies, traditionally defined.

temporarily effected. The notion of a more comprehensive approach to change as a way to rectifying this problem was continually emerging in federal educational policy circles. This view was echoed in a number of reports, including that of the National Advisory Council on Education for the Disadvantaged in 1966. The report talked about how "Title I projects are piecemeal and fragmented efforts at remediation or vaguely directed 'enrichment.'" And it went on to suggest that a more "strategically planned, comprehensive program for change" be implemented.

It was this type of call for a program of comprehensive change which informed the reform efforts of E.S.P. The program was specifically seen as a response to the failures and shortcomings of past federal efforts at "piecemeal" or "categorical" change in a variety of educational programs conducted during the last two decades. In congressional testimony on E.S.P., the program director explained that since 1945 a number of programs of school reforms has been initiated by federal reformers but that most of these programs offered only an improvement in a small, relatively isolated part of a school—that is, "piecemeal" or "categorical" change—and that the results of these efforts "brought dissatisfaction" to educational reformers.

These programs were further described in an internal E.S.P. staff memo which explained that previous "piecemeal" efforts such as "curriculum reform projects failed because the curriculum presupposed knowledge or skills which were not present in teachers (who were not given adequate training) and the curriculum as intended was never implemented." As another example in the memo explained, new programs "were introduced without adequate involvement and/or preparation of a community which raised the normal level of anxiety associated with any change to the point where any problems encountered in the implementation of the program could be sufficient to kill it."

As an alternative "hypothesis" to reform, federal E.S.P. reformers advanced the notion that significant improvements in the outcomes of formal education were not likely to result unless there was "holistic" or "comprehensive" change; that is, unless the different "practices" or individual "pieces" were both compatible and mutually reinforcing in a "synergistic" way.

To do justice here to the significances of the failure of E.S.P. is beyond our scope, and we urge the reader to consult the Cowden and Cohen book when it is published. What we shall do is focus on a few of the aspects of the program most germane to our purposes. For example, what was the relationship between the program's "holistic" objective and its time perspective? After all, one can legislate holistic objectives but on what basis does one determine what is a realistic time perspective to achieve those objectives? As we have emphasized in our discussion of informal resource exchange networks, arranging to "put the pieces together" cannot be done by the calendar. You may see how what this person has fits in with what another person needs and how the combination of the two would open up resource possibilities to a third person, but you also know that getting these people to see that it would be in their self-interest to enter these arrangements cannot or should not be rushed. Indeed, you would be aware that bypassing processes that make for voluntary participation based on self-interest can be an exercise in futility. But an informal resource exchange network consists of individuals, not agencies, which, like school systems, are formal and have many differentiated parts, each of which has a calendar-determined objective and a recognized place in an administrative structure. Implicit in the E.S.P. rationale was more than getting school personnel to talk or plan with each other because that could result (as it did) in each part continuing to do what it did before, but with more money! What E.S.P. was after was recognition by the different parts of the system that they had something to gain by redefining themselves as resources so that they could see that their own goals would be better achieved by voluntary, "giving and getting" interconnections. Leaving aside for the moment who could oversee this process and how, it should have been obvious that this would be a slow and inherently problematic process in which even partial success would be satisfactory.[2]

It was no secret that school systems consisted of a variety of subsystems more related through conflict, controversy, and competitiveness than through any felt need of mutuality. That may be regarded by some people as an exaggeration, and undoubtedly there were exceptions, but not in regard to urban school systems of large or middle size. We say "It was no secret," and yet there were

[2]One of us (Sarason) was a two-time consultant to the E.S.P. in its earliest phases, and he is not exercising hindsight when he says that two things were obvious: (1) that the time perspective of the school systems was amazingly but predictably unrealistic and (2) was matched only by the unrealism of the Washington planners. In fact, the Washington planners grossly underestimated how much time would be required of *them* if they were to achieve the program's objectives. It would be a contribution of sorts if the grant applications for E.S.P. funding would be published. It would require many volumes but nothing would convince the reader more that E.S.P. was doomed from the beginning, because neither in Washington nor in the local school systems was there any recognition that the interrelationships among three factors had to be conceptualized as a basis for action: networks, resource exchange, and limited resources.

precious few indications that the program planners took the knowledge into account. They knew that planning by the school systems
would be necessary, and they provided planning grants, *ranging from
three months to one year,* to help the school system to put the pieces together; that is, to get the community groups and the different parts
of the school system to agree about how they would use future federal funds (which would not be small) to increase synergy among the
parts, to impact and change fractionation of effort and resources.
Why a planning grant of three months? Six months? One year? How
do those intervals derive from the diagnosis of what was wrong and
form a conceptual rationale for action? Where did the time perspective come from? The answer is in two parts: The school systems saw
money and did not need very much time to come up with a grant application that said all the things Washington told them to say ("the
right things"), and Washington was under pressure to get started because they had told Congress that E.S.P. was the wave of the future;
that is, it would provide the answers to the problem of how to change
total systems. The school systems wanted money, Washington
wanted to spend it, and the clock was ticking away.

In focusing on the derivation of time perspective, we are not
advancing an explanation of the failure of the E.S.P. but rather indicating two things: first, how calendar-determined thinking and action, whatever the reasons, can stand in the way of redefinition of
roles, relationships, and resources, without which change will not occur, and, second, that formal agreements by formal heads of formal,
highly differentiated agencies (such as schools and human services
agencies) are formidable obstacles to the use and development of informal resource exchange networks by means of which the transforming of individual self-interest into mutually enriching efforts
becomes possible. Neither Washington nor local school officials
could bring about the sought-for change by money, cajoling, fiats
(there were many on both sides, as Cowden and Cohen document),
and the pressures of the calendar. Within formal agencies, the
sources of resistance to redefinition are many, but among the most
effective is a view of informal, voluntary processes as inefficient in
terms of time and quick, clear decision making. But, as the tragedy
that Cowden and Cohen so well describe and discuss, the reverse is
the case for schools and human services agencies. Their formal
structure, their confusion between the orderliness of administrative

charts and the realities of their daily functioning, their dependence on "rules" and their allergy to informality, the conflicts they contain among their parts as well as between the perceived self-interest of each part with that of officialdom—these are features that cannot be ignored if your aim is to change the agency in the direction of a resource exchange rationale, and that rationale was implicit in all that planners hoped to achieve. But that rationale could not surface in an explicit fashion, because it would have brought the planners, no less than it would have the school personnel they were trying to influence, into conflict with the traditions of their agency!

Let us now turn to one of Cowden and Cohen's (forthcoming, pp. 26–29) explanations of the E.S.P. failure. We agree with their explanation, but we ask the reader to note how rampant self-interest and disinterest were among school personnel and how there seemed to be nobody or no vehicle to confront that fact. Generalists and leader-coordinators were not on the scene, or, if they were, their presence was kept a secret.

> The eventual demise of the E.S.P. program at the federal level can, to a large extent, be seen as a result of the E.S.P. federal reformers' confrontation with the dilemma of providing a program definition which was mutually understood by federal reformers and local practitioners alike. It was this dilemma which gave rise to central administrators' differing interpretations and conflicts over the program with federal reformers as well as differing interpretations and conflicts within local sites themselves. The result of these initial misunderstandings and conflicts between federal reformers and local practitioners contributed to further misunderstanding and conflict over the meaning of the program within the federal and local levels.
>
> This dilemma is best understood by two strains of differences in the federal and local world of practice. First, the reform world of federal practice requires that federal reformers view school districts and the problem of change as whole individual units of choice which make up their federal policy perspective. Federal reformers are required to formulate program policies which are seen as relevant to their experiences in regard to effecting change in schools on a nationwide basis. Typically, they are responding to this way of understanding of schools rather than an understanding of local practice within them. The notion of comprehensive change, for example, reflected an effort to rectify what federal reformers saw as the past problems of *federal* practice in effecting "piecemeal" or "categorical" change. It was not surprising that these efforts met with some of the same problems experienced in other programs—understanding what the federal program definition meant. This occurred because local practitioners thought about, viewed, and understood school life from a different perspective.

Local practitioners shared an inside view of a single local school district or subdistrict, and, rather than these views adding up to any single whole, they were seen as made up of particular, varying and fragmented parts held down by existing responsibilities and interests. Such a view, then, by its nature, invited various local perceptions and understandings in the realm of what existed and what was possible in a single school district. Local practitioners, both at the administrative and staff levels, tended to see a program of change, if they recognized or even tried to understand it, as consistent with what was occurring or what they thought could change in their school district, school or classroom. Administrators, for example, saw such a program as a wealth of opportunities to bolster and support existing services as well as encourage and facilitate existing endeavors in the school district. Similarly, teachers were usually preoccupied with their own responsibilities—managing a classroom full of students and relating to administrative requests; there was little interest in any program of reform. It was assumed to be in their best interest to ignore or eschew any involvement in E.S.P., which is what usually occurred. For those teachers who took advantage of the opportunities for change offered by E.S.P., it was related to their own personal and pedagogic needs.

There is a second strain in the difference between the federal and local world of practice which set up the dilemma of a federal program definition which would be mutually understood by local practitioners: Federal reformers assumed that E.S.P. was to be implemented in a local bureaucratic hierarchical type system of power located in the central administration office of local sites, the offices from within making application for E.S.P. funding. They tended to see their primary task as holding central administrators accountable for the implementation of the program. However, the local response to the program, from the outset of making application, was more akin to a lawn party which local practitioners participated in and attended at their own will and for their own reasons and purposes, "sometimes to serve others, sometimes to serve themselves." This also included central administrators who had their own reasons for having such a "lawn party" in the first place. For example, central administrators tended to use the program for their own local needs and reasons, such as responding to the threat of court-ordered desegregation or community pressures for a change in schools, as well as their desire to implement certain changes themselves. The result was a program of change which brought some local satisfaction but was also much less comprehensive and more particular, contributing to the lawn-party image of the local response to the program. Ultimately, in fact, any change which was able to occur was typically a result of those changes which could be tailored to a teacher's own needs and interests. These personal interests usually involved few other staff members in the school.

Rather than a centrally directed program of change, then, E.S.P. brought and aroused varied, piecemeal, and isolated local responses which were quite inconsistent, if not contradictory, to the federal vision of comprehensive change. Local efforts at implementation reflected their own widely diverse range of needs, interests and priorities. Rarely were these held together by any common theme or purpose. Rather, their response might best be described as a highly decentralized and unpredictably fragmented one which reduced the federal plans of comprehensive change to a disparate variety of piecemeal endeavors at the local level.

What the E.S.P. planners thought schools needed could not be achieved by money. Before, during, and after the E.S.P. program, the ambience of the participating schools was antithetical to a resource exchange rationale and hospitable to a "You do your thing, I do my thing" stance. "Comprehensiveness," the federal rallying point, makes no sense if it does not mean increasing interconnectedness, exchanging resources, and expanding (redefining) people's conception of themselves and others as resources. But these meanings, however virtuous their intent and sound, are worthless unless they are tied to an action strategy that specifies the conditions, timing, and leadership style by which these meanings stand a chance of being realized. And such an action strategy has to confront the social world the way it is—the ways it is connected and disconnected, the ways in which institutional cultures reward fragmentation and the narrow protection of self-interest, the obstacles it presents to confronting the implications of limited resources—and to adopt a rationale that, by altering the existing pattern of incentives and rewards, stands a chance of approaching the goal of comprehensiveness. The resource exchange rationale tied to the fact and the concept of networks is no panacea. It is *an* alternative to the present sorry, ineffective, cynicism-producing state of affairs. Informally, it works. If we have doubts that it can be adapted to the ambience of our schools and human service agencies, it is because the E.S.P. is only one of many scores of instances from which few lessons seem to have been learned, except the major one that the more things change the more they remain the same. But that major lesson can be a form of scapegoating if it is meant to imply that the culprit is the recalcitrance of people to "good" ideas. Far more often than not, the good ideas were not so good. The new math, the new physics, the new biology, and similar efforts at change were "good" ideas, but the strategies used to implant them in schools guaranteed, as in the case of the E.S.P. program, that little or nothing would change (Sarason, 1971). Good ideas, like love, are not enough. Untied to action strategies rooted in the realities of the situation you seek to change, good ideas are, at best, mischievous in their consequences and, at worst, downright harmful.

And what might one such strategy look like? Several times in previous chapters, as well as in more detail in our earlier book (Sarason and others, 1977), we have referred to the teacher center developed by Dr. William Fibkins on a resource exchange rationale in a junior high in Bay Shore, Long Island. This teacher center became connected in various ways with many individuals in the community; it was, by design, not a walled enclave within a school building. When we became aware of that teacher center, interconnections between it and the Essex Network were made, despite the distances involved. What came out of this intersecting of the two networks is best indicated in the following section of a grant proposal by two Bay Shore citizens (Marie Greene, Patricia Topitzer) who had been drawn into the Teacher Center network. Independent of their knowledge of and embeddedness in their community, as well as because of their scanning minds, which came from we know not where, was an intuitive grasp of the resource exchange rationale. What Fibkins, Sussman, Dewar, Lorentz, and Sarason contributed to them was a language for verbalizing their intuitions and, of course, access to their resources. Since a prime objective of the Essex Network was now to spawn other networks, we were getting more than we were giving! The proposal was written by Patricia Topitzer (1978a, pp. 1–3):

Bay Shore Resource Network
Rough Draft for Proposal:
A Basis for Discussion

Summary

The Bay Shore Resource Network is currently being established and coordinated by two community members as volunteer citizens. Although both Mrs. Greene and Mrs. Topitzer are trained professionals in the fields of social science and mental health, they have sharpened their current focus via their extensive volunteer activities in the Bay Shore Community.

Briefly, the scope of the project is the establishment of a citizen participation resource network which aims at improving the mesh between the *needs* of citizens and local agencies and the *resources* inherent in both. We operate from the conviction that any agency or individual possesses *both* needs and resources. Needs are not the sole property of individuals (clients, patients). Nor are resources a monopoly controlled by agencies or organizations. This creates the necessary precondition for the establishment of reciprocal relationships and opportunities for barter which can result in positive improvements in understanding of problems and delivery of services. These improvements can be measured in terms of efficiency and cost effectiveness.

The tools which the coordinators plan to introduce and utilize include the networking concepts developed by Sarason, Lorentz, and others at Yale and at the Essex Network. Its most important component is the role of the coordinator and the underpinning focus of this project is the demonstration and validation of that role. We submit that it is the full-time availability of two persons functioning in this role which will be the single most important element in developing the reciprocity of citizens and local agencies and to better elicit the resources inherent in both. In addition, the Action Research Program, explicated by Don Davies and others, of the Institute for Responsive Education, will be an inherent part of the process of developing reciprocal relationships.

Introduction

The coordinators' professional training in community mental health and fifteen years combined volunteer and leadership experience in the Bay Shore community had sensitized them to the major problem residents have in finding an easily identifiable vehicle for solving community problems.

Approximately one year ago, both women became members of the advisory board of the Bay Shore Teachers' Center, where they were exposed to Sarason's and Lorentz's concepts of networking as a mutual barter system via which individuals seek to meet each other's reciprocal needs. They experienced the successful application of this process at the Teachers' Center, which has achieved national publicity and recognition, as well as in two projects which they personally "spun off." The latter two projects, although small in size, have achieved solid success in their objectives.

These projects include a parenting education group, established and coordinated by Mrs. Greene, and run by trained volunteer parents, and a community resource minicourse project, created and coordinated by Mrs. Topitzer, and run by a group of volunteer parents at the local junior high school. The parent education group sought to bring training in parenting and group leadership skills to interested people, as well as to begin to build neighborhood networks of parents. The community resource group sought to use minicourses as a vehicle for increasing student-community interaction.

Over the past year, approximately 400 students, 100 adults, and eleven community groups have been participants in forty minicourses, sixty-three sessions of the parenting education course, and four days of leadership training which was funded and run by the Cornell University Home Extension Service at a total cost to the community of $176.

Finally, a group of concerned parents is coalescing around curriculum and parent involvement issues. Some of these people, including the leader, Mrs. Lynne Lewis, have expressed interest in exploring the application of the networking process and action research concepts to the further development of their activities. The idea of identifying reciprocal needs and resources of parents and the school staff appeals to this group as a means of finding nonconfrontational ways of achieving their goals in an already tense atmosphere. They understand that to even present their problems to school administration would be perceived as an untenable demand on a school system that is already overburdened financially. They see the existence of the network coordinators as a necessary ingredient to help them define and locate those needs and resources with minimal financial expenditure. . . .

The activities outlined above have become known to others in the community who are becoming interested in introducing the element of using the coordinators to help them develop a barter system of reciprocal relationships in order to improve the delivery of social services and help create a more positive impact on specific problems of poor integration of released mental patients into our community, and inflationary burdens on senior citizens.

The sum of all these experiences has convinced the two women that two full-time, paid coordinators are a necessity if further growth and improvement in these areas is to occur. Furthermore, they have become aware of the importance of the process inherent in the coordinator's role which creates a "middleman" who is constantly scanning and evaluating the community for both needs and resources and who can create the appropriate match and act as a support to the emerging reciprocal relationships. There are people within organizations who function in this way. However, they are limited by the parochialism of their parent organization. A neutral, community-based coordinator is required if all the resources are to be made available to each person or institution in need.

After writing brief descriptions of our assessment of the problems experienced by Bay Shore residents and our proposed solution, we discussed the idea of the establishment of the Bay Shore Resource Network with Seymour Sarason, Richard Sussman, and Mrs. Dewar, coordinators of the Essex Network; with Dr. Sanford Kravitz, dean of the School of Social Work at Stony Brook University, a member of the Essex Network; and with Mrs. Martha Mobley, Cornell University Home Extension Service. Each of these people has indicated their agreement with our assessments of our community's disorganization and with the focus of our proposed project. They have contributed ongoing consultation, training, and commitment to continue doing so over the life of the project as needed. Dean Kravitz has stated his willingness to place four M.S.W. students with us as early as this fall, if both coordinators are functioning as paid, full-time staff members. Mrs. Mobley, who is interested in the problem of the lack of coordination in the delivery of social services, is exploring the possibility of our use of a local planning agency (on whose board she serves) as a fiscal agent. Furthermore, she is interested in bringing our project to the attention of a member of the faculty at Cornell University School of Human Ecology and Development, in order that we might explore the possibility of a reciprocal relationship with that institution. In addition, ten local professional people have indicated an interest in exploring further possibilities of their involvement with the Bay Shore Resource Network, and some thirty citizens have done likewise.

Problem Statement or Assessment of Need

1. The township level of government must now concern itself with hundreds of thousands of people over a wide geographical area. Years ago, when the area was sparsely populated and largely rural or a summer resort, this unit of government sufficed. Today, with increasingly complex services demanded of local government, and a highly varied and mobile population, people are having increasing difficulty in identifying the town government as a responsive organization. And that statement must be seen as an indicator of the severity of the alienation problem rather than an indictment of a particular town administration.

2. The lack of communication between residents and the town government is exacerbated by poor public transportation and sparse local channels of communication in the area.

3. The sudden, large, unplanned growth in population which occurred after World War II, besides straining all local resources, had unforeseen consequences, such as the birth of suburban shopping malls, which contributed to the demise of downtown Bay Shore. This central shopping area had served as an informal focal point for the community and had fueled local service groups' efforts, helping to provide "clout" for Bay Shore.

4. Even salutary governmental efforts to deal with these problems, and there are several originating from all levels of government, are perceived as being emitted by large, unresponsive bureaucracies whose major effect on the average resident is to raise his taxes!

Every resident is acutely affected by this lack of a viable Bay Shore community. There is widespread agreement about the existence of serious community problems: the alarming rise in rate of property taxes and the disproportionate numbers of state mental hospital patients who have been released into Bay Shore. Since citizen experience in trying to deal with these problems has lead to feelings of frustration, powerlessness, and alienation, an unhealthy apathy is increasing. The need for a grass-roots citizen participation network where people can air their concerns and discover the resources inherent in themselves for some solutions is becoming increasingly evident. Currently, there are individuals and small groups, even isolated committees, working alone on pieces of individual problems. The vision and motivation is "out there," along with the frustration and apathy. The vehicle for citizen participation is not.

It should be noted with particular interest that this problem of citizen alienation and the individual's inability to find a niche in his social and political surroundings from which he can operate to successfully affect the problems impinging upon him is by no means peculiar to the small community of Bay Shore. As Dean Kravitz pointed out, this problem is endemic to a large part of Long Island. Clearly, the disorganization afflicting Bay Shore, as well as many other Long Island communities, has two levels: (1) the obvious problems that many residents perceive and complain of and (2) the lack of an easily identifiable social or political pathway toward finding or creating solutions. The needs and often even the resources exist. The linkage between them, in many cases, does not. Nor does the person or agency currently exist who is available to uncover or forge the connecting link or path. This, of course, is precisely the proposed role of the network coordinator.

We do not feel it necessary to instruct the reader about the significance of what these women have already accomplished (let alone what they want to accomplish) for the E.S.P. fiasco. Several things are deserving of brief emphasis. First, there are few communities and few school systems that do not have a Fibkins, a Greene, a Topitzer. Second, it is tragically wasteful, and ultimately self-defeating, to view school system changes independent of community problems and change. Third, the interconnecting of informal networks (between those in schools and those in the wider community) is a way in which the assets—not only the deficits—of individuals in schools and the community can be identified and effectively used. The resource exchange rationale emphasizes potential and existing resource assets. Fourth, informal networks can become an influence on formal organizations. Fifth, the resource exchange rationale presents a pattern of incentives and rewards to individuals quite different from that of the formal agencies in which they work. Sixth, by its very nature the rationale makes it difficult for the developing network to fall into the trap of defining resources as those which one pays for and, therefore, controls. Money is not the carrot stimulating action, and the pressures of money and time are not the sticks without which action ceases.

Now for the sequel to the proposal written by Mrs. Topitzer. She and Mrs. Greene have two goals: to obtain formal community recognition of the network coordinator role and to receive salaries. They are not asking funding for what they have already done but for far more time-consuming activities of which the community has great need. Each of the women can get a job. That is not their problem. What they want is the kind of job described in the proposal. *They have been remarkably unsuccessful, even though several of the human serv-*

ices agencies are solidly supportive and a few even have funds. One of the obstacles is that agencies have funds for circumscribed, specialized activities for which one can write a job description stating boundaries, formal relationships to other agency activities, specific responsibilities, and position in a line of command. And implicit in every job description is the idea that the development of interagency relationships is the responsibility of the agency director and that all those below him or her are not free to make arrangements with other agencies. From the standpoint of the formal agency, the network leader-coordinator is a "non-job"; that is, it simply does not fit the usual conception of a job. By its very nature, it is a "job" without clear boundaries in time, place, and focus. A second obstacle (related to the first)—recognized by Topitzer and Greene and the supportive agency—is that, even if an agency could find the role, one had to expect there would be difficulty over time maintaining the independence of the role, organizational dynamics being what they are. A third obstacle can be put in the form of a question: "What happens when Topitzer and Greene go to a foundation, or a state agency, or some federal bureau for funding?" Two citizens, unaffiliated with an agency, describing a "non-job" are listened to politely but the answer is no, even though some of the listeners see sense in the request. But either these listeners know only how to deal with formal, legal entities or they operate under guidelines that do not permit them to make arrangements with private individuals.

What is encouraging in the Topitzer and Greene story is that a few agencies saw the crucial point: *The place for the network vehicle was between and among agencies, not in or under them.* Initially, and reluctantly, Topitzer and Greene sought piecemeal or membership funding from agencies, but when their own fears were also voiced by these agencies they gave up that tactic. There was agreement that payment of part of the salaries from several agencies would likely impose time and goal constrictions and raise issues of "ownership" that would inhibit acquisition of new members and the changing and adopting of new foci. The problem was and is, "Given the nature and goals of a resource exchange network, where does one place and how does one fund its 'intermediate' functions? In a sea of formal organizations, where is neutral ground? And what sources would be willing to give in ways that do not restrict the potentials of the resource exchange rationale?" These are crucial and thorny questions for which practical approaches are hard to come by. One such approach is taken up in a later chapter, where we discuss a new role in and among formal organization: the resource exchange ombudsman. The concept of the ombudsman, especially in the Scandinavian countries, is an old one, and we endeavor to examine and apply the concept to resource exchange.

Let us now focus on another difference between the rationale of the formal human services agency and that of the informal resource exchange network. It is the difference between a deficit-emphasizing and asset-emphasizing orientation.

Slums, Mental Retardation, Medicare, and Nursing Homes

Perhaps the most radical departure of the resource exchange rationale from conventional agency thinking is its emphasis on what people can do for themselves and with others, not on their disabilities or psychopathologies. The concept of exchange is predicated on the assumption that people have assets; that is, they are assets if one learns to look at them from a standpoint other than that of psychopathological symptoms. Immersed as we are in an age of psychology and mental health, we are unaware of the extent to which our conceptions of ourselves and others is concerned with deficits. We have read enough clinical reports of all kinds to be able to say that one has to strain to find statements about a person's assets. That, of course, should not be surprising when one realizes that the *sine qua non* of a clinician is that he or she does the best he can on the basis of knowledge, training, and experience to help someone who comes with a problem. The problem has to exist before the clinician is called in. The danger here is that, in riveting on an individual's deficits and vulnerabilities, it becomes difficult to pay attention to assets, real or potential, personal or social. This style of thinking has invaded the policies and practices of agencies and governments. So, for decades we have looked at slums and ghettos, recoiled in fear and even in disgust, and vigorously approved demolishing them and putting up new structures (into which few from the slums went, but that is another story). We could not see any assets in "those places." How could they have *any* redeeming features, *any* pattern of human relationships that would have *some* positive consequences! The fact is, as we have learned the hard way, these were not totally disabling, disorganizing areas. They did contain some sources of mutual support that permitted some sense of identity and community, and the concept of resource exchange, far from being absent, was understood by many of the inhabitants. But the inability to look for assets, to see only deficits and social pathology—implied in the statement of an infamous vice-president: "When you have seen one slum, you have seen them all"—permitted the demolishing of some of these areas, scattering their populations here and there, destroying what social assets had given the people support, and ignoring the possible absence of these assets in the areas to which they would move. It is obvious, we assume, that we are not recommending the preservation of slums and ghettos but, rather, policies and actions that try to take personal and social assets into account.

Until a couple of decades ago, society believed that mentally retarded individuals were better off living in institutions or spending a good part of each day in segregated settings with "their own kind." This belief rested, among other things, on a view of these individuals as without assets to be members of the natural community. They needed the protection of segregated facilities, without which they would be unable to survive. It was also assumed that the families of these handicapped individuals did not have, or should not be expected to have or to develop, the socially supportive assets to maintain these individuals in the home. It is not fortuitous that the National Association for Retarded Citizens was, until a few years ago, called the National Association for Retarded *Children.* As someone once said, "Calling people 'children,' regardless of age, *and* 'mentally retarded' was literally adding insult to injury." Today, public policy has radically changed in favor of helping retarded people become "normalized" in their communities. They are not seen as without assets, and recognition has finally been accorded the fact that most families wish to and can keep handicapped members at home and in the community. There is no better example than the field of mental retardation to illustrate how redefining people as resources dramatically alters the behaviors of the redefined and the redefiners. Where only deficits had been seen, there is now recognition of some assets. Whereas resources for the education of mentally retarded people had been defined as "special," both in terms of personnel and location, they came to be seen as obtainable from a wide variety of community sources; that is, these sources had much to give and much to get if only someone like a network coordinator could "put the pieces together."

In this connection, we would like to relate some experiences that are described in detail elsewhere (Sarason, Zitnay, and Grossman, 1972). The specific program we focus on was developed by Schwebel and Cook (1972) in connection with a new facility for the mentally retarded that was making a serious effort to relate its resources to those of diverse community groups and agencies. That is to say, the staff of this facility, aware that its resources were no less limited than those of others in the community with an interest in or some responsibility for mentally retarded people, were operating explicitly on a resource exchange rationale. The primary task of the staff was to be network leader-coordinators.

Schwebel and Cook were aware that a number of parents with educable retarded children in special classes expressed concern that their youngsters were unable to develop friendships with neighborhood children and generally spent afternoons and weekends watching television. Feeling that their children's needs for constructive companionship were unmet, the parents tended to blame the schools for not training their children in social skills and to blame the community for not providing adequate recreational facilities. These views were similar to those of school personnel, who also expressed concern about the quality of their special programs and complained of having few resources available to them for these programs.

What was being said was all too familiar, but what was not being expressed by the parents, except very indirectly, was their concern for the future—that their youngsters would become increasingly isolated, unhappy, and restless, and that this could have adverse consequences in family organization and stability. The parents wanted a more comprehensive program, not only for its immediate or short-term benefits but also for what they hoped would be long-term ones.

Schwebel and Cook's objectives can be seen in the following (Schwebel and Cook, 1972, p. 49):

> Given that contact had already been established with the school system and the YMCA, which had suitable facilities, the present authors began to consider how a program might be designed in conjunction with these agencies which would also meet the objectives set forth in and critical to the philosophy of the CCRC [Central Connecticut Regional Center]. After as-

sessing the resources and facilities which were likely to be available, the authors began to plan a tutoring program for special-class children which would be sponsored jointly by the school system, YMCA, and the center. This program, it was thought, could involve the high school students in service clubs and could be designed to meet several objectives:

1. To provide a constructive experience in relationship building for educable mentally retarded children
2. To demonstrate the value of using supervised nonprofessional volunteers in helping build relationships
3. To develop constructive relationships between the center and those local agencies which had traditionally focused on specific and narrow aspects of retardates' needs
4. To study the processes by which such a program develops and to draw relevant conclusions about its worth to the community

Schwebel and Cook describe in detail the issues and problems that arise in organizing a program requiring the cooperation of several community settings, the preparation and use of nonprofessionals (high school students), detailed planning, and eternal vigilance. As they indicate, these are not technical details arranged in some kind of time sequence that can be described in an organizational chart. Rather, they are aspects of a never-ending process in which means are constantly judged by the desired ends. For example, it is clear from their description that it would have been far simpler for them if their goal had been only to provide certain experiences for the special-class youngsters. But as important to Schwebel and Cook as that laudable aim were the depth and quality of the experience of the tutors. The following excerpt from their report (Schwebel and Cook, 1972, pp. 50–52) provides a glimpse of the kind of planning required as well as the attention given to the experiences of the tutors:

Twenty-eight girls volunteered for the program and were matched with twenty-eight children from the special education classes. Fourteen pairs were asked to come on Wednesdays and fourteen on Thursdays. The tutoring took place for an hour and was followed immediately with an hour of group supervision for the tutors.

A good deal of thought and discussion went into preparing for the first tutoring sessions. We considered the kinds of things which might happen which would help or hurt the program, thinking that, by heightening our awareness of these possibilities, we could maximize the program's value. We also wanted to develop a plan of action in the event a crisis developed (such as a child running away or having a seizure). . . .

Our efforts in thinking through what was likely to happen if we followed different courses were helpful and important in that we managed to avoid major pitfalls and to set up workable mechanisms for implementing and coordinating the tutoring. To a certain extent, however, we still failed to anticipate some key factors. For instance, related to the above examples, we had prepared complete lists indicating the tutor-tutee pairs we had made, which children were to be tutored on the first day and which on the second. The list also had phone numbers and addresses of all those involved in the program. We did a careful job for we planned to give copies of this list to the school people. On the first day of the program, we personally delivered the lists to the principal and to the teachers involved. We felt this would be important in terms of the kinds of attitudes they would develop vis-à-vis our program. It never occurred to us, however, that the bus drivers needed a copy of this list as well and that their attitudes about the program might also be related to those that the children would develop.

It had occurred to us that the tutors as well as the tutees would want to explore the YMCA building during the first session. We expected that they would want to become familiar, on the first of many visits, with their surroundings and the resources available to them. Therefore, we began the first sessions with a tour of the facilities, led by the YMCA's program director. Although there was confusion during the tours, chaos did not exist because, from the outset, the tutors took their responsibility seriously. After touring the building, most of the tutors sat down with their tutees and began some school work. There were, of course, a few children who would not sit down after the tour and who began to wander around the building. Their tutors followed them faithfully, pursuing their goal of gaining some control of the relationship in order to begin to develop it. In all but one instance, the tutors managed to begin to get some response and had an opportunity to spend at least a few quiet moments talking to or working with their tutees during the first session.

The supervision meetings which followed the first sessions moved slowly. The tutors were somewhat hesitant to ask questions and initiated little of the discussion. Similarly, they tended to respond briefly to questions which were posed to them by the supervisors. It was clear, however, that the tutors had a great deal of interest in what had happened in their tutorial relationships and wanted to know what was likely to occur in the future. Informally, before and after the meeting, lively conversations did take place. The issues which were discussed during the meeting were (1) how the children differed from the tutors' expectations, (2) how to best utilize the hour of tutoring, and (3) the kinds of goals the tutors should work toward. Clearly, related to these issues the tutors were expressing their concern with whether their tutees were going to like them and whether they felt they were competent enough to be good tutors. In keeping with our plan, we did not provide the tutors with answers, but rather limited ourselves to posing alternatives and aiding the group in the evaluation of these.

During the second week, the tutoring sessions had a much more settled quality to them. In fact, for most of the periods, the rooms were quiet, and the tutors were helping the children with school work. The tutors had apparently been reassured during the first supervision session by fellow group members, and to some extent by us, that as tutors they had the prerogative to suggest activities and that by exercising this they would not destroy their opportunity to develop a meaningful relationship with their tutees. . . .

The supervision meetings at the end of the second sessions were strikingly different from those at the end of the first and were a preview of the kinds of meetings which were to take place during the following weeks. Undoubtedly surer of themselves and their roles, the tutors began to raise issues pertaining to tutoring, to discuss problems they were experiencing with their own tutees, and to feel free enough to comment on their co-workers' problems. The thread which ran through these sessions and several which followed was the issue of how much time should be spent in play versus in work and the extent to which the tutor should maintain control over the selection of activities. The concern related with these issues was still the question of what was involved in getting the children to "like" the tutors.

By the third and fourth sessions, the tutors began to believe that their children cared about them; this realization led the tutors to redouble their efforts. . . .

When the tutors began to realize their competence in tutoring (assessed by them in terms of their child's liking for them and his willingness to spend a good portion of the hour working), a qualitative change took place in the supervision sessions. The tutors became freer to discuss problems which occurred during the hour and experienced less of a need for "lectures" from the supervisors. Concomitantly, the supervision was benefited by the fact that the girls began to see that they as a group could examine aspects of the tutee's behavior and begin to understand some of the dynamics which might be involved and that on the basis of this analysis they could suggest alternative ways of working with the child so that this type of problem would not interfere with the relationship. . . .

In terms of its educational impact, the girls were exposed to a type of learning situation which, for most, was new. Our efforts as group supervisors were directed toward drawing from the girls their emotional as well as their intellectual reactions to each experience. We tried to help them clarify their decision-making processes by asking leading questions and supporting explorations of alternative approaches. This part of the experience seemed sufficient in and of itself to elevate the present program's impact from the level of baby sitting or sibling experience. . . .

The tutors gave us several indications of the value they placed on this program. Attendance was impressive and absence well-founded. The girls took the responsibility of looking out for unaccompanied children and would work with these children or find someone to work with them. Moreover, they would report these children's activities and reactions to the absent tutor at the following session. One indication of the girls' positive attitude came in a more disguised form. In the fifth week of the program, we broached the issue of placing a newspaper article and photographs of the program in the local newspaper. The tutors' reactions were mixed: We had succeeded in convincing them of the value of making the community aware of the tutoring program, but they held to their first feeling that they did not want to be seen or referred to by name. Although at first we wondered if the girls felt ashamed or ambivalent about their involvement with retarded children, we eventually were convinced by them that they genuinely felt they were doing something for someone else which deserved privacy and which could be spoiled if lauded publicly. Not unlike their adolescent feelings about many kinds of relationships, the girls perceived the dyadic tutorial relationships as "something special" and something unique which could be ruined by public scrutiny. Yet another indication of the girls' involvement was the extent of the girls' sadness in preparing for termination. Many asked about the fall and working with the same child. Three seniors about to start full-time jobs asked to be included in the following year's program, saying that they'd skip a lunch hour at work in order to make up the time that they would spend in tutoring their child.

Several months after the program's conclusion, we learned that as a result of their experiences in the tutoring program, at least three girls had changed their vocational plans and were preparing to become special education teachers. We felt that in at least some ways all of the girls would begin with greater eagerness to try new techniques in relationship building as a result of their budding confidence and competence and that in the future, as a result of their tutoring and other experiences, they would build upon that history and would become more responsive and sensitive mothers.

More were involved than tutors and tutees. The parents, a group of women volunteers, the classroom teachers, and staff of the YMCA played crucial roles, and Schwebel and Cook present observations, self-reports, and other data to support the conclusion that important segments of the community had become conscious of how they could assume some responsibility for mentally retarded individuals. At the very least, Schwebel and Cook's efforts demonstrated to individuals and agencies in the community that mental retardation was not, indeed could not, be the sole responsibility of the regional center. To the extent that this was demonstrated, the possibility was increased that the community would develop those resources and programs that could prevent some of the adverse personal and familial consequences that follow the social isolation of the mentally retarded youngster.

It is, according to our values, no less important that to achieve this goal requires the achievement of still another goal: the heightened awareness in the community's individuals and agencies that their horizons and resources expand as they engage in the helping process. One engages in the helping process not only for others but also for oneself, and when this twofold objective is met one experiences a sense of community that is all too rare. The most poignant part of Schwebel and Cook's report is their discussion of how *they* benefited and changed from their program. Their satisfaction inhered not only in what they had helped to provide for others but also in what they had provided for their own development.

And now to Medicare. It is ironic that at the same time that the place of mentally retarded people in the community was being redefined in a positive, asset-emphasizing way, our society pushed vigorously for the implementation of a deficit-emphasizing policy for older people. The very word *Medi*care focused attention on disability and illness, and, fatefully, the legislation spawned a large, profit-making, nursing home industry. At the same time that it was being demonstrated that mentally retarded individuals could be part of the community and did not necessarily have to live in segregated settings, the incentives and rewards contained in the Medicare legislation worked to put older people in segregated settings. In addition, those incentives and rewards worked against any tendency families may have had to keep their senior citizens with them or in the community. In point of fact, families were financially "punished" if they kept their senior citizens at home. And, needless to say, many senior citizens precariously living by themselves were urged and sometimes railroaded into nursing homes.

From one standpoint, the Medicare legislation must be viewed positively because it recognized that many older people were not receiving or could not afford life-maintaining services. From another standpoint, it has been viewed negatively because it was solely concerned with the deficits of people and did not confront the question, "What were the existing personal and social assets of senior citizens, and how could these assets be a basis for services that would allow them to continue to live in the community?" Just as we used to look at slums and ghettos and say we must get rid of them, regardless of the personal and social consequences to their inhabitants, we looked at the precarious existence of senior citizens and concluded they should be moved elsewhere. They had no personal and social assets that could be the focus of services that would maximize their chances to live an independent existence! There was amazingly little recognition of the possibility that many of these citizens wanted to remain in the community rather than go to the spanking-new nursing homes that could not be built fast enough to meet the needs as defined in the legislation. There was such righteous concern for the fragile existence of many of these people that few people asked, "How come they manage? What indigenous family or neighborhood or friend support systems are aiding them? How can we beef up these support systems? What do we have to do that will permit them to enjoy some sense of freedom and independence, which is ruled out by institutionalizing them?" Medicare was literally antisocial in that it diverted attention away from the obvious fact that older people were always embedded in some kind of social fabric or network that rarely was without any assets to the individual. Medicare was about people's bodies, not their social embeddedness. Their bodies had or would have disabilities, and that deficit-emphasizing stance determined how other aspects of their functioning would be perceived or ignored.

The Medicare legislation had one other major built-in problem, a kind of time bomb that, when it exploded, exposed the culture of nursing homes. That problem, a basic one confronted in the resource exchange rationale, was that over time, and not too long a time, there would not be sufficient resources, fiscal and otherwise, to keep the program going. Given the increasing numbers of old people and the bonanza of incentives and rewards to medical personnel, hospitals, and the private nursing home industry, it did not take long before the fact of limited resources was confronted and cutbacks were made, the main victims being old people in nursing homes or elsewhere. The nursing home scandals, if they demonstrated anything, showed how effective segregated institutions are in robbing people of whatever personal and social assets they may once have had.

Only recently have governmental and human services agencies come to see the catastrophic consequences of focusing on older people's deficits. It is beyond our scope to try to answer why these agencies have such a focus or why it has been "outsiders" who have forced them to see assets where before they only saw disability, pathology, and deficits. Few people have played a more productive role in bringing about this change than Claude Pepper, chairman of the House of Representatives' Select Committee on Aging. Here are excerpts from an article of his in the *New York Times*, May 20, 1978 (p. C19):

A great deal of energy has been spent in trying to figure out how to make nursing homes more efficient, economic and responsive to aging Americans' health care needs. It is now time for an infusion of imagination and new ideas to provide adequate, compassionate medical services to the elderly, at a price we can afford. I am more convinced than ever that the answer to such essential services lies in an effective home health care program.

Over a period of time, the government unwittingly has adopted a costly, counterproductive institutional bias toward elderly citizens who need health care. We think of home health care for the aging as an alternative to institutionalization. That's a tragedy—a tragedy that goes against traditional American values of independence and personal dignity.

After several hearings on home health care, the House Select Committee on Aging concluded, "It only stands to reason that in the natural order of things it should be just the reverse. Institutionalization should be an alternative to home health care."

There will always be disabled people who require full-time institutionalization in nursing homes. But those who are able to remain in their homes should be given the right to make that choice. Even putting aside logic and compassion, and if costs were the only consideration, home health care is still the way to go. A report prepared by the General Accounting Office shows that "until older people become greatly or extremely impaired, the cost of nursing home care exceeds the cost of home care, including the value of the general support services provided by family and friends."

Medicare regulations affecting home health care are too stringent. To be eligible, an elderly or disabled person must have been hospitalized for three days, the plan of care must be prescribed by a doctor, the care must be "skilled," and the patient must be considered "home-bound." In addition, home visits are limited under hospital insurance to 100 per spell of illness and under supplementary medical insurance to 100 per calendar year.

Those requirements ought to be liberalized, and legislation to make important changes has been offered. The prior hospitalization limitation should be removed. The visit limit should be deleted. The arbitrary "home-bound" requirement should be eliminated. And the definition of home health care should be interpreted to include homemaker and periodic chore services.

Representative Pepper puts "skilled" and "home-bound" in quotes and refers to "general support services provided by family and friends." Representative Pepper is quite aware that older people are inevitably embedded in a network of relationships that—in varying degrees, to be sure—interacts supportively with whatever assets the individual possesses; and he is also aware that by defining services only in professional or credentialing terms the individual may be denied help from those who do not possess credentialed skills but who can help him or her the most. There *are* natural support systems but one would never have known that from Medicare and Medicaid legislation. Representative Pepper is also bothered by the fragmentation of the "delivery of services," a fragmentation in the federal bureaucracy that has its counterpart among human services agencies in the community. The following are excerpts from a speech he made in Congress on September 20, 1977 (U.S. Congress, House, 1977):

> Many of our committee's hearings have revealed that one of the major problems in getting necessary benefits and services to the elderly is the fragmented delivery system itself. The proliferation of uncoordinated programs creates a situation in which older persons are shuffled from office to office only to emerge confused, degraded, and still without the help they need.
> When an older person has a need for a particular service, for example in-home health services, where can he turn for help? The answer, unfortunately, is "it all depends." Home health and supportive services are provided under Medicare, Medicaid, the social services program under Title XX of the Social Security Act, home health demonstration grants under the Public Health Service Act, two different titles of the Older Americans Act, the senior companionship and RSVP volunteer programs under Action, the older Americans community service employment program, senior opportunities and services under the Community Services Act, and other statutes. All of this adds up to a bewildering maze of programs and regulations that is a nightmare for the elderly person trying to find a way through it. . . .
> These remarks represent an update on the status of efforts to accomplish these objectives.
> Before discussing specific recommendations, it is important to note that there is no single best way to reorganize the federal government. This might best be understood through a homely analogy. If a person wishes to purchase a pair of sneakers, there are a number of different retail outlets from which he can get them—shoe stores, sporting goods stores, a PX, stores specializing in selling sneakers, department stores, or a general store. Who is to say which is the best at providing goods to the public, since this will vary depending on such factors as whether it is an urban or rural area and the type of sneaker desired? Similarly, we approach efforts to streamline the

federal government's delivery system by recognizing that to be successful it must combine a variety of approaches. On the one hand, we cannot simply expect the elderly to fend for themselves in trying to get needed services and benefits through programs that aim not just at the elderly but other segments of the population. Such an approach is ruled out by their specialized needs and frequently by the added problem of lack of mobility. At the same time, we cannot simply construct a series of specialized delivery systems and individual bureaucracies for the elderly. That approach would in fact increase, rather than decrease, the kinds of proliferation of federal programs that we are concerned about. For example, one large-city administrator of aging programs told me that, because of differing federal programs, statutes, and regulations, his city must operate completely separate "meals on wheels" services for the home-bound elderly, disabled, and other groups. The absurdity of a situation in which buses delivering meals pull out of a housing project after serving the elderly and pass another bus about to provide the same meals to other residents of the same housing project is evident. Clearly, the utilization of a combination of these mainline and specialized—as well as other—approaches, depending on the situation, is the only way of maximizing federal efforts to aid the elderly. . . .

It is also not fortuitous that Representative Pepper regards Daphne Krause's Minneapolis Age and Opportunity Center as a model of what coordination of community services should mean (Chapter Two) if one is asset oriented. Few people understand as well as Daphne Krause does the tie between the resource exchange rationale, the emphasis on assets, and exploiting the existence of social networks. In her one-stop/all-services agency, coordination was not achieved by fiat but by choosing personnel, not in terms of credentials or professions but in terms of actual or potential assets and a willingness to act both as network leader-coordinator or Perkins' generalist, to ferret out the resources of existing networks, and, if need be, to transform existing networks, to bolster an individual's competence to maintain some degree of independence in the community. On the level of action or services, it is a difference that makes a difference if one looks at people and their interconnections in terms of assets.

At the beginning of this chapter, we said we were not out to prove that the resource exchange rationale could not be developed and maintained within and among human services agencies. Our purpose was to illustrate several points. First, human services agencies are governed by a view of self-interest, professionalism, and autonomy that guarantees a kind and degree of competitiveness within and among agencies that is wasteful of existing and potential resources. Second, the ideology of these agencies, together with that of their funding sources, reinforces a pattern of incentives and rewards that in practice works against redefinition of roles and resources. Third, although there has been recognition that resources are limited and that better and more coordination among agencies is essential, efforts at change have been remarkably unsuccessful. Fourth, human services agencies, by virtue of their history and clinical orientation, are deficit oriented, not asset oriented, in regard to their clients as well as to the utilization of nonagency personnel. Fifth, informal processes and relationships among agencies that threaten existing boundaries and structure, or that cannot be controlled or judged by the usual ties between accountability and the calendar, are looked on with suspicion and hostility.

To conclude, as we do, that human services agencies (their pattern of interrelating and the ways they are connected to governmental agencies and funding) are not, nor should they be expected to be, hospitable to a resource exchange rationale should occasion no surprise. We do not offer that conclusion as a moral judgment or a psychological explanation. The people who populate these agencies are, as people, no better or worse than the rest of us, and, like the rest of us in some parts of our lives, their thinking reflects the adverse consequences of concepts and practice maladaptive to the welfare of themselves, others, and the larger society. They have not willed this state of affairs, and many of them seek, albeit unsuccessfully, ways out of the self-defeating entanglements. To "explain" their thinking and practices in terms of psychology is to trivialize the issues, because we would then be ignoring the cultural and social historical processes within which what seemed to be "right, natural, and proper" emerged. Human services agencies, like schools, were and are creatures of society, not vehicles alien to society. And when, over time, they changed, it was in response to changes in the societal *zeitgeist*, as the Levines (1970) and Bledstein (1976) so well describe. So, when the Great Depression enveloped this country and spawned the creation of myriad social programs and changed the relation of the individual citizen to government, scores of new human services agencies were created, with societal blessings. Precisely because this was taking place in the context of a national crisis, speed of response (against time) was of the essence, and few people were disposed to examine the implicit assumptions governing action. And those implicit assumptions were, among others, that resources were far from limited, that money and national resolve were the major ingredients for achieving desired goals, that professionalization and specialization of agencies were unalloyed blessings, that coordination and efficient use of resources could be legislated, and that a clinical (deficit-emphasizing) approach to human services would be as effective as it was thought to be in medicine.

When the turbulent 1960s arrived, those assumptions received added reinforcement, but only for a time, because for the first time there were articulate groups, not all of them in the client category, who said that our human services agencies, and the professionals who worked in them, were part of the problem and not the solution. As we described in earlier chapters, disillusionment with traditional thinking, programs, and agencies is now general, and, with differing degrees of clarity, one of the outcomes has centered around informal arrangements, resource exchange, and networks. We have to say frankly that we do not know to what extent this outcome is, so to speak, in the air or, better yet, beginning to filter into the world of action. We resist indulging optimism by looking at these outcroppings of new thinking and predicting an abundant harvest. We have great respect for the staying power of the status quo, far greater respect than has been accorded it by well-intentioned reformers in recent decades. Also tempering our optimism is the observation that the fashionableness of the network concept, tied or not to a concept of resource exchange, has tended to obscure rather than clarify the present state of affairs. Too frequently, proclaiming an effort at coordination a "network," implying a more efficient use of resources, is no more than that: a proclamation. What is missing is a rationale that states the relationship between assumptions and goals, on the one hand, and, on the other hand, strategies for action—a rationale that is also diagnostically explicit about the obstacles that will be encountered. The current disillusionment will be productive to the extent that it stimulates new rationales that go beyond expressions of hope (or despair) or new ideas to the arena of action. In the next chapter, we shall focus on such action strategies.

8

An Emerging Consensus on Networks

It is obvious, but nonetheless deserving of emphasis, that on the level of action the future of the resource exchange rationale will depend on the growth in the numbers of people who can tie that rationale to the development of networks. Typically, when a shortage of people for certain roles is said to exist, training and educational programs are developed, credentialing criteria are formulated, and the program is advertised to attract "students." This, very likely, would be the kiss of death for the role of leader-coordinator, for several reasons. For one thing, formalizing a program in a formal educational institution immediately constricts the pool from which "teachers" and "students" can be selected, and, in addition, the traditions of such institutions will require that the new program conform to these traditions. This is not meant as a criticism of these traditions, at least most of them, but rather as an emphasis on the strength of educational traditions to require a degree of conformity from new programs that dilutes their innovative intent. A second consideration rests on the generally shared experience that many who apply for admission to specialized educational programs are not appropriate for them and that admissions procedures are far from good in selecting those individuals who would be most appropriate. A third consideration, and one that is crucial for network leader-coordinators, is that one cannot learn the role in *a* place but in the arena of action. For example, you learn to do research by doing it with people actively engaged in research, and, as some eminent researchers have emphasized (Taylor, Garner, and Hunt, 1959), the picture of the research process you get from reading research reports bears little relationship to how it is actually done. Generally speaking, colleges and universities do a poor job in preparing people for the world of social action, if only because their traditions (and, therefore, structure and organization) were not developed to be appropriate to the world of social action (Sarason, 1978a, 1978b).

But another reason we would resist formalization is that we have no good basis for estimating how many people are functioning in a role similar to that of the network leader-coordinator or how many could perform the functions of that role if they had a modest apprenticeship experience. Putting it that way can be misleading, however, if it is not understood in the context of how a resource exchange network develops and elaborates. In the five-year-old Essex Network, described in our earlier book (Sarason and others, 1977) and in Chapter Three of the present one, several leader-coordinators have surfaced, as much because finding them has been a major goal of Mrs. Dewar and Mr. Sussman as because of a self-selection factor in who was attracted to that network. Without exception, they all, explicitly and almost formally, asked Dewar or Sussman for help, or support, or consultation. "Will you help me if I go ahead and do it?" was the way one of the people put it. "You'll have to hold my hand!" was the way another put it to Sussman in relation to her proposed effort to develop a network and to connect it to the Essex one. But, inevitably, the Essex Network early became interconnected with other networks, in the course of which process other leader-coordinators emerged. It was through this type of interconnection that Fibkins, Topitzer, and Greene were "found" on Long Island, and they in turn, through their network interconnections, will locate and relate to other leader-coordinators. Inherent in the implementation of the resource exchange rationale is the process of redefining people as resources, and one of the consequences of that process is the encouragement it gives to performing the role of leader-coordinator. And behind that encouragement is the belief that there are people who possess the assets necessary for the leader-coordinator role.

The Creative Minority

The title of this chapter and section, "The Creative Minority," is from a section of a draft of an unpublished paper by Derek Sheane (1977), an industrial executive in Ulster, Northern Ireland. We learned about this paper in a series of discussions on networks with an urban planning group at the University of Pennsylvania. We are indebted to Sheane for permitting us to quote liberally from this paper. What is remarkable about it is how many points of similarity there are to our own position. Living in Ulster, observing and experiencing fratricide and the squandering of human and natural resources, the seeming impotence of government and the political system to defuse the conflicts, and the flight of "the creative minority" from the country, Sheane is able to make observations and conceptualizations about networks, leader-coordinators ("the creative minority"), and the relative merits of informal versus formal strategies for action. As the reader will see, Sheane assumes that the leader-coordinators exist, and he would obviously be opposed to formalizing their role or "training." Implicitly, he is raising a central question: "How can you capitalize on the existence of *informal* resource exchange networks so that they grow and interconnect and indirectly affect formal politices and agencies? How can this come about? If Sheane does not provide answers, at least he is crystal clear about what *not* to do if we are to be spared further disillusionment. That clarity is important, indeed crucial, because it should sensitize us to how prepotent a tendency it is in all of us to be unwitting prisoners of traditional forms of thinking and action. The following excerpt is from Sheane (1977, pp. 9–12):

> The ultimate force of darkness is the flight of the creative minority. In Ulster, pockets of creativity exist at all levels, in all pursuits and in all communities. Yet from time to time the sources of this creativity are threatened by alternating tides of apathy and violence, which tempt them to give up. Civilizations have always been made and saved by creative minorities. Civilization is not—repeat, not—made or saved by governments, reports, or marches. Civilizations are held together by linkages between those groups and individuals who share civilized values. They must be resolute, definite, and concentrate their energy and efforts.

> *First Steps for the Creative Minority*
> The first somewhat obvious conclusion is the need to multiply the impact of the creative minority. This implies that the forces of light must be

dynamically connected. To achieve this, the Ulsterman's natural impulse might be to form a new movement or a new organization. This would not work. Instead, let me suggest the opposite. Let us think about the use of *networks*, which are in many ways powerful nonorganizations. The concept of a network, which will become clearer as we proceed, is in the opinion of many the real alternative to rigid and bureaucratic forms of society and organization. This feeling is present in many societies: U.S.A. and India, to mention just two where much is being accomplished through the use of networks. There is a growing theory and practice that Ulster can use. Networks are spontaneous forms of communication and action that have developed as a reaction to the excessive centralization of Western societies and their institutions and organizations: the bureaucratization and dehumanization of large industrial firms: the lack of creativity, innovation, and energy in modern organizations: the feelings of powerlessness, lack of impact, and lack of self-worth that many individuals experience at work and in society at large. Observations which the reader, using different words, may already have made for himself.

Processes such as these have been developing for some time, indeed writers throughout this century have been drawing attention to these factors. What is new is that many more people experience these factors as real. It is not just the misfortune of people at the bottom of the pile. Middle managers in industry and public service experience it. Most significantly, the more able and thoughtful people in high-ranking jobs in industry and public service are finding their roles constricting, leaving them no personal space or freedom, even to change or modify their own organizations. The real feelings of individuals about their jobs, roles, and organizations are very different from their public statements, and well they know it. The 'quality of working life' is as much a slogan of the manager as the managed. As a result, commitment and loyalty to the formal organization has declined. People are putting their energy elsewhere. They are starting to live in networks. Networks are informal organizations. They are nonorganizations in the sense that they are largely leaderless, formless, and have very loose boundaries. They are informal sets of linkages that traverse modern institutions and organizations. Perhaps a diagram helps.

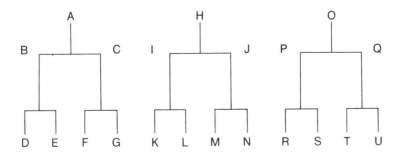

The diagram represents three organizations, say, a business firm, a local council, and a university. A, H, O are the works manager, the chief executive of the council, and the vice-chancellor, respectively. The other letters represent heads of functions, department heads, professors, and so on. "Lower down" you have workers, subordinates, and so on. This is the old society that is breaking down. The words used to describe it are *hierarchy, rank, rules, order, structure.* Its characteristics are rigidity, unresponsiveness, unimaginativeness. It is only capable of obtaining partial commitment: It gets the commitment of your head but not your heart.

But A, J, and S are also members of an informal organization. They are networked. They have a relationship because all three have a basic interest in the problem of, say, youth unemployment in their local community. Their interest stems from a personal commitment rather than the company, council, or university policy. Their "organization" evokes very different words: It is rankless, cooperative, energetic, spontaneous, creative, and real. Note how the network reflects a task, a common interest, and shared values. Note how the criteria for membership are *rational.* For example, in a formal organization heads of departments get together on a problem: This is typical in most industrial firms and public services. But this is *irrational,* as rank is the unspoken but actual criteria. And as any experienced member of an organization knows, rank has no direct relationship to skill, knowledge, and enthusiasm in solving a problem. Add to this that some departments are more decentralized than others; then bringing people together on the basis of the traditional hierarchy is indeed irrational.

The informal grouping of individuals around a task is a network. The concept of a network can be applied on different scales. Networks can be within an organization, between organizations, national or international. Networks can also differ in substance: business, social, political, academic, and so on. It is among the members of these networks that the creative minority is found. In Ulster, the social fabric is probably already held together by an unconscious network system that is invisible to the outsider. Certainly many of Ulster's problems can be solved by the use of networks to trigger and support useful activities. They can also be used to compensate for the inadequacies of formal organizations. They can also be used to neutralize or lessen the impact of ineffective interventions made by individuals acting in their formal roles. Networks are the key instruments and mechanisms for creating total change processes that impact on all aspects of society.

But what kind of individual can build, live in, create, and contribute to networks? They have many variations in personality, style, political interest, but they also have some of these unusual characteristics:

- They have overcome the "authority" problem. They can tolerate the anxiety of confronting their own power system—they will have freed themselves from slavish submission to outmoded reward and punishment systems in their own institutions.

- They are very aware people: At some critical point in their lives, they have gone through the pain barrier. They know what their mission is and what their values are.
- Although they acknowledge the need for a core structure and constitution in society, they have learned to make life up as they go along. They no longer feel threatened by a lack of structure and "disorder." They lead untidy lives.
- They have developed an open, and nondefensive, style of discussion and conversation. They can be forthright and feel comfortable with a very frank discussion. They welcome and use feedback about their behavior.
- They are aware of their own needs and motivations and know the difference between their personal needs and the needs of the situation. When they intervene, they do not work their personal agenda. They don't let ambition mock their contribution.
- They have understanding of mature leadership and help. They are concerned with helping people help themselves. They do not just give a starving man a fish. They also teach him to fish for himself. They keep their egos under control and avoid creating undue dependence in the group they lead or the people they are helping.
- They have a clear understanding of the total institutional crisis. They will be able to perceive the totality of problems. For example, they will take an interest and be able to see the interconnectedness of political, economic, and social problems in Ulster.
- They are change agents in society. They are action oriented, and when they intervene they know why they intervene. They are purposeful.

People who approximate (no one could be this ideal!) some of these characteristics naturally aggregate into networks and new institutions. As they have a high degree of empathy they can often recognize each other—not in any formal way—just as fellow spirits. But they are not unthinking rebels, wreckers, or in any way negative. They are, however, rational rebels and constructive challengers of the status quo. If and when they revolt, their revolt is informed and knowledgeable, not blind or ignorant.

But not all individuals in networks have these characteristics. Many profess the values but many are Hamlet-like, unable to act and unsure of themselves, anxious about their competence and role in society. And quite frankly not aware enough to know this. In consequence, they fail to meet the toughest test of life in formal organizations: the ability to take personal risks. Taking personal risks means laying a lot on the line: reputation, image, credibility and a lot of other things dear to the ego. Then there are careers, family. Thus networks can only be effective if the individuals can take personal risks when acting in their formal roles.

The growth of networks is related to the pain of existence that the creative minority feel. For this reason, the potential for effective network activities in Ulster is high. Indeed, already much has been accomplished. But there is a need for networks to straddle, traverse, and penetrate *all* of Ulster's organizations.

Informal networks can be used to help achieve various practical aims. Networks can be connectors in that they create bonds between individuals and groups who are working towards similar objectives. Networks can provide the overlapping group membership so necessary to counter the gang mentality. In particular, the use of networks can minimize the tendency of people to compete destructively or in some way cancel each other out. One imagines this applies very much to community groups and peace movements. Networks can act as "umbrellas" for new projects. It is well known that formal structures and organizations tend to inhibit, if not strangle, new projects at birth. In effecting change, experience indicates the need to build an "umbrella" over the project to prevent individuals in their formal roles intervening to threaten the project or reduce the resources being allocated to it.

Sheane (1977) is obviously impressed by the potential of the resource exchange rationale, its "spreadability," and the importance of the "creative minority": the leader-coordinators. It seems equally obvious that he would like to see informal networks impact on formal organizations without being coopted by them. How would this impact come about? Sheane does not really address this question but, rather, lists a number of issues that could serve as a substantive focus for network development. The unanswered question, however, is too important for action to be bypassed or to be answered with the hope or belief that out of the "creative minority" will emerge the ideas and opportunities that will have general impact. A close reading of his paper suggests that Sheane is not clear about several aspects of network development that may give a partial answer to the question. The first aspect has to do with the role of leader-coordinator in the development of a resource exchange network. The second aspect has to do with the ultimate goals of the leader-coordinator in regard to a network that begins with a single, substantive focus. Is the single focus a starting point or a means to an end? That is to say, is it the aim of the leader-coordinator—is it part of his or her rationale—to look at resource exchange *across* substantive foci so that, for example, the initial focus may be on aged people but this is seen as an opportunity whereby the needs and resources of other groups (such as students or handicapped people) can be interrelated? The beauty of informal networks is that they need not be confined in their scope the way Sheane recognized formal agencies are. *Resource exchange networks can intersect with a freedom that the formal agencies cannot.* But for networks to intersect, however diverse they may appear in terms of focus, requires that network members unlearn the habit of remaining riveted on a single focus. From the standpoint of limited resources, the single-focus network constricts the resources available to it. No less important, the single-focus network prevents its members from exploiting how their resources may be helpful to and exchanged with other networks.

We are here emphasizing an aspect of resource exchange networks that we discussed earlier in this book, namely, that the resource exchange rationale is based on and encourages the process of resource and role redefinition. Once that process takes hold, once network members begin to see themselves and others as differentiated resources useful in a variety of ways and with a variety of groups, networks grow and intersect. And so we have to ask Sheane what he means by "creative." From our standpoint, the creative network member or leader-coordinator is one who constantly scans the social world for new arrangements and exchanges; that is, someone who can "dream up" new opportunities for implementing the resource exchange rationale, someone who can see behind labels and traditional role definitions. One of the clearest criteria for judging the degree to which a network is exploiting the resource exchange rationale is the extent to which it intersects with a diversity of networks. And by intersect we mean that individuals in these different networks relate to and exchange resources with each other.

But why should an emphasis on intersection be expected to impact on formal organizations? One part of the answer, implied in Sheane's paper (1977) and explicit in our presentation, is that, although the informal resource exchange network consists of individuals, many (if not most) of whom are part of formal organizations, what they learn and experience informally can become an influence in the formal organization. Another part of the answer is suggested in a book by Friend, Power, and Yewlett (1974) based on extensive and intensive observations in England. The title of their book *Public Planning: The Inter-Corporate Dimension* does not, unfortunately, communicate the direct relevance of its contents to anyone concerned with networks and leader-coordinators (whom they call "reticulists" = networkers).

The Reticulist

Friend, Power, and Yewlett (1974, pp. xxi–xxiii) begin their book with these words:

> *Corporate planning is not enough.* That, distilled into as few words as possible, is the central thesis around which this book is built. Especially in the public sector—with which we shall be primarily but by no means exclusively concerned—the making of strategic decisions must be considered not merely as a corporate but also as an interorganizational process. The point may be familiar enough to many of those most deeply involved, including politicians, political commentators, urban and regional planners, and senior administrators in both local and central governments. However, the increasing dominance of large corporate bodies in both public and private affairs has brought with it pressures to introduce more formal structures and techniques for the coordination of planning activities within the corporate setting; and this in turn has led many people toward an implicit assumption that planning at the corporate level somehow represents a clear pinnacle toward which all those engaged in other forms of planning within an organization should aspire.
>
> To many managers and consultants, there is considerable appeal in a view of planning as an activity that can be organized entirely in a given hierarchical framework, wherein objectives can be clearly formulated and then methodically pursued. All too often, however, the goal of purposive corporate planning is found to be an illusory one. The more comprehensively those in large corporate organizations seek to plan, the more they find themselves dependent on the outcomes of other agencies, both public and private; also, the more aware they become of the many subtle relationships—economic, social, political, and ecological—that extend into other parts of their environment which may be less clearly structured in formal organizational terms. Demands for participation from the grassroots become more vocal as the technical and organizational obstacles to such participation appear to proliferate; increasingly, therefore, questions of how to develop effective systems of democratic guidance over the course of local and national affairs seem to become uncomfortably intermeshed with issues of global survival.
>
> In essence, our aim will be to move toward a richer understanding of the interorganizational—or "intercorporate"—dimension of the planning process and to contribute toward the development of practical working guidelines for use by those who must operate within this general field, including those concerned with the design or adaptation of relevant institutional forms. We shall attempt to work toward this aim through a focus on problems arising in that broad field of public affairs that may be described as "the management of local and regional change"; in other words, the whole range of possible actions by local authorities, by national or regional agencies of government, and by other public bodies whereby the richly interactive processes of change in local communities can be regulated, influenced, and planned.

Most of our case material will be drawn from observations of decision making in relation to different aspects of the planned expansion of one small English town in order to accommodate population and industry from a nearby metropolitan center, in accordance with regional policies for the relief of urban congestion. Our interpretation of the regional and local processes concerned will then be used as a basis for articulating some more general propositions relating to the processes of interorganizational planning. These will provide a basis from which we can consider the opportunities for innovation that may be open to those concerned in the development of planning processes in any given institutional setting, taking as a specific illustration the challenges facing Britain as it enters a period of exceptionally sweeping reforms in established governmental institutions.

Most of Friend, Power, and Yewlett's book (1974) is an unusually detailed description and analysis of "the planned expansion of one small English town in order to accommodate population and industry from a nearby metropolitan center, in accordance with regional policies for the relief of urban congestion" (p. xxiii). It is not easy reading, because the authors do not try to oversimplify the realities and complexities of the problem and process: the scores of actors, agencies, and interests at work; the many and changing facets of the problem and process; the centripetal and centrifugal interests represented; and the different types of decisions, formal and informal, that were made. Friend and his colleagues describe an evolving complexity (wheels within wheels, dramas within dramas). Instead of simplifying, the complexity becomes more complex. It is like mapping one individual's social network: It may seem simple at first, but it does not take long before the map or graph becomes bewilderingly complex. When Friend and his colleagues start out by italicizing the sentence *"Corporate planning is not enough"* (p. xxi), they mean that planning is not an antecedent of action but a long action process that does and should involve individuals, groups, and agencies—heterogeneous and large in number over time—who can affect or will be affected by a stated goal. Indeed, as they make clear, unless planning is conceived as complex action, a means by which ends are periodically changed as the differing perceptions and interests of the participants are confronted and accommodations sought, coordination is impossible and subversive conflict guaranteed.

Friend, Power, and Yewlett (1974, pp. xxvi–xxvii) develop a series of general propositions about planning in complex organizational environments, the flavor of which can be gleaned from the following:

These concern the inescapability of interagency processes; the strategies people adopt in responding to complexity; the influence on decisions of the interactive learning processes that take place; the inevitability, given limited resources, of adopting a selective approach to the formation and manipulation of decision networks; the dependence of such an approach on the exercise of local judgment wherever problem linkages do not follow foreseeable patterns; and the types of skill and organizational resource that are relevant to such network-forming or "reticulist" judgments. It is argued that the degree to which planning processes exercise an effective influence on decision making is very much dependent on the disposition of reticulist skills and resources among different publicly accountable agencies, local, regional, and central; and, from this standpoint, some practical guidelines are suggested for those who are concerned to bring about innovation in the ways in which public planning is done.

Friend, Power, and Yewlett leave no doubt in the reader's mind that central to the success of the planning process are "reticulist skills and resources." More specifically, crucial in the process are the presence of a few people who possess many of the characteristics of leader-coordinators in resource exchange networks. Let us listen to excerpts from what the authors (1974, pp. 364–367) say about "the characteristics of reticulist skills":

The making of reticulist judgments—in other words, the mobilization of decision networks in an intelligently selective way—depends on a capacity to appreciate both the structure of problem situations and the structure of organizational and political relations that surround them. The actor concerned, whatever his formal status, must first be able to appreciate the patterns of formal status, must first be able to appreciate the patterns of interdependence between those present and future problems which may impinge significantly on his own current field of concern, so that he can weigh up the alternative ways in which the focus of exploration might be extended. At the same time, he must be able to appreciate the structure of relationships, formal and informal, between roles in the decision process, so as to understand the political costs and benefits of activating alternative forms of communication with other relevant actors, both in his own and other organizations.

Such capabilities may be regarded as providing a necessary foundation for the cultivation of reticulist skills, yet other personal attributes will clearly enter into the success or failure of an actor in maintaining and exploiting relevant channels of communication. This question may indeed be one which merits more widespread and far-reaching research, with an orientation toward social psychology. More systematic attempts might be made to learn from the differences in "reticulist style" between actors who occupy similar organizational roles in a variety of comparable local situations—for instance, between the political leaders of different district councils, between the chief executives or planning officers of different counties, between leaders of social work teams for different areas, or between engineers who must coordinate the site operations of contractors and public utility authorities for different local projects. Social scientists have, of course, already given much attention to developing frameworks for understanding differences of style both in management and in politics (Davies, 1972, 1973). It could be fruitful to discover whether the concept of reticulist judgment throws any additional light on this general area—for instance in helping to appreciate differences in decision-making style between those who have become drawn into political, administrative, technical, or community service roles. Returning to our main proposition, however, the evidence of our case studies suggests strongly that the understanding of both problem structures and political structures, at however intuitive a level, is a necessary foundation for the development of network-shaping skills, whether the primary role of the actor concerned appears to be essentially technical or political in its orientation. . . .

The political skills of the reticulist must include a sure grasp of modes of behavior relevant to different types of relationships between agencies and between actors. He must appreciate when to bargain, when to seek to persuade, and when to confront, in situations varying from those where there is a high degree of consensus to those of inherent conflict between different constituency interests, as typified by the case of Droitwich town center. In this process, he must learn to work within the context of formal role relationships which vary from that of servant to master—as in the case of the group administrator and his committee—to that of manager to line staff—as in his relationships with other officers within the group. The political aspect of reticulist skill, as Power argues, must be considered essentially as a *craft*; but it is a craft which cannot realistically be viewed without taking into account also those other elements of skill that are concerned with the appreciation of problem structure.

When Friend, Power, and Yewlett (1974, p. 364) say that "the making of reticulist judgments . . . depends on a capacity to appreciate both the structure of problem situations and the structure of organizational and political relations that surround them," they seem to be saying that the reticulist literally does not see problem situations but rather contexts in which he or she discerns a variety of self-interests, begins to figure out how and to what degree they can be made compatible with each other, and the specific steps by which this compatibility might be approached and achieved. What is distinctive about the reticulist is not that he or she sees problems and their structures—many people can see them—but rather the prepotent tendency to seek the basis whereby differing self-interests (or agency interests) can be made to be seen as compatible with each other to some degree. And in seeking that basis the reticulist reveals another of his or her characteristics: He or she knows "the territory," its actual and potential linkages, and the ways in which people's (or agencies') perception of self-interest can be altered without being threatened. The reticulist thinks in terms of opportunities for new and more reciprocal linkages. Unlike the politician, who lives with and even creates polarizations, the reticulist, like our leader-coordinator, is constantly trying to figure out how to avoid and over-come polarizations, how to forge reciprocal network connections, not to sever them.

There are two major differences between the reticulist as Friend, Power, and Yewlett describe him and our description of the leader-coordinator in the informal resource exchange network. The first of these differences is that our description is that of a role de-rived from a resource exchange rationale in which the fact of limited resources is basic, whereas that rationale is recognized but by no means prominent in the discussion by Friend and his colleagues. Their reticulist deals, so to speak, largely with getting and disseminating information and with suggesting or devising more open channels of communication. Information is a valuable re-source that, when taken together with extensive knowledge of link-age networks within and among agencies, can be very facilitating and lead to other types of resource exchange, a point that Friend and his colleagues recognize. But resource exchange is not central to the reticulist's role.

The second major difference is a more obvious and fateful one: The reticulist has a formal role in a formal organization, and Friend, Power, and Yewlett have few illusions about what that means. Here is what they say about "the reticulist and his organizational environment" (1974, pp. 367–369):

Moving on from our concern with the nature of reticulist skills, our penultimate proposition states that the opportunities for an actor to develop and deploy skills of this nature are influenced by the configuration of organizational resources that are at his disposal. As a qualifying statement, it is necessary to add that the disposition of organizational resources within and between agencies cannot by itself be expected to guarantee the develop-ment of any required patterns of exploratory activity, or any required level of reticulist skill on the part of particular actors. Rather, it can only serve as an enabling or, often, an inhibiting factor, but one which, as we shall argue, can be highly influential in practice.

One significant organizational resource, especially in the light of our discussion about the role of "mixed scanning" in the mobilization of decision networks, is the granting to an actor of formal rights of *access*; that is, the opportunity to attend meetings of relevant decision-making groups, or to approach individuals in order to ask them questions about current problems, or to have access to documents which are not generally available. Such a resource must, however, often be skillfully utilized and husbanded if it is not to become dissipated through the fears of other parties concerned that they may lose control over politically sensitive or valuable information. Here, it may be important that the rights of access should be supported by the *political authority* that stems from the actor's formal accountability to a representative group which is recognized as reflecting some constituency interest—or set of constituency interests—that is relevant to the problem in hand. Such an accountability carries the implicit threat that, unless that interest is adequately represented in the way the exploratory processes are managed, recourse may be made to opportunities for formal expressions of dissent. Such expressions might take the form of public protests after a decision has been irrevocably taken, or possibly of objections at a public inquiry, where the commitment might not be quite so final, yet the opportunities for effective intervention may still be severely constrained.

In the years prior to the Droitwich town center inquiry, for instance, there was always an implicit threat that the borough council could, in extreme circumstances, appear as an objector, carrying considerable political authority as the body elected to serve the collective interests of the town's population; while the chamber of trade, which in the end carries its opposition to these lengths, presented its case at the inquiry in a way which placed much emphasis on the cohesion of constituency of local traders whose interests it could claim to represent.

However, if an actor is to be made accountable specifically for his achievements in mobilizing networks of exploratory activity, as well as in performing any more clearly defined tasks he may have, then another important organizational resource has to be considered. This resource concerns the degree to which the organization to which he owes primary allegiance gives explicit recognition to those aspects of the role that involve the exercise of reticulist skill, together with the marginal costs of developing such aspects more fully and the kinds of marginal benefit that may ensue. This point can be illustrated in the case of the group engineer at Droitwich, who—like many of his fellow officers—felt constrained by an accounting system geared almost exclusively to the implementation of specific capital projects. Any time spent in group meetings or other activities offering reticulist opportunities had then ultimately to be accounted for either as part of the design expenses of individual projects or as general administrative "oncosts." Both these heads of account were subject to external pressures for economy, despite the persistent demands from borough representatives for more information on the choices open to them. Of course, it would have been by no means easy to design a formal accounting system that was sensitive enough to assist rather than inhibit the seeking of those levels of exploratory activity most appropriate to each of the tasks in hand. Nevertheless, even an agreement to provide, and to keep under review, some continuing budgetary estimate for general planning activity (such as indeed existed in the early years of the Droitwich program) could have formed a significant resource to assist the search for appropriate levels of exploration within and beyond the group.

This passage cannot be more clear about the difficulties the reticulist encounters in his or her formal organizational environment. Friend, Power, and Yewlett are so knowledgeable about the constraints on the reticulist that they recommend that he or she be given *political authority*; that is to say, granted formal powers. That recommendation rests on the authors' sustained observations of the workings within and between formal organizations. What is surprising about the recommendation, however understandable it may be in terms of the reticulist's frustrations, is that the authors do not pursue the implications of giving the reticulist formal powers. From their own account, the reticulists they were able to identify stood out not because of their role or formal powers but because of how they tied a way of thinking to action. They surfaced not because they had power (the bulk of people who had power were not functioning as reticulists); they were influential on decision making not because of the nature of their job but because they thought and acted as reticulists. Given the fact that reticulists were few in number and that the rest of the people Friend, Power, and Yewlett observed were not, one might say that these few people were reticulists despite the organizational environment! And by the authors' own account the skills of the reticulist were in informal rather than formal processes. To grant formal power to the reticulist could have the major consequence of engaging him or her in power struggles that would make it difficult to form linkages, thus diluting his or her effectiveness. To fight power with power may produce victorious battles while the war is being lost. The recommendation is a dangerous one because it could escalate rather than decrease the level of organizational conflict within and between agencies. We say "could" rather than "will" because despite our reservations we would be in favor of studying how implementation of the recommendation would actually look in practice.

In concluding the previous section, on Sheane's paper, we asked, "How can informal resource exchange networks impact on formal organizations?" One part of the answer we gave there was that the informal network consists of individuals, many if not most of whom are part of formal organizations, and, therefore, what they learn and experience informally can become an influence in the formal organization. Friend, Power, and Yewlett (1974) provide still another part of the answer: There are people in formal organizations who are receptive to and function in ways similar to the reticulist and leader-coordinator but who are not identifiable by job title. To the extent that they are identified by and linked to the informal resource exchange network, the opportunity exists for mutual enhancement. Both can be sources of support and resources to each other. What is so encouraging and interesting about the Friend, Power, and Yewlett book is that they see the reticulist as the crucial person without whom "coordination" becomes at best devoid of practical meaning and at worst a deception. What is discouraging is the ambience of organizational climates that constrain the potential of the reticulist role. The more the reticulist in the formal organization is linked with informal networks from which he or she can get support and resources, the possibility exists for his or her influence to increase and, no less significant, for being able to cope better in the formal setting. What we are in effect suggesting is that, if one of the aims of an informal resource exchange network is to influence and alter formal organizations, it will have to locate the reticulist in those settings. It takes scanners to locate scanners.

The penultimate chapter of *Public Planning: The Inter-Corporate Dimension* contains some "free-ranging conjectures about the opportunities for further experiment in the development of outwardly connective styles of planning" (Friend, Power, and Yewlett, 1974, p. 475). The authors present a scenario about what the steps and contents of such a process would look like. Two of the chief actors are Nettlefold, a civil servant, and Webster, an academic and a consultant. Nettlefold relates to Webster his anxieties about various current sources of conflict within the region he works. Webster responds by expounding his views "about ways of improving the disposition of network managing skills within the region. . : . Nettlefold is able to relate much of what Webster says to the types of intuitive skill that he himself is continually calling upon to exercise. Also, they find it possible to identify a number of other regional actors, known to them both, who possess reticulist skills of a high order, and have been able to deploy these skills to bring about some crucial adjustments across the interfaces with other agencies" (p. 481).

Both actors discuss the reticulists they have known, and Webster argues that many of the conflicts that worry Nettlefold may be due to people with inadequately developed reticulist skills. Nettlefold thinks the problems are far more complex than Webster's explanation indicates (pp. 482–484; italics ours):

By the next time Webster and Nettlefold meet, we shall suppose that Webster has been able to develop some more specific ideas for an experimental process. . . . First of all, he argues that the most promising level at which to concentrate the experimental process could be just below that of the county district council, where there exist a number of "successor parish" councils and other less formal representative groups which are highly motivated to exercise influence over decisions affecting their constituents but have few if any direct powers themselves. He sees the possibility that explicit designated "community reticulists" could be placed at the disposal of a limited set of local representative groups operating at this level, who could be offered technical and other forms of support from the regional office, with the blessing of the regional council. Forestalling Nettlefold's next question about the danger that such an innovation might be considered subversive by the county and county district councils for the areas concerned, Webster argues that he knows a number of officers and members personally whom he believes would probably welcome any move that helped them act in a less erratic—and at times obstructive—way than they do at the moment. In some, at least, of the counties and districts of the Outland Region he believes that a majority of members could be won round to this view, given some evidence or assurance that such an unfamiliar being as a "community reticulist" could be a stabilizing rather than a disruptive influence. He concludes, however, that there will probably be some counties or districts that he would expect to remain implacably opposed to this kind of experiment. This might well place a stringent limitation on the number of communities that could be involved in the experimental process, at least in the first instance.

Provided that many of the initial costs of this kind of experiment could be underwritten by central or regional funds, Webster sees an exciting possibility, in the longer run, that many of the communities served might come to see the continuing retention of at least one full-time "community reticulist" as something well worth supporting through the local rate account, as a means of enhancing the collective influence of citizens on more remote yet powerful public agencies. Indeed, the whole success or failure of the experiment would depend on whether this point of takeoff could be reached in some at least of the localities taking part. This in turn could depend on whether or not a number of necessary supporting conditions could be maintained. On the one hand, the community reticulist would have to relate to his constituents in a sufficiently open way to demonstrate that his services were directly useful to local people. On the other hand, he would have to work through a representative group who would expect him to amplify rather than usurp their powers, and he would have to maintain sufficient trust among officers and members of other authorities to prevent them obstructing his channels of access to their ongoing decision processes. In maintaining this difficult balance, the existence of a "mutual support network" of some kind could be a crucial factor, and it is in this respect, argues Webster, that the regional office could provide a very important reinforcing influence. Further, it could in this way ultimately perform a vital connective role in the wider processes by which local experiences are diffused throughout wider social networks and appropriate forms of societal adaptation are induced in changing environmental circumstances.

Nettlefold is attracted, but wary. Webster has now touched on the ground of each of the four hypotheses . . . relating to questions of external orientation, of contextual reinforcement, of mutual advantage, and of societal adaptation respectively. But how credible is the whole proposition in terms of the practical politics within Outland? Also, how likely is it that Nettlefold will be able to mount a case to central government to release the necessary resources and provide the official endorsement to get such an experiment off the ground? Webster reminds him that government departments have already been prepared to back such experiments as the community development projects and the urban guidelines studies and quotes parallel innovations in a number of other countries, ranging from India to the United States. He argues that the cost required to support one "community reticulist" in each of half a dozen localities could be a comparatively modest one. Indeed, a quick calculation shows him that, for a "successor parish" council of, say, twenty thousand population, the annual expenditure would work out at only a small fraction of the permitted expenditure limit for discretionary parish purposes. He believes it would be necessary for most of this cost to be met externally for a period of two, three, or perhaps four years, while each local community reticulist built up his basic knowledge of the locality and its problems. After that, he believes the parish council or other representative group should be in a position to make a judgment for itself as to whether or not the services of a full-time (or possibly part-time) officer of this kind should continue to be borne as a direct charge to the local rate.

In the italicized sentences of this excerpt, Friend, Power, and Yewlett are solving in fantasy the dilemma of Mrs. Topitzer and Greene—two people who can and want to be "community reticulists" in Bay Shore, Long Island—discussed in the previous chapter: How do you obtain funding for roles that by their nature and aims must be independent of the usual organizational constraints? In their emphasis in their scenario on autonomy for the reticulist, Friend and his colleagues seem to be backing away from their earlier optimism about the reticulist in formal organizations. If our interpretation is correct, we would have to conclude that their solution in fantasy is less unrealistic than the one they offered earlier for dealing with the realities of formal organizations.

The reticulist and leader-coordinator share overlapping characteristics. The differences between them reflect differences in rationale and setting. From the standpoint of action and potential impact, the differences are less important than the fact that, in different places and from different perspectives, serious efforts are being made to put flesh on the bone of the imagery of networks. The creative minority, reticulist, leader-coordinator—call them what you will, distinguish among them as you must—they signify increasing recognition that alternatives to the traditional modes of functioning of formal organizations exist and are working.

9

The Ombudsman:
A Key
to Resource Exchange

Few people would disagree that currently the dominant mood in our society is one compounded of puzzlement, frustration, and anger at the failure of a myriad social programs to have intended, ameliorative effects. What we thought would be solutions, even partial ones, are viewed as either total or relative failures. Some people place the blame on faulty leadership and an insensitive, large bureaucracy; other people blame the recipients of these programs as helpless, hopeless, and unworthy; and there are those who indict what they consider the basic features, economic and cultural, of the entire society. And it is a mood that has a large dose of felt helplessness.

It is a mood both unpleasant and dangerous, leading some to retreat psychologically from the social scene, or to seek new lifestyles that blot out the unpleasantries of engagement with their societal surroundings, or to view the world of work as something to be tolerated: an interlude to be kept empty of personal meaning and involvement. There are others, such as the economist Heilbroner (1974, p. 110), who begins his inquiry with "Is there hope for man?" and whose analysis leads him to some chilling possibilities.

Yates (1977, pp. 18–21)* points out that in contrast to state and federal government, urban government deals in more direct ways, in face-to-face ways, with its citizens.

The basic function of urban government is service delivery, and urban service delivery is a distinctive function. Urban services are daily, direct, and locality-specific. Fire and police protection, garbage collection, and public education are delivered to particular people in particular neighborhoods on a regular basis. With many of these ordinary urban functions, citizens can immediately tell whether a service has been delivered: They can see whether the trash has been picked up or whether the pothole, broken traffic light, or ruptured water main has been fixed. In these cases, urban services are also distinctly tangible and visible. . . .

Urban policy making grows up from the street, and it is the street-level service relationship between citizens and public employees that makes city government distinctive. . . .

Urban service delivery often involves a street-level relationship between citizens and public employees that is not only direct but personal. Consider the relationship between citizens and city government in police, education, welfare, and health services. In these arenas, the character of service delivery is heavily dependent on the attitudes, values, and behavior of the particular citizen and public employee involved. To this extent, urban service delivery tends to be distinctively individualistic, even atomistic. Unlike their bureaucratic counterparts in the departments of state or national government, policemen, teachers, and social workers are often required by the logic of their jobs to become involved directly in the personal lives of their clients. Effective urban service delivery depends ultimately on the establishment of what Albert Reiss [1971] calls a "civil relationship"—a mutually supportive relationship between the servers and the served. It is well known that teachers assume a nearly parental role in working with their students, and policemen and social workers have to deal with all sorts of personal problems and difficult social relationships in the course of their daily work. For policemen, the most dramatic example of this facet of service delivery is the task of handling what are politely called *domestic disputes*—fights between husbands and wives or between parents and children.

There are many other equally sensitive disputes that street-level bureaucrats are called on to deal with: street fights between juvenile gangs or between different ethnic racial groups in a school lunchroom or on a school bus or between friends in a bar. There are others, too: a student who persistently disrupts a classroom, a student who is chronically truant, a runaway, a former husband who returns to his family from time to time and insists on being taken in, a son who regularly shows signs of being beaten up by someone, a Saturday night drunk, a former mental patient who occasionally

* All excerpts from *The Ungovernable City* by D. T. Yates reprinted by permission of the MIT Press, Cambridge, Massachusetts.

"goes off" and is viewed by neighbors as a "public nuisance." The list is long; some street-level bureaucrats would say endless. The point is that handling the problem requires a direct personal intervention in the life of a family, apartment building, classroom, or block.

Yates' analysis leaves no doubt about two things: Every approach to more effective ways of dealing with "street pluralism" not only has failed but also has added new administrative structures on top of old ones and contributed to greater fragmentation. Whether and how cities survive will depend on how they develop vehicles more responsive to street pluralism. It is easy, Yates (1977) notes, to argue for decentralization, but attempts at decentralizing have been made but with little or no success, and part of that failure has been the inability to overcome the tendency to separate problems that are very much interrelated. The word *fragmentation* occurs repeatedly in his book, but Yates emphasizes that the answer is not in the concept of centralization or in proclamations of coordination. Although Yates illuminates the direct and personal service relationships between citizens and city government and indicates that these services must be decentralized, he offers no specific rationale that would help avoid the worst features of past efforts at decentralization.

In addition to emphasizing the direct and personal nature of the service relationship between city government and its citizens, Yates (1977) also notes the fantastic increase in the number and variety of citizen associations calculated to represent and protect self-interests. The diversity of these associations presents problems to city government because each exerts its own pressure on city officials, who tend to respond in an unreflectively reactive fashion, thus contributing to the fragmentation. But these associations indicate, in contrast to Heilbroner's view that people have a need to obey and to be dependent on authority, that people can and do come together to further and protect their interests. Yates (1977, pp. 24–25) says,

> At the height of community organization in the late 1960s, many blocks on the Lower East Side of New York City had two or three different community organizations on the same block. In 1970 I counted over two hundred different community organizations in a twenty-square-block area of the Lower East Side. This is not a new phenomenon. According to Sayre and Kaufman [1965] writing more than ten years ago, "No careful census of [these] nongovernmental groups has ever been made, but the number seems to run at least to tens of thousands. This estimate comprises only those groups sufficiently well organized to have letterheads, telephones, and/or to appear in some published directory." Some of these groups are

traditional and well known: church associations, neighborhood chambers of commerce, as well as Rotary, Kiwanis, and Lions clubs, PTAs, police precinct councils, NAACP and CORE chapters, ethnic associations (be they Hibernian Societies or Attillean Associations), and neighborhood social clubs ranging from youth gangs to senior citizen centers to the storefront clubhouses where older men congregate in Italian and Spanish neighborhoods. More recently, a new generation of neighborhood organizations has grown up and added to the fragmentation of urban politics at the street level. Some of these organizations—community action agencies, neighborhood health councils, and neighborhood service centers—were direct outgrowths of the War on Poverty and provided the main impetus behind what Daniel Bell and Virginia Held have called the "community revolution." Bell and Held [1969, p. 142] argue that there may be "more participation than ever before in American society, particularly in the large urban centers such as New York, and more opportunity for the active and interested person to express his political and social concerns." They continue [Bell and Held, 1969, p. 143]:

"Forty years ago, a Tammany political boss could give an order to a mayor. Today, no such simple action is possible. On each political issue—decentralization or community control, the mix of low-income and middle-income housing, the proportion of blacks in the city colleges, the location of a cross-Manhattan or cross-Brooklyn expressway, and so on—there are dozens of active, vocal, and conflicting organized opinions. The difficulty in governing New York—and many other cities as well—is not the "lack of voice" of individuals in city affairs, or the "eclipse of local community," but the babel of voices and the multiplication of claimants in the widened political arena. In this new participatory democracy, the need is for the creation of new political mechanisms that will allow for the establishment of priorities in the city, and for some effective bargaining and trade-offs between groups; without that, the city may end in shambles."

Such organizations as block associations, tenants' councils, neighborhood associations, decentralized school boards, food cooperatives, organizations of welfare mothers, taxpayers' groups, drug prevention groups, citizen street patrols, and protest groups of all shapes and sizes further reflect the participatory mood of the late 1960s.

Not all of these groups still exist; some were in operation for only a few weeks or months; some were never more than paper organizations operating out of the living room of a single neighborhood activist. If it is hard to find out who is in charge in city government, it is that much harder to find the voice of the community in the many voices that rise from it. One thing is clear, however: If policemen, firemen, and teachers are the foot soldiers of city governments, then members of these neighborhood groups are the foot soldiers of the community in dealing with city government. They take the lead in pressing complaints and in fighting city hall. They are the principal neighborhood combatants in the many-sided contest of urban politics.

So, at the same time that it is true that the societal mood has a definite dysphoric tinge we cannot gloss over the willingness of people to form associations in order to pursue and protect their interests. It used to be said that "You cannot fight city hall." Today, as Yates describes, city hall feels beleaguered because so many groups are fighting it.

From all that we have said in previous chapters, it should not be surprising that we regard Yates' analysis as encouraging precisely because he draws our attention to the direct, personal, face-to-face nature of urban services as well as to the growth of street, block, and neighborhood associations. Nor should it be surprising that the latter feature is characterized by a fragmentation so marked an aspect of the former. In regard to both features the incentives and rewards reinforce the single focus or, to put it in another way, keep people from acting on the perception of the interrelatedness of problems. Yates (1977, pp. 110–111) again provides us with examples:

> Historically, the most familiar service issues also had the characteristic of being relatively independent of one another. The task of building a school in one neighborhood had nothing to do with the task of policing the street or fixing a pothole. Separable issues of this sort present clear advantages to urban policy makers, for they can be rather easily sorted out, assigned, and monitored. In contrast to these simple urban issues, those that confront policy makers in the new urban politics are increasingly intertwined, so it is hard for even the careful policy analyst to figure out where one dimension of the issue begins and another ends. Such issues involve not only multiple problems but also impinge on the work of several different urban bureaucracies. A good example of an intertwined issue is lead poisoning, or street crime (as related to drug addiction), or educational problems (as plausibly related to health, housing, and nutrition problems), or problems of discipline and crime in schools (which are at once problems for teachers, policemen, and often social workers). Because urban issues are increasingly intertwined, it is more difficult for urban policy makers to cut into a problem and develop a policy response. Hence they are faced with the difficulty of choosing which facet of an issue to attack and of trying to figure out whether they can treat just one part of it.
>
> In her account of the controversy over lead poisoning in New York, Diana Gordon shows how the fact that the problem involved issues of housing, health, public education, and medical testing fragmented policy making and frustrated both a clear definition and a sustained policy initiative. In addition, Gordon's study of New York's welfare hotels also illustrates this point. The intertwined problems of welfare policy, housing policy, and government regulation and inspection (of the welfare hotels) led to a policy-

making fiasco in which city departments wound up blaming each other for the welfare hotel problem, ignoring the fact that the problem arose in the first place because the departments had not worked together on a joint problem.

It would, we think, be more correct to say that the departments had not worked together, not because of stupidity or callousness, but because the incentives and rewards powering their activities worked for, not against, fragmentation.

The difficulty for people in generating optimism about the future bespeaks many things, chief among which is a widening discrepancy between the interrelatedness of social problems—their diversity, scale, urgency, and ramifications—and the traditional ways with which we have been accustomed to think about them. On the one hand, the social world has changed dramatically, while, on the other hand, some of the basic assumptions by which we comprehend that world has not changed. When people say that we are living in an era of rapid change, they are both right and wrong: right in the sense that in their lifetimes they have literally seen dramatic social changes and wrong in the sense that their categories of judging and dealing with these changes have changed to a far lesser extent. If we are at odds with these changes, if the actions they require us to take seem inadequate, if we are puzzled by the failure of our good intentions, we tend to place the blame outside of ourselves, unaware of the possibility that some of the assumptions basic to our thinking are contributing to our pessimistic outlook. There are causes enough in our external world to justify worry and pessimism, yet that should be no warrant for passivity but rather for a searching reexamination of our accustomed ways of comprehending our worlds.

It is such a reexamination that has led us and others to changes in thinking and action. The fact of limited natural and human resources, the potentialities of the resource exchange rationale, the intertwining of that rationale with the network concept, the emphasis on informal and voluntary approaches—in these regards, our thinking and actions changed markedly as we reexamined the past inadequacies of our thinking and social actions. And as this reexamination proceeded we better understood why so many people doomed themselves to disappointment despite the best of intentions and what seemed to be huge sums of money. In fact, it is fair to say that what has come to puzzle many people is how to explain why in and of itself money has not led to "solutions." In our society, it has long been an accepted tenet that national resolve and money are sufficient to cope effectively with any social problem. Yates' discussion of this tenet represents a truly new note that people are hearing but are having trouble dealing with (Yates, 1977, pp. 38–39):

> The proposals for a domestic Marshall Plan and for the creation of "federal cities" were similarly based on the assumption that what the city basically needs is more money. In fact, it is plain that many urban problems cannot be approached, much less solved, without a large-scale commitment of new funds. There is no way to build new housing for low-income urban residents without buying bricks, mortar, and the services of the construction trades. It is impossible to construct new highways, public transit systems, hospitals, schools, and parks without substantial capital outlays. Although cities have been able (at least until recently) to undertake significant capital construction every year with the funds derived from municipal bond issues, city halls lack the fiscal resources to develop new housing and adequate schools and parks throughout the city.
>
> If Newark, New Jersey, had an extra billion dollars a year, it would have no difficulty applying it fruitfully to its most pressing problems. But even if Newark had even far greater resources at its disposal, it would quickly find that many of its most critical problems were not amenable to direct fiscal solutions. The city would build many new homes and schools and hospitals; but, having done so, it would still be confronted with the perceptual problems of service delivery. If public employees were thought to be unresponsive, insensitive, arbitrary, and inefficient before the windfall fiscal bonus, it is not clear that hiring more employees would address the core problems. These problems are not fiscal ones to begin with; they are social, political, and administrative ones. More precisely if, as is so often the case, problems arise from the fact that services do not match the needs of residents in a particular area and that citizens lack the information about services and access to those who deliver them, the problem is one of responsiveness in government. The responsiveness problem is also manifest when citizens complain that the city takes too long to respond to their request or that city administrators still evade or get tangled in red tape in the course of dealing with their complaints or requests. The extreme case of the responsiveness problem exists when citizens complain that they cannot get a hearing—that no one in city government will listen to their concerns.
>
> If urban public employees do not follow the policies and procedures designed by city administrators to control and improve service delivery, the problem at the street level is one of regulation, not of inadequate fiscal resources. If policemen sleep in their cars or use unnecessary force in dealing with suspects or harass certain groups of people, the problem is that they are

failing to do what they have been told to do. If sanitation men do not follow their routes or do not meet their schedule, the problem again is one of administrative regulation and control. If city health inspectors, housing inspectors, or building code inspectors fail to report residents' problems or fail to follow up on them, the problem again is regulation.

If there is deep hostility and little communication between the servers and the served, the problem is one of trust, not money. Citizen complaints that public employees are racist, hostile, indifferent, or dishonest reflect a deep lack of trust in the mayor's foot soldiers. When policemen, firemen, teachers, and social workers feel that residents do not understand the difficulties of their jobs, or refuse to cooperate with them, or treat them with disrespect, the other side of the trust problem in service delivery is manifest.

In the remainder of this chapter, we shall endeavor to make some concrete suggestions deriving from our thinking about and experience with the resource exchange rationale. They are not presented as "solutions" in the natural science sense; that is, the problems they address will not go away. The force and the scope of the problems would, hopefully, be diluted, but more important in the long run is the public focus it could give to the rationale. One of the major defects, as Yates' book documents, of efforts at social change has been the emphasis on administrative rather than on substantive changes. To be sure, these administrative changes were informed by substantive concerns; they were not intended to be ends in themselves, but that is precisely what they tended to become, because the administrative form for the intended change was inappropriate to the preexisting functions and the ambience of the administrative apparatus. Insofar as the implementation of a resource exchange rationale is concerned, the very nature of the rationale precludes an emphasis on administration and formal authority.

The Advocate

This and the next section are prefatory to a concrete suggestion about how one might approach the seemingly intractable problem of "coordination" in the public sector. The suggestion involves a variation in the role and concept of the ombudsman. Although our suggestion will be based on the concept of the ombudsman, we shall first discuss the concept of the advocate, because what has happened to that concept will help the reader understand the rationale for our suggestion. The concepts of the ombudsman and (especially) the advocate have, in our society, been transformed (*mutilated* would be a more appropriate term) in ways that obscure their origins. And that transformation says as much about organizational parochialism and arrogance as it does about the devaluation of the historical perspective.

The terms *advocate* and *ombudsman* have become familiar, and their entry into everyday parlance is a direct reflection of two perceptions. First, many individuals are treated unfairly, are unable to obtain the services and respect due them, and are impotent to cope with the maze of rules, regulations, and agencies in the effort to get what is coming to them. They may be poor, or handicapped, old people, and so on. In the absence of someone who becomes their advocate, they remain unheard, neglected, and robbed of their rights. The second perception is that, in the ever increasing size and complexity of organizations in the public sector, with conflicts and injustices affecting both the servers and the served becoming more frequent, there should be an impartial person skilled in fact finding and conflict resolution. The advocate is supposed to be a partisan for an individual; the ombudsman is supposed to be impartial, much like an arbitrator called in by opposing sides to settle a dispute. The two titles have become symbols of virtuous intent. Appearance and reality, however, are not the same. Let us begin with the concept of the advocate because it is a role that unlike that of the ombudsman has been sanctioned in federal, state, and local legislation.

The use and popularity of the advocacy concept has to be seen in the context of the civil rights movement, which exploded into national awareness with the 1954 Supreme Court desegregation decision. In rendering the "separate but equal" doctrine unconstitutional, the decision had the effect of contributing to heightened awareness in different groups about their legal rights and the use of courts to clarify and secure those rights. Women, gays, and diverse ethnic minorities fought against discrimination in education and employment. These groups advocated for themselves. But there were many other groups who were not as able to advocate for themselves, such as physically handicapped people, mentally retarded people, old and infirm people, and people in mental hospitals. Others advocated for these people, by seeking new protective legislation and increasingly using the courts to force remedial actions. The fact is that, beginning in the mid 1960s, hardly a week went by without some public institution being put under court injunction to clean up scandalously inhumane conditions. The nursing home scandals of the early 1970s captured the national imagination, but the same conditions had been exposed earlier in regard to other dependent, handicapped groups. For example, in 1970, Blatt and Kaplan published their famous photographic essay *Christmas in Purgatory* illustrating the horrors contained in institutions for the mentally retarded in several states. Few things were as symbolic as the change that was occurring as when the National Association for Retarded *Children* changed its name to the National Association for Retarded *Citizens* (italics ours). And few things expressed the change more concretely than Public Law 94-142, the Education for All Handicapped Children's Act (Sarason and Doris, 1979). That federal legislation, as well as others, incorporated the idea that handicapped individuals required advocates whose task it was to make sure that the spirit of these laws would not be subverted by institutional practice.

Wolfensberger (1972) was, without question, the first person to treat systematically the issues surrounding advocacy. His writings and the action programs he mounted have been recognized, but it has been a strange recognition, in that neither his basic position nor his programs have been accepted. Wolfensberger wrote about *citizen* advocacy, by which he meant that the advocate had to be a private citizen dedicated to *a* handicapped person and independent of the agencies and institutions with which that person had to deal. *One could not trust the advocacy role to those agencies and institutions that, directly or indirectly, had contributed to the scandalous conditions that necessitated remedial legislation.* And it has been precisely to these agencies and institutions that the advocacy role has been given.

The conclusion we draw from this discussion is not that the personnel in human services agencies and institutions are evil or morally inferior to the rest of society. They are not. What we do conclude is that these agencies and institutions are interconnected and interdependent in so many ways (financial being one of the most important) as to result in conflict of interests if any one of them seriously and uncompromisingly takes the advocacy role. To advocate for an individual, as a legal advocate does for his or her client, can produce an adversarial situation in which you pull out all the stops to get for the individual what is coming to him or her as a human being and citizen. However, as Wolfensberger has shown, by virtue of his independence, knowledge, and commitment, the citizen advocate's informal status can be productive of results without rancor or adversarial polarization. His or her informal status gives the citizen advocate a degree of flexibility, the freedom to seek information, to explore avenues of approach, and to act with a minimum of concern for the niceties of administrative status and power that do not obtain for an advocate who is part of "the system." Our experience clearly confirms Wolfensberger's earlier expectation that, if the advocacy role is given to agencies and institutions, the spirit of the advocacy concept is for all practical purposes subverted. One dictionary defines an advocate in this way: "(1) One who pleads the cause of another, as before a tribunal or judicial court; a counselor. (2) One who defends or espouses any cause by argument; a pleader; as, an *advocate* of free trade; also an intercessor. Synonym: *backer, proponent.*" To be able to plead and intercede for another human being is extraordinarily difficult to do well (if at all) if it means that you will be criticizing your own agency or institution or criticizing another agency or institution with which yours is interconnected.

Let us take an actual example, one of many we could have chosen. As a result of federal developmental disabilities legislation, each state has had to come up with a plan for advocacy. In one state, a planning group was convened by the chief officer of the state department of mental retardation. It was a mixture of state employees, some representatives of the more traditional social service agencies, representatives of parent groups, and a few "unaffiliated" individuals.[1] After many meetings, they came up with the following recommendations:

---

[1] We do not feel it necessary to describe all of the events in this story, because they all illustrate the main point. Suffice it to say, in this example it was egregiously clear from the outset that the commissioner would have the final say on the advocacy program. The commissioner was not being arbitrary, because according to the federal legislation he could come up with any advocacy program he deemed appropriate. The commissioner could have made the advocacy program relatively independent of the state apparatus, but he did not. How many people in that position want an independent watchdog?

1. There should be a fifteen-member board, consisting of five people representing the interests of the physically handicapped, five for the developmentally disabled, and five members at large.
2. The board will have policy-making responsibility and power.
3. The director of the program will be chosen by the board and his or her chief function would be to implement board policy.

It was no secret that some of the planning group wanted the board to be as independent of the political process as possible and to place responsibility with citizens rather than state agencies or community agencies dependent on or interconnected with governmental functions. This is not to say that the planning group went as far as it could toward such a goal but, rather, it went as far as it thought "practical." And that is the point: Created as this board was by public officials who were part of the problem with which the board was trying to deal, some of the members quickly saw that there would be resistance to a truly independent advocacy function. The worst fears of the planning group were realized: By the time their recommendations were digested by the governor's office and then locked in legislative and administrative concrete, it was the governor who would choose the director and the advocacy board; that is, the director would have the most important policy role, not only because he or she would be responsible to the governor but also because the board would be likewise appointed. It is axiomatic in political life that what you cannot control can control you and is to be avoided. This in no way should be interpreted as a derogation of people in public life but simply as an acceptance of what it means to enter and remain in political life. (Let us bear in mind that what we have said about the political world is no less true for the world of private business and industry.) When it is said that we should put our trust in laws and not men, it is because so much of human history has taught us that over time principles are more trustworthy than motivations.

Is there a way of institutionalizing a role in the public sector that would be relatively insulated from the character and demands of the political system as well as from intra- and interagency crossfires and yet would stand a chance of increasing the impact of the resource exchange rationale? Throughout this book, we have expressed skepticism about the viability of that rationale within and between formal organizations. In the next section, we take up one affirmative way of answering the question that, far from contradicting the basis of our skepticism, is itself a response to the characteristics of organizations we have described. The concept of the ombudsman is far from a "solution," but it is an ingenious way of dealing with the realities of formal organizations. In the Scandinavian countries, the ombudsman is a "citizens' protector," someone to whom any citizen who feels his or her rights have been infringed can go. As we shall see, the success of this type of ombudsman was the stimulus to our considering another type of ombudsman: the resource exchange ombudsman.

The Ombudsman

Historically, the cautions we have stated about the advocate gave rise to the concept of the ombudsman and the structure of that role. And when we say *historically* we are not talking about recent decades. As Gellhorn (1967, p. 5) notes, "In 1955, Denmark's first ombudsman—the *Folketingets ombudsmand,* or parliamentary commissioner, to give him his proper title—took office and began to function. This was 146 years after a similar activity had commenced in Sweden and 36 years after a Finnish version had appeared. For most of the world, however, interest in the ideas behind the ombudsman institution was all but nonexistent until Denmark's ombudsman came on the scene. Then, suddenly, the institution began to attract attention not only in the Western world, but also in Asia and Oceania." Let us note briefly the distinguishing characteristics of the ombudsman, using the Danish model as described by Gellhorn:[2]

1. The ombudsman can, if he chooses, "deal with virtually every high- or low-level exercise of governmental authority outside the courts" (Gellhorn, 1967, p. 11).

2. The scope of his responsibilities can be seen in the following (Gellhorn, 1967, p. 11):

---

[2]Gellhorn's book describes the role of the ombudsman in nine countries. There are discernible variations among these countries, but five of them (Sweden, Finland, Denmark, New Zealand, and Norway) share many of the characteristics described here.

The statute and Parliament's accompanying "general directives" command the ombudsman to inform himself constantly about the manner in which all officials within his jurisdiction perform their duty.

The ombudsman, it must be stressed, has no statutory power to change a decision he finds to be improper. He can comment on the quality of administration, but not directly overturn the results of poor administration. Later discussion will make clear, however, that the ombudsman's suggestions do frequently have the effect of reversing or modifying determinations he has found to be unsound.

3. Any citizen can bring his or her complaint to the ombudsman (Gellhorn, 1967, pp. 13–14):

If he believes that misconduct in public service has occurred, the ombudsman may order the public prosecutor to investigate further or to commence a criminal proceeding in the ordinary law courts, or, if he chooses, he may order that disciplinary proceedings be commenced by the appropriate authority. In point of fact, he has not once during the eleven years of his activity ordered either a prosecution or a disciplinary proceeding, though in a few instances he has requested prosecutors to carry on investigations.

Chiefly the ombudsman has acted in the far milder manner contemplated by Section 9 of the statute: "In any case, the parliamentary commissioner may always state his views on the matter to the person concerned."

At first glance, this may seem to be a sword without a sharp cutting edge. As wielded by the Danish ombudsman, it has proved to be a potent and versatile weapon. He himself has written that the power to voice his opinion "enables the commissioner to exercise a guiding influence on the administration and provides him with the legal basis for initiating oral or written negotiations with the ministers or the services concerned in order to have decisions which he considers erroneous corrected or, if this cannot be done, to achieve revision of the general procedure."

Furthermore, the ombudsman has not hesitated to express criticism even when the outcome of a particular case has not been at stake. A reviewing court must (at least in theory) disregard a "harmless error." Not so the ombudsman, who points out deficiencies of method, judgment, or personal manners in the hope of discouraging their later occurrence. Nor does the ombudsman confine himself to stating his views about what administrators are legally required to do. Instead, he freely states what he thinks they would be well advised to do. Unlike the courts, a leading commentator has remarked, the ombudsman "is not required to base his judgment solely on legal analysis." The ombudsman has, for example, explicitly said that an official organ cannot be criticized for what it has done or failed to do in the particular matter under discussion, because its acts were consonant with existing law—and then has outlined what he believes would be a better practice for the future.

4. The ombudsman has the power to inspect independent of any complaint. In the case of the Danish ombudsman, such initiatives have rarely been taken.

5. The ombudsman prepares an annual report identifying agencies against which complaints have been made but does not describe the complainant (Gellhorn, 1967, p. 27):

> Persons close to the ombudsman have estimated that civil servants have initiated about 5 percent of all the cases received in recent years, that 10 percent of the complaints have come from persons in detention either before or after conviction of crime, that 5 percent of the complainants have been inmates in public institutions of one kind or another, and that attorneys have signed about 5 percent of the complaints and have perhaps prepared another 5 percent to which their clients' names have been attached. The remainder have come from "the public at large," without any significant occupational or geographical grouping that has been noted.

6. The office of the ombudsman has a small investigative and clerical staff.

It is clear from this list that ombudsmen have a unique status. Although appointed by a legislative body, they are independent of it. Although they have unusually broad powers and authority, they have no statutory power to change a decision they deem improper. In practice, their influence resides in the respect accorded them by virtue of their accomplishments before they took on the role of ombudsmen, in the importance that the legislative body has given to the role, in their power to investigate, in their published reports, and in their ability to persuade and negotiate informal settlements. As important as any of these is the simple fact that the legislature willingly and overwhelmingly recognized the need for an independent force or agent within government. The office of the ombudsman is as remarkable a combination of scope, independence, and flexibility as one can get in a formal organization.

It is not surprising that the ombudsman concept encountered opposition in Denmark. Let us listen to Gellhorn (1967, pp. 25–26) on what happened.

> When the ombudsman system was first proposed in Denmark, civil servants and their organizations were energetically opposed. Existing review mechanisms, they contended, provided ample protections against mistake. To create an overseer of public administration would be simply to in-

vite harassment by cranks and malcontents. Ultimately, too, it might lead to debasing personnel safeguards and had, over the course of many years, created a professional, responsible, trustworthy Danish civil service envied by less favored countries.

When the ombudsman statute was enacted despite this opposition, it embodied clauses intended to mollify civil servants. Anonymous complaints were proscribed in order to lessen the risk of irresponsible accusations. The new law also provided that a civil servant involved in a matter of interest to the ombudsman "may always demand that the matter shall be referred to treatment under the provisions of the Civil Servants (Salaries and Pensions) Act," which meant in effect that he could insist upon being investigated by the agency in which he served rather than by the ombudsman.

This provision, added to the original bill upon the demand of civil service groups, has never been used. "In the beginning," the president of a major organization recently said, "we were suspicious. As a matter of fact, we were scared. But we have found that we were mistaken." Instead of fleeing from the ombudsman, civil servants have fled to him. Many of their cherished "protections" had in fact not been legally enforceable through the ordinary courts, and Denmark has had no administrative court specially empowered to deal with personnel disputes. The ombudsman's capacity to inquire into every type of official lapse was quickly seized upon by public servants who thought they had been ill treated by their superiors. Thus it has come to pass that over 13 percent of all the cases fully investigated by the ombudsman in 1962, 1963, and 1964 involved controversies about personnel matters. The share of his time devoted to this type of problem seems all the more remarkable when one recalls that the group from which the cases arise numbers only a little more than 100,000 in a population of 4,500,000.

We are now ready to offer a suggestion that attempts to bring together the concept of the ombudsman and the resource exchange rationale in relation to the intractable problem of "coordination." The specifics of our suggestion are less important than the significance they give to the creation of an independent office headed by a person who understands resource exchange, informal and formal networks, and the realities of bureaurcacies. In short, the person will have characteristics of the network-coordinator or reticulist.

The Resource Exchange Ombudsman

The resource ombudsman (ombudswoman) would be appointed by the legislature (local, state, federal) for no less than a five-year term. He or she would have no formal power to force anybody to do anything. In the most general terms, the ombudsman's responsibility concerns the ways in which agencies define and utilize resources, the ways in which they can share resources, how informal networks among agencies can be developed to increase resource exchange, and identification of the barriers that prevent public agencies from locating and utilizing existing community networks with which some form of resource exchange would be mutually enhancing. This scope of responsibility would in practice take two major forms. First, *any* citizen, in or out of government, could come to the ombudsman with any suggestion or complaint about resource utilization and exchange. The ombudsman is obligated, if he or she deems the complaint or suggestion within the substantive scope of his responsibilities, to investigate the complaint (or to pursue the suggestion) in whatever ways he or she deems necessary to accomplish the aims of the office. The second major form is the ombudsman's right to scan and investigate, independent of a complaint, any administrative unit where he or she has reason to believe there are practices inimical to resource exchange, to forming relations with other administrative units, and to utilizing nongovernmental resources, be they information or anything else. Just as any citizen has the right of access to the ombudsman, so the ombudsman has the right of access to any individual in the public service. But in all that he or she does it is made clear to everyone (as the legislation could state) that the ombudsman has no formal decision-making powers. His or her influence resides in the fact that a representative legislative body has expressed its concern about resource utilization and exchange and has created a role whereby this concern can be dealt with in an informal, nonbureaucratic, noncoercive manner; that is, whatever gets accomplished has a voluntary flavor. The second major source of influence is the annual report, a document available to anyone, in which the ombudsman describes his or her activities, accomplishments, and failures, and offers opinions about issues that the legislature should consider.

The resource ombudsman is not an administrator, head of a task force, or a time- and focus-limited investigative unit. It is not a role for which the usual job description is appropriate. One cannot say that he or she should have a certain educational background, or be a certain type of professional, or describe how the person will spend his or her time, or the techniques and procedures used, and to whom he or she will be responsible in daily activities. One can say that the person's experience clearly reflects a breadth of knowledge about public services, active participation in formal and informal community networks and functions, a reputation for fairness and firmness, and the capacity to scan the scene to see potential linkages and exchanges that surface appearances and differences prevent most people from perceiving. In short, the ombudsman has the characteristics of the reticulist or network coordinator we described in earlier chapters. And he or she is a person in whom these cognitive skills are in the service of a resource exchange rationale. The role of the resource ombudsman is a "quiet," not a muckraking, publicity-oriented one.

In the course of this book, we have described individuals who could perform in the role of the resource ombudsman. Although they may be described, as Sheane (1977) did, as the "creative minority," they are not so few in numbers as we once thought.[3] It would be the rare community where one could not locate a member of this minority. They are not a minority in the elitist sense but in the sense that, for reasons we do not understand at all well, integrated in them is a cognitive rationale powered by a committment to certain values that has propelled them to engage in definable ways in the arena of community affairs.

Throughout the course of this book, we have centered attention on the fate of the resource exchange rationale in formal and informal settings and networks. If our preference was for the informal route, it was not because it was without limitations or obstacles that could seriously constrict growth, applicability, and impact. It was, rather, because of the more serious limitations and obstacles contained within formal organizations. The concept of the resource ombudsman struck us as a feasible way by which the resource exchange rationale could have more impact in formal organizations and between formal organizations and informal community individuals and networks. It is a concept that builds on the Scandinavian ex-

---

[3]It is Mrs. Dewar's conviction that there is some of the reticulist in us all, a conviction that receives support in the number of people she has located and supported in reticulist activity. We said that reticulists "are not so few in numbers as we once thought." Mrs. Dewar would put it more positively and, probably, more correctly: There are many reticulists, some already playing that role and many more who could be sparked into playing the role.

perience (albeit in relation to resource exchange and not citizens' rights) in relation to a set of issues plaguing every country. Although the United States is not Scandinavia, the ombudsman concept requires no special adaptation to our society. However, the difference in size of the country and in scale of the public sector—interacting with significant differences in forms of municipal and state government and, in turn, their interacting with massive, bewildering federal apparatus—would undoubtedly affect the role of *an* ombudsman. One starts with where one can start, where a legislative body has the insight and courage to create the office of the resource ombudsman. What could happen if the office becomes more frequent? Can the local, state, and federal level ombudsmen develop their resource exchange network? We realize that the wish-fulfilling element in fantasy tends to blot out the negative consequences that can follow from acting on fantasy. In this case, however, given the informality and powerlessness of the role, it is hard to see how any envisioned negative consequences would be greater than the positive.

The form of the suggestion is simple, inexpensive, and quite the opposite of efforts at change using fiat, or rhetoric, or administrative reorganization, which, like war, is the continuation of politics by other means. In saying this, we do not suggest that the office of the ombudsman is bathed in sweetness and light or that the incumbent is an avuncular, benign paragon before whom conflict, recalcitrance, and rigidity lose their sting or melt away. Gellhorn's (1967) description should dispel that notion. The fact is that the resource ombudsman would be, like the ombudsman for citizens' rights, a partisan for resource exchange and its network vehicles by which it can be implemented. As a partisan, he or she is both reactive and proactive, both clinical and preventive, both problem and opportunity oriented.

Hirschhorn's Review

As we were finishing this book, a review appeared of our first book (Sarason and others, 1977), in which we describe the development and functioning of the Essex Network. It was written by Dr. Larry Hirschhorn of the department of city and regional planning at the University of Pennsylvania. It is a critical, thoughtful, and balanced review that permits us to clarify our position and to make a concluding point we consider to be of crucial importance. Here are the relevant portions of his review (Hirschhorn, 1978, pp. 229–230):

> The resource scarcity argument seems to make a virtue out of a necessity. Indeed, the authors go so far as to suggest that "undermanned" settings in which people are stretched to meet the tasks faced by the setting might be more functional than adequately manned ones. People feel more useful within such settings, and there is less obsession with status and merit.
>
> This argument sits uneasily with me, not because it is wrong but because of the political economy of enforced austerity that hovers menacingly in the background. Productive responses to austerity take place within a political-economic frame of structural unemployment, falling profit rates, and capitalist disinvestment in many of our old cities, if not the country as a whole. If networking is a solution to resource scarcity, it might also be an ideological sop to frustrated service workers and managers at a time when fiscal politics is squeezing them out.
>
> But the resource argument is more complex than the authors let on, and this complexity is demonstrated in their own experience. They describe the dilemmas of success they faced as the network grew. They needed a second coordinator, but where could they find the money to hire one? Some network members felt strongly that grants would distort the network by attaching strings and requiring evaluations. The network would lose its flexibility and autonomy.
>
> This turns the resource scarcity argument on its head. Networks should not search for ultimate recognition from the official money vendors. Its goals are not to permanently expand its fiscal base. Networking is a qualitative response to resource scarcity. It cannot restructure the fiscal politics and economics of metropolitan areas; that requires a politics that goes beyond the slim capacities of small, self-activating networks. But it can begin to teach people how resources can be developed in new and productive ways. This is why I believe networking is emerging as a grass roots activity. . . .
>
> Networks evolve by integrating people who have organizational commitments yet who come together not as representatives but as interested *persons* who are looking for satisfaction and fulfillment in the roles. A network is based on a deliberate confusion between people as role performers versus people in their own distinctive "personhoods." In this context, networks emerge as general forms of social interaction that recognize this role confusion by maximizing the tension between our roles and our construction of what we authentically are. This tension in turn allows people to examine the distance between what they are and what they might be and thus enables them to find new and more satisfactory activities and cooperative relationships. Such experiences mirror the developmental pressures of postindustrial society. As we experience many more role transitions, we must increasingly rely on a concept of ourselves as persons, not role per-

formers, to give coherence to our life cycles. This, I would argue, is why the theory of networks is definitely in the air. . . .

This is an attractive model for planning. Planners who work at the community level today, particularly in the older cities, are well aware of how stalemated and restricted community action activity has become. It is tempting to think of networking as a strategic answer. Remove people from the narrow representational roles they play on neighborhood councils, community advisory boards, and the like, and network them informally. Promise no money, tell them no lies, but facilitate discussion and awareness about the potentials for resource exchange and mobilization in which all could gain. Start small, and don't think big.

It is an appealing model, slightly utopian, but the authors' experience and analysis suggest that such an approach could touch upon fertile soil. Yet there is a danger in such a networking thrust. Networking will never substitute for politics; it cannot overcome or end-run the politics of conflict. As more people get into networking—and more are—there will no doubt emerge an ideology of networking and a networking movement, which will project an image of self-managed resource allocation emerging from the grass roots and slowly taking over the power centers.

This is decidedly utopian, much like the syndicalist dreams of yesteryear. Politics remains the bottom line for the mobilization of resources, and we should not forget it. At most, networks should be seen as learning systems in which people, removed from the constraints of their roles and operating at the role-personhood boundary, learn to plan the allocation and mobilization of resources outside the inhibiting constraints of the present political setup. Networking effects, in other words, will be *indirect*. They will establish a climate for organization activity in which the narrowness and inhibitions imposed by local, state, federal, and market-determined relations can be critically scrutinized on the basis of the new and real experiences that networks provide. But if the ideologues of networking should aim for more—if they should decide to build networks, and networks of networks, beyond the point at which they can be self-sustained, if they should refuse to dissolve them when the time is ripe—they will simply reintegrate themselves back into the urban management system that thus far has proven incapable of solving the problems of postindustrial decay.

In sum, the present period presents us with a three-part configuration that adds up to the social crisis of the transition to postindustrial society: resource scarcity and massive disinvestment in the cities; a new, more diffuse, less bounded role structure; and a politics of stalemate and narrowness. Networking speaks to all three dimensions of this trinity. It offers a new vision of resource exchange and mobilization based on local planning and self-management; it presents a new way to productively structure the role confusion of postindustrial life; and it gives hope that the political stalemate might be broken in a new climate of awareness about community exchange and cooperation.

We agree with Hirschhorn. When he talks about "the ideologues of networking" he is expressing our misgivings about the popularity (fashionableness) of the network concept, a popularity that blurs the complexity of the issues, engenders unrealistic expectations, and replaces thinking with slogans and labels.

We wish that Hirschhorn (1978) had been able to expand on his statement, "Politics remains the bottom line for the mobilization of resources, and we should not forget it." From our perspective, this suggestion for a resource ombudsman rests on the assumption that our political system is capable of doing something that addresses in a limited but not self-defeating way the "three-part configuration that adds up to the social crisis of the transition to postindustrial society." Although we would agree that one can say that politics remains the bottom line for the mobilization of resources, we should not forget that a political balance sheet consists of three interrelated factors: ideas, vested interests (used non-pejoratively here), and values. If people differ in why and how resources should be mobilized and distributed, it is because they differ in what they believe people are, should be, and need.

So, for example, one could conclude from Hirschhorn's review that mobilizing and allocating resources for any social purpose would only make sense, would only be justified, if it gave "coherence to our life cycles." What Hirschhorn means by "coherence in our life cycles" we cannot say, but the thrust of his comments suggests that this coherence must reflect a greater reliance "on a concept of ourselves as persons," not as role performers. We may be unfair in saying that Hirschhorn is right but incomplete. He is right in the sense that slotting people into roles has become maladaptive for them, and this is no less true for highly educated as for less educated groups (Sarason, 1977). But in our experience a major concomitant of what Hirschhorn so pithily describes as the dilution, and frequently the absence, of a sense of community, the sense that one is part of a dependable, mutually supportive fabric of social relationships is the feeling of stagnation and isolation in the work setting. And, we assume, this is what Hirschhorn alludes to when he says "new and more satisfactory activities *and* cooperative relationships" (italics ours). If we are right, the issue, then, is not whether one regards politics as the bottom line in the mobilization of resources. That has always been the case. The issue is whether the values that inform one's politics have an explicit Janus-like quality: seeking the enhancement of the individual at the same time seeking to enhance his or her sense of social bondedness. It will not do, as past experience indicates, to pay attention to one and not the other. In a peculiarly intriguing way, we, like Hirschhorn, find the resource exchange network to have this Janus-like quality. But let us hasten to add that, although gods like Janus may be able to look in two directions simultaneously, to mere mortals it is literally a pain in the neck and ultimately an impossibility. There is and will always be a tension and gulf between what individuals feel they need for individuality, on the one hand, and their no less strong need to belong, on the other hand. Individuals are quite sensitive to this tension and gulf, far more sensitive than our political system has recognized. Indeed, the most serious criticism one can make of politics and planning is that they have not been sensitive enough, they have not been able to face and live with, the constant tension and gulf between individuality and community (Sarason, 1974).

Politics is about the mobilization and allocation of resources but to leave it at that is to beg the question, "Why mobilize and allocate resources? For what ends?" And the ends are always plural and to a certain degree, at least, in conflict with each other. That should be disheartening only to those who believe that there can be a heaven on earth, that there are solutions to these questions in the form of "Four divided by two is two." There are no such solutions. In our individual and social lives, no less than life in the political arena, the task is how to stay true to what one values. But to stay true to one's values is easier said than done, because, although values give rise to action, the content of values, however explicit those values may be, does not in any logical fashion dictate *a* course of action. To act on values confronts one with a universe of possible actions, and it is a difficult task to determine how to choose among the alternatives.

In this book, we have at some length described how staggeringly restrictive and self-defeating are the alternatives our system of politics has considered in regard to resources. This has less to do with the economic features of our society than with the failure to consider alternatives that would challenge these characteristics. The same situation obtains in countries with very different economic characteristics. Our society has come to the point where there is a general disillusionment with the way we have done things, a disillusionment that questions all forms of institutional authority, administrative gimmickry and growth, and the empty rhetoric of hope and peace. This did not come about only because of economic and political factors, and it will not go away by economic or political actions only. The tensions and gulf between the needs for individuality and community have long existed in our society, when resources seemed abundant or were discernibly reduced. But in the past there was always the belief that some day the resources would be of such a scale that these tensions and gulfs would disappear. Today, the question that alarms people is whether we will have the resources in the future that we had in the past. For us, as we hope we have made clear in this book, the important question is whether we can learn to integrate the fact of limited natural and human resources with the values and actions of the resource exchange rationale. We have made an effort at such integration by describing informal resource exchange networks and by offering a suggestion about where we might start in the public sector.

Networking, as Hirschhorn says, is in the air. That is a mixed blessing, but unavoidable. Fashions are transient, but they do reflect needs, however inchoate. In the case of the fashionableness of the network concept, the evidence is compelling that it reflects the need for individuality *and* community. But no less compelling is the evidence that we have hardly made a beginning in our understanding of the different ways and degrees by which those needs can be met by the resource exchange rationale. And that understanding will not be furthered by theorizing unless that theorizing is a distillation of experience in developing and sustaining resource exchange networks of the informal and formal varieties. Nor will it be furthered by clarification of values or ends unless they too derive from the actual practice of a theory of values and ends. To understand the world, you have to try to change it, and in the process you and the world inevitably change.

In concluding this book, we return to earlier themes in order to emphasize a feature of the resource exchange rationale that is of enormous significance and without which that rationale loses its attraction to people.

We have emphasized the difficulties people have in recognizing that human and natural resources are limited. It makes no difference, we said, if people did not believe that resources were finite as long as they realized that in practice there were serious limits to these resources. And, we pointed out, although in recent decades there is a growing but reluctant acceptance of limited natural resources, the limits of human resources have hardly been discussed. Central to our discussion of the benefits of the resource exchange rationale was the process of redefinition, which is a precondition for three desirable consequences: individuals see themselves as more differentiated resources, this enlarged self-perception alters their perception of their relationship to others, and this alteration can lead to exchanges with others that increase the resources available to everyone in the exchanges. These consequences are, of course, not inevitable or self-sustaining, but when they are embedded in a deliberately forged network of relationships, these consequences not only can be sustained but also can have a spread effect that adds significantly to the resources potentially available to each network member.

How does one account for the participation and even enthusiasm of people in a resource exchange network? We have at some length discussed the obstacles that prevent people from even starting the redefinition process, let alone altering the basis on which they interrelate with others. But how do we account for the myriad instances where people have started the process, albeit in different ways and with different consequences? More specifically, why have so many networks emerged that are based on some kind of resource exchange rationale? The reader may have noted that we gave a prominent place to the concept of self-interest; that is, by participating in a network, an individual's interests were more likely to be furthered. This was mirrored in the phrases "give and get" or "barter economy" or "exchanges." This emphasis was deliberate because we wanted to illustrate how in the redefinition process self-interest required one to change one's perception of others as resources no less than one's perception of self. To the extent that the redefinition process results only in a changed perception of self as a resource and not, concomitantly, in a changed perception of others, the individual drastically limits the resources potentially available to him or her. This may strike some as having a "marketplace" flavor: There are superficial, interpersonal contacts during which an exchange of resources takes place, each person is satisfied, and then they go their own ways, never knowing whether they will have occasion to meet again. If that were primarily what it is all about, we would be totally incapable of explaining the origins, development, and viability of resource networks we have experienced or come to know. Furthermore, we would completely miss what happens to many people over time as participants in such a network.

A member of an informal resource exchange network does not "join" the network in the sense that he or she is invited, or applies, or has the status conferred on him or her. In every instance, the person hears about the network through a friend, acquaintance, or colleague who participates in the network. He or she may hear about it because the participant wanted to pique the curiosity of the person or, no less frequently, because in the course of discussion the person senses something similar to what he or she has been thinking. The concept of resource exchange is in the minds of many people, although it usually is in a negative form: "Why can't individuals, groups, and agencies cooperate with each other instead of competing destructively with each other?" But one should not underestimate the number of people who independently have conceptualized a resource exchange rationale, almost in the nature of a pleasurable fantasy that helps them tolerate the senselessness of so much they see going on around them. Far from being passive people or thinkers, they are ever on the alert for opportunities to be more active in ways consistent with that rationale. And that desire to be active in a special way often goes far beyond the idea of resource exchange to a participation that is both conceptually and interpersonally stimulating and enriching. And we use the words *stimulating* and *enriching* advisedly, because what these people seek is a way of being with others that enlarges their commerce with ideas and their social surroundings. Far from seeing resource exchange in the context of a marketplace, they see it more in the context of a variegated, extended family.

The steps between hearing about the network and participating in it cannot be predicted or programmed. Hearing about the network can be followed by telephone calls to or from network members or coordinators or by attending minimeetings or one of the general network meetings. Obviously, there is a selective factor in who follows through from hearing about the network to some initial participation, just as there is a selective factor in who participates on a sustained basis. We have noted instances, relatively few in number, where it seemed obvious that the person was far more interested in finding out what was in it for him or her than in listening to what other people were about. (That presents no problem, because participation is voluntary, and the degree and frequency of involvement is determined by the individual.) Some of these individuals become intrigued with the character of the meetings—the range of ideas, the heterogeneity of the participants, the variety of settings with which they are affiliated, and the interconnections forged or being planned. They find themselves enjoying the experience as much for its intellectual stimulation and information value as for its potential utility for their needs.

There is an old saying, "Talk to me, and I will forget; teach me, and I will learn; involve me, and I will understand." The resource exchange network has no missionary program; it is not set up to teach or indoctrinate, and there is no curriculum. At its best, the network provides opportunities for people to involve themselves, on the levels of ideas, discussion, and action, with others. People can differ widely in the understandings they derive from their involvement (in what they think they are learning, getting, and contributing), but it is *their* understanding, not someone else's, that sustains their participation. Members' perception of their self-interest changes by enlarging. It is not only that new people become part of a person's environment, just as the person becomes part of theirs, but that this happens in ways that add new possibilities for thinking and action.

The reader will recall that in Chapter Seven we described the efforts of Mrs. Topitzer and Mrs. Greene to develop a resource exchange network in their communities. We are indebted to Mrs. Topitzer for allowing us to quote from an account she wrote (Topitzer, 1978b, pp. 1–3). It has a concreteness that our generalizations inevitably lack; for example, the first two sentences nicely differentiate between teaching (through books) and involvement.

> The conceptualizations and "putting it together" which we learned initially from our experiences with Bill Fibkins and the Teacher's Center and from reading Sarason's books were important and probably a crucial first step. However, to my mind the element that "made the difference" in Marie's and my final decision to go ahead with the Bay Shore Resource Network was our meeting with Richard Sussman and Mrs. Dewar in New York early in April. They communicated to us their excitement about what we

were thinking of doing in Bay Shore and that they would "be there" for us. We had suddenly found a "family," with all the support, acceptance, and resources that word can signify. Marie Greene and I were amazed, delighted, and truly excited.

I am aware that most descriptions of social structures do not ordinarily include the emotional experiences of their participants. But it must be recalled that I had told Marie only two weeks previously that I was "overwhelmed," "could see no financial future in this venture," and, though "still tremendously excited about its long-term prospects, I had to beg off." Therefore, to my mind there is no doubt that it was the initial outreach by the Essex coordinators that turned the tide.

Further, there was very little of a "concrete" nature offered by the Essex contingent at the initial meeting. The resources of the wider network were implied, I'm sure, but frankly, it meant as much to us as the offer of the keys to an alien planet! One might expect potential resources there, but what they might be or how they might help was certainly far from clear!

I think it is the supportive relationship that continues to grow between Essex and ourselves that remains the most important element in the linkage. And one of the strongest elements in that relationship is the reinforcement that Marie and I continually get that what we are doing and thinking is as helpful and significant to the wider network as their input is to us. In fact, it is nothing short of experiencing the dynamic method of the resource exchange relationship, as opposed to the one-way, giver-taker relationship which most of us have experienced heretofore. The fertilizing potential of this type of mutual support relationship is really amazing in its energizing effects.

As far as concrete gains, some are still in embryonic form, naturally enough; for example, Marie's parenting connection with the Essex School group, our hookup between our Y OutReach peer-group counseling project and Richard's group (in Essex). Most important is the other network members' involvement in trying to help us solve the funding problem and the contacts with various people to put us on the path to finding foundation support. Also, the mentor component, where we have Richard's and Mrs. Dewar's experience to use as a sounding board for our own projected *modus operandi,* has been invaluable in both its practical and supportive effects. For example, questions of how to approach potential network participants and the timing involved in these initiating steps do not have to be a trial-and-error operation on our part due to our "trainee" relationship. Practical advice on such matters as fiscal agents and advisory boards is much more easily come by in this setting. Finally, there is little question that our connection with the wider network has lent us a much easier credibility in our own community for our "new" venture. Although Marie (especially) and I are known quantities here, my hunch is that people's initial puzzlement is transformed the more easily into their usual pattern of enthusiastic acceptance by our ability to say that we are patterned after a similar organization in Essex that has been operating successfully, and to mention the ties to the university members. That, if you will, functions as our *imprimatur* in what is basically a conservative community. It does not mean that, in the end, people will decide that they do not want to join up, but, at least, they feel free to examine the idea and see if it's something that meets their personal requirements.

How we define people as resources and, therefore, the limits we see in people as resources is largely a function of when in a society that definition is attempted. The definition is culturally determined through processes and vehicles that start having their effects from the time an individual is born. Until recently, if the newly born child was female, the perceived limits on what that individual would "be" in life were narrow indeed. Today, those limits are much broader, and there is every reason to believe they will even be broader in the future. In fact, one can characterize our society today as one in which accustomed definitions of people as resources are being challenged, changed, or discarded. It is not simply a matter of the legal rights of individuals as citizens or of increasing their access to all levels of education. The challenge is coming from all segments in the society, from more as well as the less privileged groups. It is, for the most part, an inchoate challenge in which what is most clear is a festering dissatisfaction with life as it is lived with others, the sense that, although one is inevitably tied to and dependent on others for what one can do or be, the ties and the dependency seem too frequently to work against rather than for one. Individuals possess, treasure, and guard their individuality only to find that in winning that battle they have lost the war against rootlessness, isolation, and routinization. More correctly, they fought the battle for independence and lost the war for interdependence. It was not a war of their making, and they are not at all sure who the enemy is. All that they are sure of is that they do not get from others what they feel they need, and they do not give to others as much as they potentially can give or others expect.

There is nothing new here that has not been analyzed and commented on by countless others from the earliest days of the industrial revolution. Few social historians have communicated more effectively this theme over the sweep of history than Nisbet in *The Quest for Community* (1971) and *The Social Philosophers* (1973). It is a sad picture, not because the future is bleak and hopeless but because in the developmental dynamics of Western society the quest for individualism—however it may have been phrased in terms of liberty, autonomy, and self-determination—was in the prospect of the active person pursuing his or her destiny. And destiny was an individual matter and responsibility. It was also an illusion, because one can only pursue one's destiny with, because of, or through others. But, if these others are no less victims of the same illusion, the road to destiny becomes a mined obstacle course for everyone. How to maintain the precarious balance between the laudable desire for individuality and the needed bonds of interdependence has always been problematic. When that balance is markedly askew, people feel adrift and incomplete, powerless and fearful.

The pursuit of individuality reflected a radical redefinition of people as resources. The removal of the fetters (social, familial, political, and religious) on the thoughts and actions of people released energies that transformed societies. Initially, the redefinition of people as resources applied to very small segments of society but, as we now know, the redefinition had an allure and power that could not be contained. People generally, not only elites, clamored to be more than custom and tradition had heretofore permitted. But from the earliest days of the industrial revolution there were people who warned against the consequences of individualism for the sense of community. There was no withstanding, however, the forces giving rise to the quest for individuality.

Today, as we pointed out in earlier chapters, there is awareness that the precarious balance between the desire for individuality and the need to feel socially connected is seriously upset, and there can be little doubt that the popularity of the network concept and the resurgence of interest in resource exchange rationales reflect efforts to restore a balance. These are not efforts to deemphasize individuality nor are they a move to a smothering togetherness in which selfhood is extinguished. It is not, we think, indulging wishfulness to see these efforts as the outcroppings of a radical redefinition process in which people see each other as resources to each other. Like all previous redefinition processes that become benchmarks in human history, the substance of this redefinition is quite simple. Whether it has or will gain the power of these benchmarks, we cannot say. In this book, we have attempted to say that this redefinition has powerful consequences by increasing resources available to individuals in ways that meet intellectual and social needs and increases knowledge of the environment. At its best, the resource exchange network creates the conditions for active, productive growth and sustained learning. Our society offers few opportunities for such an experience. The resource exchange rationale is not a panacea, but neither is it the musings of noble hearts trying to deny the realities of existence in today's world. Nor is it the province of theoreticians. It is an uncomplicated conception that necessity has brought to the awareness of very different kinds of people who acted and began to exercise control over their lives. In their efforts to understand their world, they found themselves changing it.

It is fitting that in closing this book we turn again to Mrs. Dewar:

> Networking deals with conflict only as efforts toward peace deal with a trend towards war. To negotiation or arbitration, which look for areas of common interest, networking would add a search for complementary interests and needs. It would make diversity of situation and viewpoint useful rather than threatening. It would make a meeting of needs mean more for everyone, rather than less.
>
> Networking, it seems to me, can be a political tool useful to organizations, communities, and nations, to supplement or even preclude necessity for activities of the arbitration expert, the negotiator, the backroom wheeler-dealer. It is participatory by definition. It is continuing and developmental. It would not be time-bound, like periodic union negotiations or class action suits. It might deal with issues that then would never have to get to the bargaining table or the court.

These aims and claims are anything but modest. They are more in the nature of a vision. But it is said by somebody who has dealt extraordinarily creatively with the world as she finds it, and she has left her mark. Visionaries need not be impractical activists!

References

Adams, H. *The Education of Henry Adams.* Boston: Houghton Mifflin, 1974. (Originally published 1906.)

Albee, G. W. *Mental Health Manpower Trends.* New York: Basic Books, 1954.

Baker, B. L. "Parent Involvement in Programming for Developmentally Disabled Children." In L. L. Lloyd (Ed.), *Communication Assessment and Intervention Strategies.* Baltimore: University Park Press, 1977.

Baker, B. L., Brightman, A. J., Heifetz, L. J., and Murphy, D. *Read Project Series: Ten Instructional Manuals for Parents.* Cambridge, Mass: Behavioral Education Projects, 1972, 1973.

Beck, B. M. "Humanizing the Human Services." Paper presented at the National Association of Social Workers Professional Symposium in San Diego, Calif., November 19, 1977.

Becker, E. *The Denial of Death.* New York: Free Press, 1973.

Bell, D., and Held, V. "The Community Revolution." *The Public Interest,* 1969, Summer, No. 16, pp. 142–177.

Blatt, B. *Exodus from Pandemonium.* Boston: Allyn & Bacon, 1970.

273

Blatt, B., and Kaplan, F. *Christmas in Purgatory.* Boston: Allyn & Bacon, 1970.

Bledstein, B. J. *The Culture of Professionalism: The Middle Class and the Development of Higher Education in America.* (1st ed.) New York: Norton, 1976.

Boston Self-Help Center. Mimeographed descriptive brochure, 1977, available from Boston Self-Help Center, 12 Essex St., Cambridge, Mass. 02139.

Bowen, M. "Family Psychotherapy with Schizophrenia in the Hospital and Private Practice." In I. Boszormenyi-Nagy and J. L. Framo (Eds.), *Intensive Family Therapy: Theoretical and Practical Aspects.* New York: Harper & Row, 1965.

Cohen, S. B., and Lorentz, E. "Networking: Educational Program Policy for the Late Seventies." *Education Development Center News,* 1977, Fall, No. 10, pp. 1–4.

Cowden, P., and Cohen, D. *An Evaluation of the Experimental Schools Program.* Forthcoming.

Cowen, E., Trost, M. A., Lorion, R. P., Dorr, D., Izzo, L. D., and Isaacson, R. J. *New Ways in School Mental Health: Early Detection and Preventions of School Maladaptation.* New York: Human Sciences Press, 1975.

Crittenden, A. "Economist Hero Thinks Small." *New York Times,* October 26, 1975, p. F5.

Davies, A. F. "The Concept of Administrative Style." In *Essays in Political Sociology.* Melbourne: Cheshire, 1972.

Davies, A. F. *Politics as Work.* Melbourne Politics Monograph, 1973.

Dubos, R. Unpublished lecture given in a series of lectures at University of Washington, Seattle, Spring 1978.

Fibkins, W. "Teacher Centers and Professional Burn-out." Unpublished manuscript, 1978. Copies available from author at Bay Shore Jr. High School, Guidance Dept., 393 Brook Ave., Bay Shore, N.Y. 11706.

Fill, J. H. "An Epidemic of Madness. The Confessions of a Perpetrator." *Human Behavior,* 1974, March, pp. 40–47.

Friend, J. K., Power, J. M., and Yewlett, C. J. L. *Public Planning: The Inter-Corporate Dimension.* London: Tavistock, 1974.

Garner, W. R. "The Acquisition and Application of Knowledge: A Symbiotic Relation." *American Psychologist,* 1972, 27 (10), 941–946.

Gellhorn, W. *Ombudsmen and Others: Citizens' Protectors in Nine Countries.* Cambridge, Mass.: Harvard University Press, 1967.

Heifetz, L. "Professional Preciousness and the Evaluation of Parent-Training Strategies." Paper presented at the 4th International Association for the Scientific Study of Mental Deficiency, Washington, D.C., 1976.

Heilbroner, R. L. *An Inquiry into the Human Prospect.* New York: Norton, 1974.

Hirschhorn, L. "Human Services and Resource Networks." (Book review.) *Journal of American Institute of Planners,* 1978, *44* (2), 228–230.

Hurwitz, S. "The Folketingets Ombudsmand," 12 *Parliamentary Affairs* 199, 202 (1959).

Krantz, D. *Radical Career Change.* New York: Free Press, 1978.

Krause, D. U.S. Congress, House. Select Committee on Aging. Hearing Before the Subcommittee on Health and Long-Term Care, 94th Cong., 1st sess., July 8, 1975. (Available from Superintendent of Documents, U.S. Government Printing Office, Washington, D.C. 20402. Stock No. 050-070-02903-0. $1.70.)

Krause, D. "The Care of the Elderly: Meeting the Challenge of Dependency." Speech given before the Royal Society of Medicine Foundation at the National Academy of Sciences in Washington, D.C., May 17–19, 1976.

Krause, D. U.S. Congress, House. Select Committee on Aging. Hearing Before the Subcommittee on Health and Long-Term Care, February 22, 1978. (Available from Superintendent of Documents, U.S. Government Printing Office, Washington, D.C. 20402.)

Kravitz, S. "Family Development—Community Development. The Need for Integration and Coherence in Social Work Practice." Invitational paper at the annual Program Meeting for the Council on Social Work Education in New Orleans, La., March 1, 1978.

Levine, M., and Levine, A. *A Social History of Helping Services.* New York: Appleton-Century-Crofts, 1970.

London, M. "A Study of Interagency Perception and Cooperation." Unpublished senior thesis, Department of Psychology, Yale University, 1977.

Michaels, M. "Bartering, for the Things that Money Can't Buy."

Parade, August 6, 1978, pp. 18–20.

National Commission on Resources for Youth. *Resources for Youth Newsletter,* March 15, 1975, *4* (entire issue).

National Commission on Resources for Youth. Information letter "About the Commission." 36 West 44th St. New York, N.Y. 10036.

National Institute of Education. "Request for Proposals: Research on Social Networks in Education." Washington, D.C.: National Institute for Education, 1978.

Nisbet, R. A. *The Quest for Community.* New York: Oxford University Press, 1971.

Nisbet, R. A. *The Social Philosophers.* New York: Crowell, 1973.

Pepper, C. "For the Elderly, Health Care at Home, *First." New York Times,* May 20, 1978, Sec. 1, p. C19.

Perkins, D. N. T. "An Attempt at the Holistic Delivery of Human Services: Analysis and Implications." Unpublished manuscript, School of Organization and Management, Yale University, 1977.

Rappaport, J. *Community Psychology.* New York: Holt, Rinehart and Winston, 1977.

Reiss, A. J. *The Price and the Public.* New Haven, Conn.: Yale University Press, 1971.

Sarason, S. B. *The Culture of the School and the Problem of Change.* Boston: Allyn & Bacon, 1971.

Sarason, S. B. *The Creation of Settings and the Future Societies.* San Francisco: Jossey-Bass, 1972.

Sarason, S. B. *The Psychological Sense of Community: Prospects for a Community Psychology.* San Francisco: Jossey-Bass, 1974.

Sarason, S. B. "Community Psychology, Networks, and Mr. Everyman." *American Psychologist,* 1976a, *31* (5), 317–328.

Sarason, S. B. "The Unfortunate Fate of Alfred Binet and School Psychology." *Teacher College Record* (Columbia University), 1976b, *77* (4), 579–592.

Sarason, S. B. *Work, Aging, and Social Change: Professionals and the One Life-One Career Imperative.* New York: Free Press, 1977.

Sarason, S. B. "An Unsuccessful War on Poverty?" *American Psychologist,* 1978a, *33* (4), 831–839.

Sarason, S. B. "The Nature of Problem Solving in Social Action." *American Psychologist,* 1978b, *33* (4), 370–380.

Sarason, S. B., and Doris, J. *Educational Handicap, Public Policy, and Social History: A Broadened Perspective on Mental Retardation.* New York: Free Press, 1979.

Sarason, S. B., Zitnay, G., and Grossman, F. K. *The Creation of a Community Setting.* Syracuse, N.Y.: Syracuse University Press, 1972.

Sarason, S. B., Carroll, C. F., Maton, K., Cohen, S., and Lorentz, E. *Human Services and Resource Networks: Rationale, Possibilities, and Public Policy.* San Francisco: Jossey-Bass, 1977.

Sayre, W., and Kaufman, H. *Governing New York City.* New York: Russell Sage Foundation, 1965.

Schumacher, E. F. *Small Is Beautiful: Economics as if People Mattered.* New York: Harper & Row, 1973.

Schwebel, A., and Cook, P. In S. Sarason, G. Zitnay, and F. K. Grossman, *The Creation of a Community Setting.* Syracuse, N.Y.: Syracuse University Press, 1972.

Sheane, D. "Ulster: The Leading Edge." Informal discussion paper, 1977. Copies available from Mr. Derek Sheane, Central Personnel Department, Imperial Chemical House, Milbank, London SW1P3JF, England.

Shoreham-Wading River Central School District. "Children and Their Community." Middle School Friday Memo. No. 4-77. Randall Road, Shoreham, N.Y. 11786.

Skills Exchange. "Adult Education: Meeting the Challenge." Handout from organization, 1977. Information available from 482 Brunswick Avenue, Toronto, Canada M5R-2Z5.

Stapleton, C. *Barter.* New York: Scribner, 1978.

Taylor, D. W., Garner, W. R., and Hunt, H. F. "Education for Research in Psychology." *American Psychologist,* 1959, *14* (4), 167–179.

Topitzer, P. D. "Bay Shore Resource Network." (Rough draft for proposal: *A Basis for Discussion).* Unpublished manuscript, May 1978a. Copies available from author at 103 South Bay, Brightwater, N.Y. 11718.

Topitzer, P. D. "Initial Interactions between BSRN and the Wider Network." Informal report, 1978b.

U.S. Congress, House, *Congressional Record,* 95th Cong., 1st sess., 1977, *123* (146), 1.

Veysey, L. "Who's a Professional? Who Cares?" (Review of M. O.

Furner, *Advocacy and Objectivity: A Crisis in the Professionalization of American Social Science, 1865–1905). Reviews in American History,* 1975, *3* (4), 419–423.

Washington Consulting Group. *Uplift: What People Themselves Can Do.* Salt Lake City: Olympus, 1974.

White, D. E. "Minds in a Groove." *The Chronicle of Higher Education,* May 22, 1978, *16* (13), 40.

Wildavsky, A. B., and Pressman, J. L. *Implementation: How Great Expectations in Washington Are Dashed in Oakland; or, Why It's Amazing that Federal Programs Work at All, This Being a Saga of the Economic Development Administration as Told by Two Sympathetic Observers Who Seek to Build Morals on a Foundation of Ruined Hopes.* Berkeley: University of California Press, 1973.

Wolf, T. H. *Alfred Binet.* Chicago: University of Chicago Press, 1973.

Wolfensberger, W. *Normalization: The Principle of Normalization in Human Services.* Toronto: National Institute on Mental Retardation, 1972.

Yates, D. T. *The Ungovernable City.* Cambridge, Mass.: MIT Press, 1977.

Zax, M., and Specter, G. A. *An Introduction to Community Psychology.* New York: Wiley, 1974.

Index